I0531820

Running in Slippers

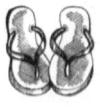

Running in Slippers

ANGIE HAWKINS

Divine Sol LLC

Copyright © 2022 by Angie Hawkins

All rights reserved. No part of this book may be reproduced or transmitted in any form or by any means without written permission from the author.

This is a work of nonfiction. Nonetheless, some names, identifying details, and personal characteristics of the individuals involved have been changed.

Printed in the United States of America
First Printing, 2022

ISBN 979-8-9858996-0-3 (print) | ISBN 979-8-9858996-1-0 (ebook)

Divine Sol LLC

www.runninginslippers.com

*In loving memory of my father, Randy,
and to my mother, Colleen.*

Author's Note

WHEN I was a little girl, I thought adults knew what was up. Like, maybe there was a rite of passage where you were given an instruction manual:

How to be an Adult! A Step-by-Step, Easy to Follow Guide.

What a hilarious realization that none of us know what the hell we are doing! This trial-and-error-laced experience creates a rollercoaster adventure through life. The ride can be fun and successful. It can also be extremely painful and ridden with mistakes. Sometimes we are the only ones who suffer from our mistakes. And sometimes we take down others with us.

As human beings, we are all flawed, and we all make mistakes. That's okay, as long as we learn and grow from those experiences. That learning and growth may take time, and at any given time, we are all doing the best we can with the tools and knowledge that we have at that moment.

This is a work of nonfiction. I wrote this book from my point of view at the time the facts unfolded, not from hindsight. Many events have been consolidated and edited for brevity only. Most names and identifying pieces of information have been changed for anonymity.

Running in Slippers

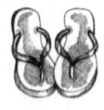

INTRODUCTION

JANUARY 31, 2020

ONE perk about living in Hawaii is that I only wear shoes when working out or going out. Any other time, I wear slippers. I have lived here for just over a year now and am still not used to using the word slippers to describe flip-flops, but I do everything I can to assimilate to local life, so slippers it is. Another perk about living in Hawaii is that if I want to go to the beach after work in January, I can. It's a far cry from my former Chicago life, and quite frankly, I don't miss feeling dead inside all winter with the obscenely cold wind blowing across frozen Lake Michigan. Oddly enough, I think that I still suffer from Seasonal Affective Disorder in Hawaii. But I can't tell if I am depressed from the shorter hours of daylight, or because my life has been an uphill struggle for the better part of the past three years.

When does this end?

When will I be happy again?

I have been thinking about Dad a lot lately and still have a lot of regrets. And my remote Chicago job is draining the life out of me. I feel that the new management is pushing out the old management, which I am a part of. Many key people from the old administration have been let go and my manager, Rick, resigned last month. I set up a call next week with my new manager, Brian, to explain how valuable I am and how much I deserve a raise. I am nervous because I feel like I'm on the chopping block anyway and will look like a fool by having the nerve to ask for a raise. If I lose my job, I am screwed because local companies don't pay as much as my Chicago job and the prospects for remote work are few and far between. It doesn't help that I haven't found a solid friend tribe here. Yes, I have some friends here and there but there is a clear void of love and connection. Since I feel stressed and lonely today, I came to the beach after work to journal my feelings and relax.

Leaving the beach, I see an unkempt, barefoot man with unruly, dirty blonde hair who has his eyes fiercely focused on me. I pretend to ignore him.

Please don't talk to me. Please don't talk to me.

He doesn't receive my subliminal message. "You know what? When your girlfriend plays you, you just have to move on with your life."

I don't stop walking. I intend to ignore him, but I am so dumbfounded by his uninhibited comment that I accidentally make eye contact with him. And because I have no boundaries around not engaging with him, it feels awkward not to say anything. "Yes."

I have no other words. Plus, even though his statement should not be a hard opening to a conversation with a stranger, it was very logical and, yes, I agree that he should move on with his life. Fortunately, I still have the walking pace of a Chicagoan. Unfortunately, this dude is so intent on talking to me that he matches my pace, which might as well be sprinting in Hawaii. He raises his hand to get my attention. Not that he has to do anything to get my attention. Despite my closed-off body language, which he clearly does not know how to interpret, I haven't stopped paying attention to him since the second I noticed him. I don't even turn my head toward him, but he desperately needs me to listen and he will not let this go.

"Can I ask you a question?"

"No."

Okay, maybe I do have some boundaries. I don't stop walking. I hope I don't have to start running because I don't want to run in slippers. With all of the hardships over the past few years, I feel like I am running through life in slippers anyway. I'm exhausted from the struggle.

When will I be happy?

Chapter 1

I wake up at 5 a.m. to run along the Chicago lakefront before work like I always do every weekday, but this time I have a missed call and voicemail from Mom from last night after I went to bed. And a text. And an email. They all have the same message.

`Hi Angie, call me when you get a chance. I need`
`to tell you something. Love you.`

Shit, this is not good.

Mom never initiates calls to me. And she doesn't like to text. I know her tone, and the tone in the message is somber. It's 6 a.m. Mom's time in Fort Wayne, Indiana, and she is not a morning person. I will call her when I get back from my run. I feel responsible for Mom's emotions, so I don't want to upset her if I wake her up with a phone call. I have no idea when she leaves for work. Hopefully, I can catch her this morning because I am going into the office today, and areas to have personal calls are limited. I don't want everybody in the vicinity of my desk to hear this bad news conversation. I usually work from home, but working from home is too isolating right now as I am grieving my breakup with Marc. I need to be around people, even if it's my co-workers.

I bundle up in my three layers of clothes and two pairs of gloves and run along the lakefront starting at North Avenue Beach. The serenity of frozen Lake Michigan, twenty-degree, crisp air, and the city lights in the darkness before dawn stir my intuition.

Grandma or Dad died.

My logical mind is in denial, blocking any more incoming messages. I am already devastated about Marc dropping me on my ass for Julia that I can't handle anything else right now. But I don't know why else Mom would leave me so many urgent messages. I pause along the lakefront. The air is freezing my nostrils. I look up at the sky. There is too much light pollution to see the stars. I take a deep breath and sigh it out as I look at the John Hancock building.

I'm thirty-six years old and have been through shit before. I can handle whatever life throws at me.

I run home, take a warm shower, get ready for work, and call Mom before leaving.

"Hello?"

"Hi, Mom."

"Hi, Angie. I have something to tell you."

It's typical of Mom to avoid a soft opening. This would normally trigger me, but I cannot wait for another second to hear the news. I hold my breath and brace for what she is about to say.

"Dad died."

I think I am still standing in my kitchen, but I don't know. I am physically, mentally, and emotionally numb.

Forget what I said along the lakefront. I can't fucking handle this. I can't handle anything else on top of losing Marc to Julia, especially Dad dying. Why now?

She tells me that she went to check on him at his house, which is my childhood home that we all lived in before they got divorced, and I went to college. She thought he was sleeping on his recliner, then realized he wasn't breathing.

He died alone.

I haven't talked to him much in the past ten years. I am drowning in regret.

M Y earliest childhood memories are of Mom dropping me off at preschool. I never went directly into the classroom because I was too painfully shy. I would timidly stand outside the door until I was emotionally ready to go in. I especially hated class performances. I always lip-synched. To my childhood logic, if I couldn't physically hide, then I could vocally hide. The weird part about this was that my grandparents in the audience always seemed to know.

"We couldn't hear you singing!"

Could they really pick one voice out of the whole choir?

Even at that young age, I was ashamed of who I was. I thought something was wrong with me because I don't remember ever getting hugs or words of encouragement. I don't remember anyone in my household exchanging acts of unconditional love. Mom liked to keep up appearances, so everything seemed normal, whatever that means, but on the inside, Mom, Dad, my half-sister, Amy, and I were emotionally disconnected strangers. As I grew up, I wrapped myself up in school because having perfect grades earned me conditional, short-term displays of affection from my parents. Plus, grades were the only thing in life I felt I had any control over— until high school.

In my junior year of high school, I saw a Paula Abdul dance VHS at Target. I was a fan of Paula during her peak, but this was several years after she peaked. I have no idea what intrigued me about that video. Maybe it was the merchandising magic of anything sold at Target. Every day, after school, I would immediately change clothes and dance with Paula in my bedroom before starting my homework. It was fun! And as an unintended consequence, I started losing weight. I wasn't overweight to begin with, probably one hundred and twenty-five pounds, but being an overachiever, I soon became addicted to seeing the number on the scale creep downward. I don't remember when it became unhealthy and out of control, but I weighed only a gaunt eighty-five pounds the summer before my senior year. I was miserable— yet oddly comforted that my internal world of disconnect and lack of love now matched my external world. Living with an emotionally closed-off family who swept everything under the rug, my skeletal appearance and obsessive eating habits were the elephants in the room. One day, during the fall of my senior year, Mom approached me to say that she had scheduled an appointment for me with a therapist.

She was finally concerned about how I was feeling!

Just kidding. But my friends' parents were concerned. They had asked Mom about my emaciated appearance, and the questions were too embarrassing for her. Her words, not mine. My friends and boyfriend, like my family, swept it under the rug and pretended nothing was wrong. I felt disconnected in all aspects of my life. As much as I didn't want to go to therapy, I was miserable and wanted things to change. My therapist, Rose, was just as emotionally cold as the rest of my family. And for some reason, she wanted me to go to an all-girls college, which was horrifying because I fantasized about finding a hot boyfriend in college. She seemed to prefer militant interrogation over the getting-to-know-me type of conversation. Her direct style quickly revealed that I was hurting about Dad being an alcoholic and emotionally unavailable. At the next appointment, she invited Mom to our session.

"How do you feel about your husband's drinking?"

Mom was silent. I started crying. I don't know if it was because my emotional pain was coming to the surface or because I was absorbing Mom's embarrassment and discomfort.

"Would you feel comfortable having a family conversation about his drinking habits and how they affect the family?"

Tight-lipped, Mom was silent. On the way home, we stopped at Dairy Queen. I think it was an attempt to feed me high-calorie food to gain weight. We sat on the curb and, as I was eating my Oreo Blizzard, she interrupted the silence of me shoveling ice cream into my starving body. "I didn't know Dad's drinking bothered you."

At this point, I had zero experience having difficult conversations. On the other hand, I could chim chiminey any damn thing under the rug. Thus, I had no response and stayed silent and dissociated by concentrating on the cold, sweet ice cream melting on my tongue. It was in this pause that Mom acted upon the realization that my eating disorder was more than something within me that could be fixed and was a larger problem that would require her to do hard work too. "Do you want to keep going to therapy?"

It was emotionally painful and awkward to talk to Rose, the rigid, all-girls school interrogator. Of course, I didn't want to go back. "No."

"Okay."

"Chim chim cher-ee!"

But the problem was that my anorexia was still very present. By this point, I felt a lot of anger toward my parents, so much so that I counted down the days until I could go away to college and move out. Mom, of course, realized this. I gained the weight back fast, under Mom's threat that I would have to live at home and go to community college if I didn't gain weight. Fear is a great motivator. In less than two months, I gained forty-five pounds by stuffing my face with everything in sight. Mom was happy, but I felt fat, disgusting, and out of control. I went back to counting down the days until I could escape to college.

But I couldn't escape. I was still under my parent's financial rein. After I first moved away, I was enjoying my freedom. It didn't even occur to me to call my parents because we never really talked to each other when I lived at home, so why did we need to talk now? But one day, Mom called me in a tizzy. "Why haven't you called?!"

I don't know, probably because I'm having fun without you.

Not to mention, she hadn't called me either. She went on to demand that I call her every single week so that we could talk. She meant that she wanted me to call her so that she could talk about herself and I could listen. To this day, Mom never calls me and insists that I call her at least once a week. When I call Mom: *Let me tell you every single detail about my week. Afterward, it will be your turn to tell me about your week, but I will loudly yawn and constantly interrupt you as you speak.*

My parents divorced when I was in college and living in Indianapolis, Indiana. Complying with Mom's demands to call her every week, I also began to call Dad every week in an attempt to form a relationship with him, even though we'd never been close before. When I was growing up, he would come home from work, sit in his recliner, and drink until dinner. Then we would eat, he would drink some more, and then usually fall asleep in his recliner while watching television until Mom nagged him to go to bed. He was physically present, but mostly a warm body in the house. Mom was always angry, presumably about how little of a role he played in the family, but instead of leaving, she constantly criticized and nagged him. Amy and I picked up on this resentment, and we mostly just ignored him as he did to us. Until I started calling him every week after the divorce. Some weeks went well. Other weeks, I could tell he was uncomfortable and wanted to get off the phone. Other weeks, I could tell he had been drinking too much and would go on drunken rants about how much he hated the government or whatever else was pissing him off. For the most part, like the calls with Mom, I was the only one putting in the effort to initiate. As an adult, in hindsight, I think he was depressed. And I know now that both of my parents did the best they could with the knowledge and resources they had, but growing up, I took their behavior personally.

I don't deserve to be loved.

There is something wrong with me.

After college, I was still living in Indianapolis, but wanted to move to Chicago. I loved the idea of getting lost in the crowd. I liked to hide. In Chicago, I could remain largely unseen in a big city and nobody could easily criticize me like Mom and extended family members did. I had been searching for jobs in Chicago for about a year, and finally, I was offered a job that was a good fit for me at Sara Lee. I was moving to Chicago! I called Dad to tell him the good news.

He knows this is what I want, so he will be excited for me, right? Wrong!

"Chicago is expensive. You're not going to be able to afford it."

"It's the armpit of the nation."

"There's too much traffic. I'm not visiting you."

"You're going to hate it there."

"I'm not helping you move."

I cried myself to sleep that night and stopped calling him every week. I would see him a few times each year when I would drive home for holidays, which felt uncomfortable and forced. I didn't initiate a call to him for ten years and that was only because Mom told me his health was failing. As a nurse, she suspected COPD, but because he didn't have health insurance, in an attempt to stick it to "The Man," he didn't go to the doctor much, especially not for a life-threatening diagnosis, because that would mean the doctor would tell him to stop smoking and that was not happening, even after he had to have a section of his tongue removed for cancer. His quality of life was so bad that he was forced to retire from his handyman job at the age of sixty because he was physically unable to do much other than sit. Out of love and guilt for not talking to him anymore, I called him to check in on him. Even then, he seemed uncomfortable talking to me and rushed to get off the phone.

That was six months ago. I didn't get to say goodbye.

Chapter 2

I'm a horrible daughter. I should have called more. I could have done more to repair the relationship.

As my critical inner voice barrages me, my logical voice kicks into gear. I don't know much about planning funerals, but I assume we need to start this weekend. I let Mom know that I can come home this weekend.

"You don't need to come home this weekend. Since we are getting him cremated, there is no rush. Enjoy your weekend and come home the following weekend. We'll keep in touch."

Um, what? Aren't we supposed to grieve together as a family?

Oh, that's right, we don't display emotions in this family, so I will isolate myself and go through it on my own like I always have with any difficult event in my life. I will put on my soldier facade, so everyone can see how strong I am and be proud of how well I resiliently handle life, even though I am a disaster inside and don't know how to regulate my intense emotions. I know these feelings are normal for an adult whose childhood emotional needs weren't met, but it still rips me up inside. Even though my family is emotionally cold and I hate going to Fort Wayne, because it holds so many uncomfortable memories, I want to see Mom. It seems comforting, even though it's doubtful my current emotional needs will be fulfilled. I tell her that I will come home on Saturday after my writing class to figure everything out.

I signed up for the writing class a month ago, when my life was normal. By normal, I mean when I still thought I had a chance of getting back together with Marc and Dad was alive. I have an idea for a blog to write backstories about random street findings, but I haven't written since high school, so I want to freshen up my skills. I was a prolific writer as a child and won the Young Author award out of the entire elementary school when I was in fifth grade. The last real writing I remember is a creative writing class in high school. In college, I studied finance and became disconnected from my creative side. I had been looking for a writing class on the weekends and the only one I could find that was offered on the weekend was a sketch comedy writing class at The Second City, an iconic sketch and improv comedy theater and training center. The thought of taking a comedy writing class is terrifying, but this is how determined I am to start writing again. I feel guilty for staying in Chicago to take the class on Saturday, but it's the first day, and comedy is what I need right now. Still, it feels like my heart has been ripped out of my chest and there is nothing that could be funny to me right now.

Even though we are talking about making arrangements for Dad's death, Mom is formal and unemotional on the phone. After we hang up, I start walking to the Red Line station to catch the subway to work. The weather is bitterly cold, which I usually hate, but right now it feels refreshing as the sting of the cold air numbs my feelings slightly. I try not to disturb my makeup as I wipe away my tears, but my makeup doesn't stand a chance with the flood of tears running down my face. I need to talk to someone for emotional support. I call my friend, Joe, my family of choice, big brother. "You will never guess what happened."

"Oh no, what?" I know he probably thinks I am about to unload more drama about Marc, but thankfully I haven't been in touch with him. He's probably too busy fucking Julia.

"My dad died." Niagara Falls starts all over again and I am glad the temperature is not less than thirty degrees or my cheeks would be covered by a sheet of ice, which has happened to me more than once crying outside in winter. Talking to Joe is so comforting, that I walk two miles to work instead of taking the crowded, noisy Red Line.

I wasn't thinking clearly after talking to Mom, but I am now that I have talked to Joe, and I feel like it was a bad idea to come into the office. But as I progress through the day and have multiple meetings, I know that I would have been too isolated at home. Even though I am walking my IT counterparts through boring, financial spreadsheets, it's comforting to be surrounded by people.

WHEN I was about six years old, my parents bought a timeshare in Fort Myers, Florida. We drove down for a family vacation, along with Mom's sister, Cynthia. It's all hazy, but from what I remember of Cynthia during this time is that her boyfriend, Brock, broke up with her, and it was so devastating that she was depressed all of the time, so whenever any of Mom's two brothers or other sister did anything eventful, they would invite Cynthia. My Aunt Donna and her boyfriend, Robert, who would always take Amy and me on a horse and carriage ride in downtown Fort Wayne around Christmas, invited Cynthia that year. Looking out the carriage window, Amy innocently exclaimed, "That guy looks like Brock!" This sent Cynthia down the rabbit hole of sadness that foiled Operation: Cheer Up Cynthia. But here she was with us on our vacation in Florida and seemed happy. One evening, Mom, Dad, Cynthia, Amy, and I drove down to the boardwalk. As soon as we got out of the car, Dad walked off and disappeared. Amy and I kept asking about him, and Mom deflected our questions by taking us to Dairy Queen. When we left the boardwalk, Mom got in the driver's seat. We were still missing Dad.

"How is Dad going to get home?" Mom didn't seem to care, so we kept our mouths shut. Until later that evening, when he walked through the door. I had been so worried about how he would get home that I ran up to him, excited to see him back.

He pushed me away. "Where's Mom?"

I was devastated. I was so happy to see him and he discarded me. Mom had stepped out. I assume to avoid his wrath, but she eventually returned, and all hell broke loose. I don't remember what they argued about. All I remember is watching Dad assert his dominance as Mom backward walked through the doorway of the bedroom, and he marched in front of her. A lot of arguing ensued inside the bedroom and I was happy that Cynthia was there because she comforted Amy and me during the fight. The result was that my parents declared they were getting divorced. Mom said that the three of us and Cynthia would fly home, and Dad would drive home. The entire situation was scary enough, but the fact that we didn't have the comfort of our own home was terrifying. Plus, once we got home, what would that home look like now that Mom and Dad were getting a divorce? Amy was upset too, but we were always both disconnected from each other, so we grieved separately. Amy and I were never close. She seemed to resent me, so I kept my distance. Amy is the child of Mom's first husband, Gary, but even though she always felt more like a full sister than a half-sister, neither of us knew how to connect. This rift continued into adulthood.

I'm not sure what happened between my parents after the fight, but the next day Mom announced that they weren't getting divorced, and we all pretended everything was okay and none of it ever happened. This was the beginning of a more than thirty-year tradition of isolating myself and sweeping shit under the rug. I was praised for playing the role of the strong one, even though inside, I was a whirlwind of intense feelings with little outlet or support.

Chapter 3

I am working from home on my kitchen island, and a smell brings me out of my work trance.

Who is smoking?

The scent is pungent enough to sting my nose, so it has to be close by. But my windows are closed because, duh, it's winter in Chicago.

The hallway. Someone is smoking in the hallway, and it's coming in through the crack under my front door.

Because I am Treasurer on my condo association's Board, I feel obligated to tell whoever is smoking in the hall to stop. We can't afford to fumigate the hallways. I rashly swing open the door. Nobody is there.

They went around the corner to hide from me because they know they have been caught!

I walk around the corner to face the elevator bank. Nobody.

What the hell? Who was smoking?

I no longer smell the smoke, but there is a lingering sting in my nostrils. I'm not crazy. I know I smelled a cigarette. I slowly walk back to my kitchen, where the realization hits me. It wasn't the smell of someone actively smoking. It was the smell of someone who had just finished smoking. And it wasn't the smell of anyone who had just finished smoking. All smokers have their own distinct scent. I whisper into an empty room. "Dad?"

An ice-cold chill runs through my body. I can feel my heart violently thudding in my chest, while hearing the heartbeats loudly in my ears and reverberating in my skull. I am terrified because my father, who is dead, was right here in my kitchen. I am terrified that I have the ability to smell him. I am terrified because I assume he left so quickly because he hates me for being a horrible daughter. I am terrified because I have to deal with his passing by myself because my family is so emotionally unavailable. I am terrified because he and Marc have abandoned me at the same time, and it's so fucking unfair and painful that I can't stand it and have no idea how I am going to get through this. I collapse on the floor and sob hysterically until I don't feel anything except my raw heart and the warm puddle of tears on the cold wood floor under my face.

January 2017

I thought I needed this trip alone to finally detox from the breakup with Marc, but I'm not feeling it. This is my seventh trip to Hawaii, and the weather has never been worse. I mean, it's not horrible, but I've never seen it rain so much here, not even during the rainy season. This isn't helping my mood. Hawaii is usually magical and I depended on the amazing weather to lift my spirits. I got up this morning to go hiking, but it was raining, so I decided to wait for the weather to clear and work out in a nearby park instead. Walking to the park, I notice the rain has stopped, but I can tell by the foreboding sky it will start again at any time.

Maybe it was a mistake to come here by myself. I feel so lonely and disconnected right now.

My phone is on vibrate and buzzes in my bag. It keeps buzzing. It's a phone call, not a notification. I take my phone out of the bag and see that it's Kimberly Parke.

Kimberly was my real estate agent when I bought my condo. Incidentally, ten years ago, her friend, Julia, dated Marc. Through meeting Kimberly as my real estate agent, I learned that she has a raging Saint Patrick's Day party every year. At least it used to be raging. It's pretty tame now. I know because I have been on the guest list for two years. I have even met Julia. Kimberly and I generally don't talk outside of the annual party.

My intuition is on high alert, and I feel my heart drop to my stomach like a brick. Something is up. I don't feel like answering, especially since I need to get this workout in before it starts raining again. I have come a long way from severely disordered eating and workout habits, but I don't think it ever goes away. I still have the critical inner voice that barrages me if I miss a workout, which is why I am working out on vacation in the first place. My phone buzzes with a voicemail notification. I am still walking to the park, so I read the voice-to-text message.

> Hi, Angie! I just wanted to call you about the party this year, you know, with Marc and everything. I wanted to make sure you were comfortable coming. Anyway, give me a shout later!

My intuition sends me a crystal clear message.

Marc is dating Julia again, and they are going to be at the party together.

My obsessive need-to-know overrides my obsession to work out. I call Kimberly back. "Hi, Kimberly! How are you?"

This is so fake. Let's cut to the chase.

"Good! What are you up to?"

"I'm on vacation in Hawaii."

To detox from Marc, so don't ruin this for me.

"Oh! Are you there by yourself?"

"Yeah, I needed some time to myself."

Cut. To. The. Chase.

"Oh well, I just wanted to call you about the party. You know Marc and Julia are together, right?

I think I am still walking down the sidewalk, but I don't know. I'm not even sure if I am still breathing.

We just broke up. He must have been with her while we were still together.

I try to hold it in, but I can't. The shame explodes in my chest. I start crying.

Shit, I don't want Kimberly to know how heartbroken I am.

"Oh honey, I thought you knew."

How the hell was I supposed to know? Plus, I told her I was in Hawaii by myself. Why would she drop this bomb on me right now?

I came here to recover from Marc. Now, I am four thousand miles away from anyone who can hug me. My workout turns into me laying in the park in the fetal position sobbing helplessly by myself. The shame is so paralyzing that I lay there for an hour. My self-discipline forces me to peel myself off the ground, but I end up going to the beach and crying by myself for the rest of the day. Any hope that I had of Marc and me getting back together has been obliterated.

Why do I have to suffer through life alone?

CHAPTER 4

THE heartbreak and shame of losing Marc and the guilt of not having the opportunity to make amends with Dad are squeezing my heart like a vice. It's so debilitating that I can't do anything right now, except sob hysterically and beg God to make the pain disappear.

Is there a God?

My first writing class is in an hour. I manage to pull myself together and get ready, but pure terror replaces the extreme despair.

What the hell am I doing taking a comedy writing class?

I'm going to be in a class full of twenty-something dudes who are hilarious and have tons of experience with comedy and writing. I don't belong there.

I'm not a writer.

I'm going to make an ass of myself.

I should stay home and cry.

On the other hand, I need to get out of the house for my mental health. At least get some fresh air. And The Second City is only a four-block walk from my condo. I'll go, and if it's horrible, I won't go back. There, I just made a deal with myself. I enter the classroom with regret, still feeling like a numb zombie from my emotional breakdown earlier.

This is too scary. I should have stayed home.

But, wait. There are people older than me! There are females! I instantly feel more relaxed. Our teacher, Jim, is immediately funny, and we go around the room introducing ourselves. I am not the only person without formal comedy experience! We do some im-

prov exercises to warm up the creative parts of our brains. At one
point, we get paired off to do writing exercises with partners. I am
partnered with Andy, who said that he is a practicing stand-up
comedian in his introduction.

*He is probably hilarious and doesn't want to be paired with an
amateur.*

We both write stories based on our given prompts. When it is
time to read, I go first. My story is about a hiker who is accosted
by a serial killer. The serial killer smells the hiker's trail mix and
panics, as he has a fatal peanut allergy. The hiker senses this fear
and starts throwing trail mix as a weapon against the serial killer,
which chases him away. As I read this short story, Andy laughs
out loud several times. This is music to my ears and boosts my
confidence. I leave the first class of Sketch Comedy Writing with
a vigor I haven't felt in many years, especially in the past few weeks
now that my world is in a different dimension. I love writing. I love
laughing. I love this class. My heart is overflowing with pure joy.

Luckily, this gets me through the drive to Fort Wayne after
class. Mom and I are making arrangements tomorrow for Dad's
funeral next weekend and I need to figure out what to do with his
house. I don't know anything about any of this. Because Amy and I
have different fathers and my parents are divorced, I am next of kin,
so all of this is my responsibility. I already feel like I am wearing a
backpack full of rocks, and it keeps getting heavier.

The drive to Fort Wayne is boring as usual. Amy hasn't even
reached out to me to offer her condolences. Mom said she isn't
coming home from Los Angeles because she has to work. This
strikes me as odd because I know Mom largely financially supports
Amy, so I wouldn't think money would play a factor in the decision. As I make my way to Mom's house, the familiar anxiety sets
in. I hate this city. It's so boring and has so many isolating, lonely
memories of my childhood. At Mom's house, it's cold, emotionally
and physically. She keeps the thermostat on, at most, sixty-five
degrees, which I think is inhumane. Every time I visit, I beg her
to turn it to at least seventy-two degrees, which is technically
room temperature, but she's too cheap, I mean frugal, to pay for

the extra heat, even if I ask her to when I visit. For that reason, I usually make it a goal to only spend one night at her house before I bounce back to Chicago. During my time spent at her house, I usually stuff my face with food, to fill the emotional and physical discomfort. I have to spend two nights this time, which adds to my frustrations. The funeral isn't until next weekend, so I have to do it all over again next week.

I wake up sweating in the little twin bed in Mom's guest room. The space heater provides too much heat, but it was better than freezing my ass off. I slept like shit because what adult can get a good night's sleep in a twin bed? Mom and I drive to the funeral home. I usually hate her lack of boundaries by needing to have control over things that are none of her business. Still, I have no idea how to do any of this, and even if I did, I don't have the emotional capacity right now. The worst part is that I have to hold it in because that's what we do in our family. If I cried in front of Mom, it would make her uncomfortable, and she never knows what to say, so she usually gets frustrated with me for being too emotional.

The funeral coordinator, Ryan, is perfect for his role because even though it seems like a sleazy job to be selling overpriced coffins and urns while customers are experiencing some of the worst days of their lives, his words are surprisingly tactful. I feel at ease with his suggestions. I feel guilty because Mom and I have on our emotional armor, so we don't seem like we are grieving at all. I am worried that Ryan thinks we are heartless. Little does he know— I would love to do the fetal-position-on-the-floor-crying-hysterically thing right about now. We make the preparations and schedule the funeral for the following Sunday.

The next stop is Dad's house. Mom has already been there, and she says it is not clean. I know he was a hoarder, but this is not enough description to prepare me for walking into the childhood home that I haven't lived in since 1998 and haven't been to in many years. Mom's sister, Donna, volunteered to meet us at Dad's house and help because one thing I value about my family is that we truly step up and help each other out in times of need.

Years of embedded cigarette smoke sting my nostrils even before I get a foot in the door. Mom has already stated that we are only staying an hour because that is all she can stand. I am on board with that. I can't believe how small this house is and that all four of us were living under this roof at one time. There is junk and trash everywhere. It's not as bad as some homes that I have heard about with animal feces and whatnot, but there is a lot of dirt, dust, and the wretched stench of cigarettes. And, for whatever reason, there are coins everywhere. The furnishings are the bare minimum, making me happy because that is one less thing to deal with. The temperature in the house is cold. The air becomes even colder when we open the windows to the winter breeze to relieve the stale cigarette smell. Dad's best friend, Steve, has also been working on cleaning up the house and making necessary repairs. Steve and Mom are going to do all of the preparations to put it on the market so I won't have to drive back and forth every weekend.

We start in the kitchen, cleaning out drawers and cupboards. Donna is extremely efficient, and it turns out it is because her boyfriend, Robert's mother, recently passed away, and she's had practice. We follow her system of organizing into the trash, donate, and keep piles. The only things that make it into the keep pile are two box cutters because these seem like an easier way to open my Amazon boxes. I am cleaning out a cupboard and the nostalgia hits me like a ton of bricks. In the 1980s, restaurants like Pizza Hut and McDonald's would have limited edition glass tumblers. Dad still had The Flintstones, Scooby-Doo, and Care Bears collections. I think those are from Pizza Hut. There are also some Charlie Brown glasses that I think are from McDonald's. My flashback to what seems like simpler times is interrupted by Mom. "Tell Donna how Dad visited you."

My chest tightens.

If I wanted to tell Donna about it, I would have told her.

$\mathcal{I}$N 2016, Mom and her siblings planned a 90th birthday party for my grandma, my last surviving grandparent. I usually don't visit Fort Wayne on non-holidays, but ninety years old was a milestone. It was in the banquet room of an Italian restaurant. After the meal, everyone who wanted to speak took turns sharing their favorite memories. I don't like to be the center of attention, so I remained silent. I was sitting at a table with Donna. She kept nudging me because she wanted me to tell the story about how one time Grandma rushed me off the phone because Judge Judy was about to start. I didn't want to tell the story. I didn't want the spotlight and it was embarrassing that Judge Judy took precedence over talking to me. I told Donna that I didn't want to tell the story. After every speaker, she nudged me to tell the story. Each time, I told her that I didn't want to tell the story. Donna took the wheel. "Angie has a story that she wants to tell!"

NO! What the hell is she doing?

I shook my head, wondering which shade of red my face was. The heat told me it was more than just a blush. Because I refused and Donna wouldn't rest until the story was broadcast, she took control of the situation. "One time, Mary was talking to her granddaughter, Angie, and she rushed to get off the phone because Judge Judy was on."

Like a bad game of telephone, she left out a lot of details. And because it was so short and to the point, the whole thing seemed extremely anti-climatic and unnecessary.

Was it really that important to violate my boundaries to tell a petty, one-line story?

My uncle, Dan, and his wife, Janet, were at our table. Dan urged Janet to tell a story. Janet is even more quiet and shy than me, which should speak volumes to Dan that she wouldn't want to speak. But he wanted her to tell a story. She told him she didn't want to tell a story. Unlike Donna, he didn't volunteer and tell the story himself, but he let it be known that his need for her to tell the story was more important than her need to not be seen. "I'm disappointed in you, Janet."

I felt a strike to my heart as if the words were directed at me.

She didn't do anything wrong! YOU want her to speak up, not her!

Then, I did something that I'd never done before. "Janet, I'm proud of you for doing what feels comfortable for you."

I stuck up for her, right in front of my controlling, boundaryless family. Donna gasped in the horror of my betrayal while Dan's jaw hit the floor, but I didn't give a shit.

Why can't I do that for myself?

*U*NFORTUNATELY, I still don't have the courage to enforce my boundaries, especially with Mom. I oblige and tell Donna the story about how I smelled Dad in the kitchen.

The drive back to Chicago is a relief. A relief from the emotional pain of being in Fort Wayne. A relief from the emotional and physical coldness of Mom's house. A relief from the emotional pain of seeing Dad's house in that condition. Unfortunately, I don't have relief from the heartbreak of Marc or the guilt of Dad's passing, and I have to put on my brave face and go through this whole dog and pony show again next weekend for the funeral. At least in my own home, I can express my emotions without judgment from anybody else.

*W*HY *am I going back? I don't belong there.*

It's Saturday at noon, and I am in the middle of another emotional breakdown. To make matters worse, my pre-class jitters are still here for the second week of my sketch comedy writing class.

Sure last week went fine, but it was a fluke.

I'm not a writer.

I'm going to make an ass of myself.

The second class is even funnier than the first because we had homework to write a sketch and we are using the first half of our class to act out each other's sketches. Our assignment was to write a sketch using The Second City five-point formula, focusing on stakes to drive the action. I am terrified that everybody else's sketches will be entertaining, and I will receive scathing reviews.

Even though this is the first sketch I have ever written, it receives good feedback from Jim and the other students. I can feel my shame rising to the surface during moments of constructive criticism, but I realize the comments are intended to help. My confidence is building! After acting out each other's sketches and reviewing feedback, we go into the next lesson about characters. After the lesson, Jim erases the whiteboard to document some brainstorming ideas. He asks for suggestions on personality types. As students shout out words, I cringe at the thought of allowing myself to be seen. I don't think I have ever spoken up in a classroom. Jim then asks for examples of transformations. I don't know if it's the rush from putting myself out there with writing my first ever sketch comedy, but I feel something that I rarely feel.

"Coward to brave!"

Did I just speak up in class?!

I have a low-grade high for the rest of the class. This lasts until I get in my car to drive back to Fort Wayne. The funeral is tomorrow and there is more work to be done at Dad's house. The dread of the drive to Fort Wayne feels the heaviest that it's ever been. As I step into the cool air of Mom's house, I brace for the frigid weekend activities.

CHAPTER 5

THANKFULLY, or perhaps, unfortunately, Mom has been to a funeral or two in her lifetime, so she knows what to do and has prepared some pictures and mementos that she took from Dad's house, such as trophies and awards, to display at the funeral home. Mom and I spend the evening going through old photo albums for more pictures for the picture boards. The family pictures fall off around the early '90s, so we don't have any recent pictures of Dad. I am okay with that because he looks happier in the '80s than I ever remember him. One of my favorite pictures is Dad on our old brown couch with our Great Dane, Scooby. I feel sad about how unhappy he had been all of the years since then.

What the hell happened?

I notice that there are an interesting amount of pictures of me crying as a child. There is one from the day that Dad brought Scooby home. Even though he was a puppy, it was too distressing for me. And there is a picture of me in some kind of preschool ceremony, clearly miserable and crying. Then, there is one that I think is from the infamous Florida trip because I am in our Fort Myers timeshare with red, swollen eyes, fresh from crying.

Why are there so many pictures of me crying?

Why am I being photographed instead of hugged?

It looks pathetic to see myself in the pictures crying alone and it uncovers more sadness around how misunderstood I was as an empathetic child. To distract me from the emotional discomfort, I sit on the armchair in the living room, prop my feet up on the ottoman, and start scrolling Instagram to dissociate. Kimberly posted pictures of her St. Patrick's Day party, which was today. It's multiple photos within the same post. I scroll through to the last picture— Marc and Julia embraced in a kiss. Ice runs through my veins.

Mom walks by, catches a glimpse of my feet, and reaches for the bunion on my left foot. "Oh, your bunion is so big! You are probably going to need to get that removed one day."

Rage erupts like a volcano, and dances the tango with shame and despair from seeing an actual photo of Marc and Julia.

I can't handle this! She never has anything positive to say!

And, of course, I don't say a word, stuffing my emotions even further down the black hole. Her cat, Rocco, jumps on my lap. The rage inside me wants to swat him off, but then he starts purring, and I welcome a loving, warm body in this house.

$\mathcal{I}$ am less zealous than last weekend with the space heater, and for the first night, that proves to be a mistake. I wake up freezing in the middle of the night. I get up to go to the bathroom, turn the thermostat up to seventy degrees, and crank up the space heater. Once again, I wake up sweating in the little twin bed. I am dreading the funeral and want to get it over with. Before Mom and I leave for the funeral home, I notice the thermostat is back on sixty-five degrees.

I'm not good enough for her to turn the thermostat to room temperature, even though she knows I can't stand being cold.

I am not important.

A lot of Mom's family shows up to pay their respects, which I appreciate because my parents have been divorced for almost twenty years. None of my cousins on Mom's side are there, and none of them have even reached out to me for condolences. But Mom said my Aunt Donna and her boyfriend, Robert, were originally going to be out of town this weekend, but they changed their plans so that they could support me. Dad's friend Steve walks in. I haven't seen him since high school, but I remember his face. I don't know what I would do without him helping me with the repairs and cleaning of Dad's house. He makes a beeline to me and gives me a huge, comforting hug. I choke up but manage to speak my appreciation. "Thank you so much."

Dad's brother, Jim, from Minnesota, his son, Michael, Dad's brother, Ron, and his sons, Ben and Aaron, are here too. I thought it would be awkward talking to them because I haven't seen any of them since Grandpa Hawkins' funeral in 2002, but it is comforting to have Dad's family here, and I find them extremely easy to engage with.

It's almost time for the ceremony. I am supposed to sit in the front row with Mom, but I am sitting in the second row, chatting with Donna, Robert, and Grandma until the ceremony starts. Grandma doesn't do well with not being in control. "Ang, you need to sit in the front row."

"I know. I'll move in a minute."

"The ceremony is about to start. You need to move now."

"I will. In a minute."

"If you don't move to the front row right now, I am taking you out of my will!"

I don't deserve to be loved.

The shame surfaces like the sting of bile in your throat right before you throw up. I have enough shame between Marc leaving me for Julia and not stepping up to my relationship with Dad, so I force it back down. Maybe it's the two sketch comedy writing classes I have under my belt or maybe I am too emotionally exhausted to have the energy for a verbal filter. Wit replaces shame. "That means that I am in the will if you have to take me out!"

Donna backs up my game. "You can have her junk. I don't want it."

I move to the front row. I don't give a shit if I am in the will or not, but it hurts my feelings that Grandma's love is that conditional. Mom isn't here because she is standing in the aisle, socializing with some guests, which, of course, triggers Grandma's need to be in control. "Colleen, you need to sit in the front row."

This request collides with Mom's equally unrelenting need for control. "What's WRONG with you?!?"

I wonder if my cringe is noticeable or only internal.

Oh my God, Mom, that was loud. And mean. And embarrassing.

I turn around from my seat in the front row to look at Grandma, sitting right behind me. Tears are welling up in her eyes from Mom's verbal barrage. I instinctively reach for her hand and hold it. She squeezes my hand and forces a smile through the tears. I can't wait for the ceremony to start.

And then it starts, and I can't wait for it to be over. A pastor says a few words. There is a song. And then there is an open forum for people to go up to speak. I do not want to speak because I obviously hate allowing myself to be seen. Besides, what the hell am I going to say?

Yeah, um, I haven't really talked to Dad in ten years. I don't even think he loved me. He definitely hated me because I'm a horrible daughter.

He was totally emotionally unavailable and drank himself to sleep in his recliner, but I'm sure he was a nice guy.

I don't know him well enough to say anything about him.

Luckily, a lot of other people want to speak. Steve's wife, Linda, cries as she talks about when Steve was out of town and their waterbed sprung a leak, and Dad came to the rescue. One of his friends, David, talks about the memories of working together and what an amazing soul he was. He walks away from the podium sobbing like a baby. My eyes are completely dry. My body is too tense to produce tears. I may or may not be breathing. I should probably relax my shoulders away from my ears, but I can't move.

Who is this man that they are talking about?

I had never seen this side of him. Then, Dad's drinking friends from the bar get up one by one crying, and sharing monologues about how loving, caring, and beautiful his soul was.

Why didn't we get this side of Dad?

I am frozen. I can't turn my head. I look over at Mom with my peripheral vision only. Her face is as tight and clenched as I imagine mine looks. I am certain she is having the same thoughts. After the pain I have gone through, especially with Marc and Dad, I am not sure that I believe in God anymore, but I am so desperate for people to stop getting up and talking about this side of Dad that I have never met that I silently start praying. By praying, I mean begging.

God, please don't let anybody else get up and speak.

God, please let this be over soon.

GOD, PLEASE MAKE THIS STOP.

A few more people get up. One is one of his bar friends. Either she is drunk or has an erratic personality, possibly both. She rambles on about how much she loved Dad. I can't tell if she is talking about love as friends or lovers. It doesn't matter. If anybody else gets up to talk after her, I am going to lose my shit. The pain from not receiving the love he seemed to be giving to everybody else has consumed my entire body. I am already so exhausted that I can't take this. Finally, the ceremony ends.

Thank you, God!

I take a large, white rose bouquet home from Dad's funeral. The fragrance is bittersweet on the drive home. At home, I put them on the 1960s olive green, hand-carved, wooden credenza Grandma gave to me seven years ago when she redecorated her living room. The flower arrangement was so beautiful, and I wanted it to last forever, but after about a week, that foul, stale flower smell set in, so I threw them away.

I am working from home on the island in my kitchen. The sharp smell of the roses brings me out of my work trance. I look up at the credenza.

Oh, that's right, I threw them away. But what am I smelling? Did I drop one?

The smell is so distinct that I am positive that I dropped one while throwing them away. I crawl on the floor, checking under the furniture, but come up empty-handed. I take a huge inhale through my nose to see if I am close to the lone rose. I smell nothing.

Wait, the roses I just smelled were fresh, not rotting.

I feel a thud in my chest as my heart skips a beat. "Dad?"

Why was he here again?

I'm already sitting on the floor, so it's easy to assume my usual fetal position and sob until I'm exhausted. The guilt crevasse is too wide to handle.

Does he hate me for not talking to him for so long?
Is he mad that I didn't speak at his funeral?

OVER the past few years, I have gone to workshops on manifestation and intuition, hosted by Spiritual Consultant, Luna and her partner, Celeste. There is something about the energy of their space that raises your vibration the moment you step foot inside. Their workshops feel enchanting, and I have always met amazing people in their studio. Luna also provides one-on-one medium and psychic services and is so in demand that she has a two-year waiting list. But, if you are already a client, all you have to do is text Celeste, and she will fit you in Luna's schedule as soon as possible. I feel bad about taking advantage of my existing client status, and I don't even know if I believe in mediumship, but I am desperate for answers. I hope she can connect to Dad. I text Celeste to tell her that Dad has died, and I really would like to talk to him through Luna. She texts me about a day later, which feels like an eternity, and says that she can get me in the following week. A week seems like a long time, but I don't want to ask any more favors. I agree.

Should I prepare questions? What if he hates me? Then what am I going to do?

I have no idea what to expect, and I want to get it over with. The day before my appointment, Celeste calls me. "Hi! Luna is so sorry, but she is sick and needs to reschedule for next week."

No! What about me?!

But I know Luna, and I don't want her to try to connect to Dad if she is not feeling her best because she probably won't receive clear messages. Even though I'm not convinced about the whole medium thing, I am convinced I need help. And hope. Both. And soon. But I know Luna wouldn't call off the session if her illness weren't serious. I endure another week of torture, on edge the entire time because I am afraid that Celeste will call again to reschedule. Dad hasn't visited again since the roses incident, so I think he hates me. The anxiety feels like a black hole in my chest, sucking away any hope of happiness ever again.

What if I feel like this forever?

The day of my appointment arrives, and even though I have been looking forward to this day for two weeks, I am scared to death. I have no idea what the hour with Luna will reveal and have a bad feeling that I will not like what I hear. Celeste greets me at the door and gives me a huge, comforting hug. Luna is soon to follow. They both give off such amazing energy. It's like when you visit a beautiful place in nature, like a waterfall or the top of a mountain, and you can feel the magic in the atmosphere. I know I am in good hands. I have chills as Luna takes me into her back room, which feels more magical than their public space. I see a Kleenex box next to the chair where I sit down.

I hope I don't cry.

Luna doesn't say a word. She closes her eyes to get connected to her Spirit Guides. She doesn't even have to open her eyes or say anything, I can feel the energy in the room shift, and I break down into tears. I reach for a Kleenex as she opens her eyes to start our session.

Do I need to tell her what's going on in my life?

"Oh, Angie, the heartbreak."

Apparently not.

Luna cringes, and her nose wrinkles. "Your Dad has a specific smell, doesn't he?"

"Yes!"

"What does he smell like?"

"Cigarettes."

She nods. I can tell by her face his smell is revolting to her, but I am not offended. I'm just glad that she was able to connect with him. "Your dad says that he forgives you. He understands why you needed a break from him and knows what you did was best for you. When he was on this side, his true self was masked by his addictions, and he says he is sorry that he couldn't be there for you."

She pauses to receive more information. "Your dad is funny. He doesn't believe in people like me, so he keeps trying to pull away, but I'm like, 'We're already doing this, so let's keep doing it.' Does that sound like your dad?"

I laugh because that totally sounds like Dad. "Oh yeah."

"Tell me about the shirt."

"Shirt?"

"Did you take a shirt from his closet?"

"Yes! I took a sweater from his closet!"

When Mom and I were cleaning out Dad's bedroom, I found an old sweater he had from high school. It was a big, heavy wool sweater and I knew I would never wear it, so I don't know why I took it. I think I just wanted something of his other than box cutters. The only other person besides me who knows I have the sweater is Mom. Any doubts I had about mediumship have been extinguished. I find it comforting that even though I can't see him or hear his messages, Dad is involved in this interaction.

"He wants you to know that while he couldn't be there for you while he was alive, he is here for you now. That is why he visits you."

What a relief! He doesn't hate me!

She gives me a few more messages from Dad and then moves to Marc. "Tell me about the other heartbreak."

I reach for more Kleenex and give her the Cliff Notes version of Marc— the trauma bond, my co-dependency on him even though he didn't treat me the way I deserved, how he always gave me the silent treatment, and how he ultimately kicked me to the curb for Julia. Up and down, around and around, and off and on for the better part of eight years, but the last four being the worst because instead of accepting that he wasn't capable of being in a loving, committed relationship, I tried to convince him to change. Luna basically tells me I need to get over him, which I already know, but can't and don't want to accept. We are almost at the end of the hour session, and I haven't asked any questions yet, but there is one burning question that I am desperate to know the answer to. "Why didn't Marc choose me?"

"Do you really want to know?" Her tone is challenging.

Shit, maybe I don't.

Curiosity killed the cat. I nod yes.

"Because you didn't accept him for who he is. She does."

I have a breakdown right in front of Luna. I don't think I have ugly cried in front of anyone before. The worst part is, I know she's right. Instead of walking away, I wanted to change him into someone who loved and accepted me unconditionally. Even though I have the closure I need with Dad, my heart feels even more damaged and raw than it did before. Before leaving Luna's, she gives me a carnelian bracelet, an orange crystal for courage, vitality, and confidence.

I go home to work for the rest of the afternoon. Before logging back in, I go to the bathroom. As I splash cold water on my face, a tornado of emotions erupts and is so intense that I collapse on the floor. The shame is debilitating. I feel shame for the role I played in the dysfunction with Marc. I feel shame for not accepting him for who he was. I feel shame for not having the self-respect to walk away on my own. The cold, hard truth is that it's my fault I am grieving Marc and Dad at the same time because even though my hands were raw and bleeding from holding on, I didn't have the courage to walk away from Marc a long time ago because I was too afraid of being alone. I'm not grieving Marc. I am grieving being alone.

I fucked up. This is why I don't deserve to be loved.

The shame comes to the surface but doesn't leave, so I wallow in it on the bathroom floor for two whole hours.

When does this end?

Chapter 6

Two months ago, I reached out to my friend, Lily, to tell her about Dad's passing and invited her to lunch over the weekend. The intention behind the lunch invitation was to get out of the house and be around someone comforting and familiar and, hopefully, share a laugh to feel something other than sadness. Lily and I have been friends for ten years. We met when I started working for Sara Lee. We both worked in Finance on different teams, but bonded immediately. Over the years, we have ebbed and flowed through different jobs and phases of hanging out from quite frequently, to not much at all. But because she was one of the first friends I made in Chicago, I always feel a special pull to her. We haven't been hanging out much lately, but we do have lunch about once a month. So when I texted her about Dad, her response was unexpected.

> Hi, Angie. Sorry for your loss. I'll check my schedule and get back to you.

I know texts can be weird, but this sounds really cold.

I gave her the benefit of the doubt and assumed it was my misunderstanding of the tone of the text. But my suspicions were confirmed when she never got back to me on the lunch offer. A month ago, one month after I texted her, she sent a group text to me and two of her other friends, who I know from hanging out with Lily, but definitely would not consider them friends of my own. The group text was an invitation for all four of us to have lunch.

Is this a joke?

My heart, already broken into a million pieces, felt one more jab. I get it that we haven't been super close lately, but I don't understand why she blew off one-on-one lunch when she knew Dad had died. Plus, she knows Dad's passing was on top of the Marc grief. I was so hurt that I muted the group text and didn't engage. An entire month has gone by, and today, Lily sends me an individual text, responding to the text I sent two months ago.

> Hi, Angie. Sorry for not getting back to you about lunch. I can be available on Sunday. Let me know what time works for you.

I'm at a loss for words and don't know how to respond. Usually, I would sweep my feelings under the rug, but I don't have the energy to pretend everything is okay. It's morning, and I am working, so I will wait until later in the day to respond.

Evening rolls around, and I still have no words. I wake up in the morning, and I am still speechless. My inner voice is not.

I don't want to be friends with her anymore.

I have never intentionally cut off a friendship. Usually, one person moves away, or the friendship slowly fades on its own. Is it a thing to break up with a friend? I contemplate this concept. I'm not sure how I feel about it. Because I take several days to go through this thought process, Lily sends me another text.

> Hi Angie, just checking in to see if you have decided on lunch.

The hurt is replaced with anger.

Oh, she didn't respond for two months, and now she is getting all impatient because I am taking a few days to respond?

All of my other friends have been supportive about Dad's passing. I don't understand why she isn't.

Why would I want a friend like that in my life?

I don't. A feeling creeps in that I have only felt a few other times in my life— inner strength. This friendship isn't serving us anymore. I have never ended a friendship, so I am unsure how to do it. I start crying as I text her.

What if she hates me? What if this is a mistake?

> Hi Lily, after thinking about it, I have decided that I no longer wish to continue this friendship. Thank you for all of the good times and I wish you the best.

Should I be doing this over the phone instead? I have no idea how to communicate. She is going to hate me.

> Hi Angie, I consider you a really good friend and don't want to lose the friendship. Can you please re-consider?

Shit, she's right. What am I doing?

> I'll think about it and get back to you tomorrow.

I sleep on it, but my intuition is still saying no when I wake up. I start crying all over again. When I text back, I feel the need to explain myself.

> Hi Lily, I have thought about it and I stand firm on my decision. I was there for you when you needed a job referral from Sara Lee and couldn't rely on anyone else because you had been fired. I don't understand why you couldn't be there for me when my dad died.

> Oh you just had to bring up that I got fired. You knew the situation was unfair.

She continues on a rant about how I am rubbing it in her face that she got fired. I don't give a shit that she got fired. That's not what this is about. I instantly regret bringing it up because she totally missed my point that I was there for her, but she wasn't there for me. And now that I think about it, bringing it up feels like a quid pro quo statement anyway. In hindsight, I wish I would have ghosted her because I don't think there is anything I can say that will make her understand why the lunch diss bothers me so much. I stop engaging in the text thread, and she sends me one last text.

> Well, this tells me what kind of person you are. You gave Marc a million second chances. You will get what you deserve in life. Take care.

Another stab in my heart. I get what she is saying, but Marc is why I don't give second chances anymore. I don't have the emotional strength for this. Dad fucking died, and all I wanted was to have lunch with her, and now she hates me.

How am I going to get through the rest of my life?
I don't know what the hell I am doing.

Chapter 7

*I*T's an odd-numbered year and summer, so that only means one thing: it's time for Will's bi-annual rooftop party. Will is a member of the gym and has earned a name for himself by hosting a next-level rooftop party every other year. Unlike Kimberly's St. Patrick's Day party, it's guaranteed to be a hardcore throw-down every single time. It's classy, with all attendees showing out, a full buffet, a professional DJ, and a real dance floor laid out on the rooftop deck overlooking the Chicago skyline. Everybody always talks about the event until the next one rolls around. It is a highly-touted honor to be on the actual guest list, but it's not completely exclusive, as guests are welcome too, making it fun to mingle with a different dynamic each time. The mingling and the dancing are playful, yet intimate. For that reason, Will's rooftop party is the kind of party where couples go together and, if you are single, you are not under any circumstance going home alone. I used to go with Marc. Two years ago, we were fighting, so I went with big brother Joe and his friend, and went home with Marc.

I received the email invite from Will a few months ago. I RSVP'd Yes, hoping that Marc and Julia would be broken up by now and he and I would reconcile and go together. I am afraid to go now.

What if he is there with Julia?

I would be so humiliated and heartbroken if I saw them there together. I text Joe to see if he is going. Maybe if I can go with him again, he can be my emotional support if Marc and Julia show up together. My phone vibrates with a text from Joe.

> I am going to be in Brazil. You shouldn't go.

> Why? Is Marc going to be there with Julia?

Obsessive minds need to know.

> I don't know. Don't go.

> Is Marc going to be there?

> I don't know. Don't go.

He knows that Marc is going to be there. I just know it.

> I'm going. I'll bring a friend.

Most of my friends are married with kids, so my friend options for this event are limited. Lindy from sketch comedy writing class and I have been getting chummy. She seems wild. I am positive she would like this event. I text Lindy, and she is down.

My confidence is high until the day of the party. I am terrified of seeing Marc and Julia together. I couldn't even handle seeing a picture of them kissing on Instagram.

That was five months ago. I am much stronger now.

I go to the beach to relax. My phone vibrates with a text. It's Lindy.

> Hi Beautiful, I can't go to the party tonight because my son is leaving for college on Monday and I have to buy him a car.

Um, she is just thinking of this now?

> Sure, no problem!

Now, I have a dilemma. Should I go to the rooftop party alone? That would be a bold move considering Marc and Julia will likely be there together. For some inexplicable reason, I am feeling bold today. By bold, I mean crazy. I am going. I don't dare tell Joe that Lindy bailed on me, or he will try to talk me out of this.

I wear a short royal blue skirt because I get a lot of compliments that I look good in blue and I also get a lot of compliments on my legs, presumably from all the years of running marathons. I am craving a hit off Marc. Even if he is with Julia, I want to see him in person. I haven't seen him since January. My stomach is so tight that I can't eat anything before getting ready for the party. Will usually has ribs and other good food on the spread, so I will eat when I get there. I know that there will also be a ton of alcohol, but I need something to calm my nerves. I take a shot of Don Julio before driving to Will's. I park in the parking garage of the gym. Part of me is scared to death, and part of me is proud of myself for putting myself out there. This is fearless as shit. Also, crazy as shit. Marc and Julia may be making out on the dance floor when I walk in. I may go psycho. Who knows?!

It starts to drizzle as I walk the four blocks to Will's building. With all of the ruminating thoughts, I didn't even notice that the weather looks questionable. I hope that the rain doesn't put a damper on the rooftop party. I brazenly walk in the door to the building, even though my hands are shaking. I get in the elevator to the fourth floor with a group of people going to the party. This calms my nerves. Until the short ride to the fourth floor is over. We step off the elevator. They head to Will's apartment. I skip the bullshit and head down the hallway that leads to the stairwell that leads to the rooftop. The sound of my heels hitting the metal stairs echoes against the walls as I travel what feels like the death march to the rooftop.

If Marc is with Julia, I will politely say "Hi" and then head downstairs as if I am going to the bathroom and then get the hell out of here.

I feel the thud of the DJ's bass in my chest.

Oh wait, that's my heart.

I can't hear the music until I timidly crack the door.

Screw it.

I swing it open. Surprisingly, the rooftop is not as crowded as it usually is, probably because of the rain. The sparse crowd makes Marc effortless to spot. His six-foot, five-inch muscular frame sticks out like a sore thumb. His eyes instantly meet mine, as he smiles and struts over to hug me. I melt in his arms. I am getting a hit, but like a junkie, I want more.

Wait, where is Julia?

I cautiously look around. She is tall and has curly blonde hair, so she should be easy to spot. I don't see her.

Is she downstairs?

Marc still has his hand on the small of my back as he leads me to a table to chat. I assume that Julia is not here, or he wouldn't be touching my back like this. At least, that is the story I am telling myself right now. We make small talk, and I am dying to know if he is still with Julia. We chat for awhile, and then he asks me if I want to dance.

Um, YES!

I have no self-control. I have wanted to see and touch him for so long. We don't even talk about how fucked up it ended or that I know about Julia.

"Chim chim cher-oo!"

The night wears on, and Julia is definitely not here, and Marc has his hands all over me, so he is definitely not with Julia anymore. His friend Shawn Dolla is here, and he is flirting with a girl from Spain. She is pretty, in a plain way, but keeps trying to smoke a cigar, making her seem rough and unattractive. But not to Shawn. I know that he is hooking up with her tonight. And I am hooking up with Marc. I'm on my third tequila shot of the night, and I already had one at home, and I rarely have more than two drinks. I feel kind of tipsy, but not sure if it is the alcohol or the high from Marc.

Shaggy's "It Wasn't Me" comes on. We are having so much fun singing and dancing that I have completely forgotten that we aren't together anymore and how he ended it so suddenly and how much that brought me to my knees and tore my world apart right before Dad died and left another void in my heart. But wait, here is Marc right in front of me with his hands all over me, and everything is better now. It's almost midnight, and the party is starting to clear out due to the rain. Marc invites Shawn Dolla and the Spanish girl back to his place for more drinks before turning to me. "Do you want to come?"

Um, YES!

"Okay."

I think I am acting casual, but I'm love drunk and tequila drunk, so who the hell knows. Shawn has also had too much to drink. Marc and I are still intertwined and dancing. Shawn has his phone out and takes a picture of us dancing. I ask him to text it to me. Then, we all head to Marc's.

We all walk to Marc's black truck because Shawn Dolla is parked at Marc's house. Marc reaches for my hand to hold it. I am giddy with the thought of us getting back together. I miss him so much. We can work out together again and go to new restaurants like we used to like to do. It's already mid-August, so I'm already planning the rest of our summer together. He drives back to his place. He has moved since we broke up, so I have never been there. On the way, I practice my Spanish skills with the Spanish girl.

Marc's new place is nice. He likes the industrial look, so, as in his last condo, there are exposed vents on the ceiling. I have to go to the bathroom. It's a two-bedroom, and there is an unattached bathroom across from the kitchen, but he leads me through his bedroom to his bathroom. After I finish, I join everybody in the kitchen. We are all starving, and Marc doesn't have much in terms of food, so we eat strawberry Uncrustables, his favorite snack, and dance in the living room. Shawn Dolla starts kissing the Spanish girl, and I wonder if her breath tastes like cigars. I mean, it has to. They leave. Obviously, to have sex, but I hope he is not a danger on the road.

"Should we get them a cab? He doesn't look okay to drive."

"They'll be fine. Let's go to bed."

I forget about Shawn's safety because this is music to my ears. We head to his bedroom, but we have both drank too much and are too tired to have sex.

We wake up in the morning and start making out, which leads to groping, which leads to me mounting him, and Marc finally addressing the elephant in the room. "You know I'm with Julia, right?"

Oh. My. Fucking. God.

I think I am still on top of him, but I don't know. I can't move. I can't think. I can't even cry. The shame has paralyzed most of my body functions. My brain is telling me one thing. And by telling, I mean screaming.

Run!

I swiftly unmount him and put on my clothes.

"Now you're mad."

Mad? I'm humiliated and hurt like hell!

My heart feels like it's been savagely ripped out of my chest, carelessly popped back in, and then slashed back out. I don't respond. I can't respond. I have no words.

"I thought you knew I was with her."

The rage wants to respond, but the shame is in control. Like a robot, I walk to the kitchen and gather the rest of my stuff. As I slip on my heels, I hear his voice from the bedroom. "Ang." He's pleading as if he wants me to stay and talk it out. A part of me would love to turn around and talk to him, but I am way too embarrassed. What the hell would I even say?

Why don't you love me?

Why didn't you ever accept me for who I am?

Why did you treat me like a piece of shit and chip away at my self-respect until there was nothing left??

I don't even want to know the answers to those questions anyway. I start my walk of shame out the door and into the elevator. I exit the building and hope that he doesn't follow me. Who am I kidding? He is not going to run after me. The sun is bright, and I don't have my sunglasses. I am wearing heels, and it's probably a mile walk to where my car is parked at the gym. My phone and money are in my car because I didn't want to carry a purse to Will's. All I have are my keys. I can't order an Uber, and I don't have money for a cab.

I take off my heels for the walk. It wouldn't be so bad if there weren't pebbles and bullshit all over the sidewalk. My feet start getting tore up, but all I can focus on is getting to my car. The shame is so explosive that I am positive everybody driving by can see. Plus, I am dressed like I'm doing a walk of shame, so it's basically like wearing a neon sign with a huge arrow. When I start feeling comfortable with being uncomfortable, I walk past a fire station, and the garage doors are wide open, exposing a crew of firefighters who are sitting in chairs, enjoying the view of the City of Chicago sidewalk that I am plodding along with my raw, tore up feet. I can feel all eyes on me. The shame sets my face and neck on fire in a way that even they can't put it out.

This is so embarrassing.

I want to die.

When it seems like the walk is never going to end, I arrive at my car. Part of me is holding onto hope that Marc has called or texted me. I open the glove compartment and check my phone before turning on the car. There are texts! None from Marc. But there is a text from Shawn Dolla at 12:01 a.m. It's the picture of Marc and me dancing. I snap back into reality.

Wait, how the hell is he still with Julia?

He was at Will's party alone. He had his hands all over me. People saw us together, including Shawn Dolla. He held my hand on the way to his truck. He took me home. There were no signs of her at his house. There was one toothbrush in the bathroom. There were all-male toiletries. He had all his food in his fridge and cupboard. He made out with me, got naked last night, and we almost had sex this morning.

How was I supposed to know?

I am exhausted because I only got a few hours of sleep, but there is no way I can sleep with all of this anxiety. There is only one thing to do. I go home and get ready to go to the gym.

It's empty. Probably because everyone was at Will's party last night. I trudge through my workout, mostly dissociating the entire time to keep myself from breaking down crying. Then, I go to the beach to relax for a few hours. I am a hysterical mess. I need someone to talk to. I call Joe. I know he is in Brazil, and I know he told me not to go to the party, but he is my go-to friend for support. I hit the green dial icon and pray that he answers.

"Hello?"

I can barely speak because I am so choked up. "Hey, Joe."

"Oh no, what happened. Please tell me you didn't go to the party."

I'm so embarrassed to tell him what happened. He warned me more than once not to go. I didn't understand then. I thought he was telling me not to go because he thought Julia and Marc were going to be there together, but I now realize that he was warning me not to go because he knows Marc is a dog and it would not end well for me whether he was at the party with Julia or not. Thankfully, Joe does not rub it in my face that he was right, and I should not have gone to the party. He listens with a compassionate ear, and I cry my heart out. I'm not sure because I repressed a lot of the memories, but I think this pain is worse than the pain I felt in February. I was doing so well in my recovery, and now I have to grieve all over again. I can't take this anymore.

The usual escape and dissociation methods are not enough. I need a way out of this pain. I've been through too much in the past six months. This feels like a nightmare that I can't escape. The shame spiral is too intense. I can't take it anymore.

Nobody is ever going to love me for who I am.

I want to die.

Chapter 8

My eyes pop open. I look down at my body. My blanket is covering me, and I feel my head on my pillow.

Wait, how did I end up in my bed?

I jolt out of bed in a panic but quickly realize how messed up my equilibrium is and almost fall into the wall. My bladder is about to burst, so I rush the ten steps to the bathroom. My movement is so erratic that it's questionable if I will make it without falling. I collapse onto the toilet seat, expecting relief from the struggle, but the effort is just as difficult seated. I hold on to the counter, so I don't fall mid-pee. I look at the shower, where I laid my pillow and blanket last night.

I need a game plan for when I leave the bathroom because I know this intense head spin will prevent me from going too far. I rush to the kitchen island and sit on a barstool facing all of the pill bottles from last night. There are three bottles, but only one has pills. I dump them out. It's a combination of Clonazepam and Hydrocodone, a benzodiazepine and opiate, both controlled substances. I had meticulously placed them in specific piles to be taken in intervals so that I didn't throw up by taking them all at once. I blacked out before taking them all but somehow placed them in one bottle.

Who saved me?

Why?

What am I going to do now?

I don't know how to get out of this dysfunctional thought cycle. At this point, I at least need to get it under control, but the emotional pain is erupting like a volcano, and I feel helpless against it. It's only 7 a.m. Beach yoga is at 9 a.m. Maybe I just need some fresh air and body movement. I'm so high that all I can do is lay in my bed until it's time to leave. I briefly consider going to the hospital, but they would probably just hook me up to an IV and wait for my body to detox. I'd rather suffer in the comfort of my own home. I change my clothes, grab my mat, and walk a mile to the beach to rejuvenate. Except, I can barely walk. Luckily, it's Saturday morning, so I probably look hungover to the other pedestrians. Technically, I am, but not in the way that they think. It's Labor Day weekend. Normally, I know all of the beach yoga regulars at the Saturday morning class, but since it's a holiday, a lot of the normal people aren't here, and there are many people that I don't recognize. I set my mat up to the side because I already anticipate having trouble balancing.

Shit, I can't even set my mat up straight.

I am so dizzy that it's nauseating.

I hope we start off laying down.

We start seated with some gentle flow movements, which are entirely too difficult for my motor skills.

I wonder how long it will take for this high to wear off.

I thought yoga would calm my heart, but all I can think about is laying on top of Marc while he told me he is with Julia.

I want to go home.

But I am not a quitter. I fumble through class, losing my balance in even the most simple poses. Another cascade of shame washes through me as I imagine everybody in class thinking I was out drinking all night and then tried to go to class.

You don't understand!

Finally, we enter savasana. This is a pose I can handle. Or not. My emotions are all over the place. It doesn't help that I physically feel like shit. I feel helpless and out of control about everything in my life.

I can't do this anymore. Being alive hurts too much.

As I walk home, I feel higher than I did on the walk to yoga. I am so miserable. My mind goes back to the pill bottles on my kitchen counter. There are still some left. Because I am still so high, if I take the rest all at once when I get home, that is enough for a fatal dose.

For the next four blocks, my mind is focused on going home and taking the rest of the pills. I turn down my street. Homestretch. All I need to do is get through the front door of my building, get in the elevator, and get through my front door. The pills are still right there on the kitchen counter.

As I approach my building, Jasmine walks out. Jasmine is a personal trainer at the gym. She cat-sits for her client, my neighbor, Jenny when she and her husband go to Australia, their home country. Jasmine and I know each other well from the gym. I have been a member for nine years, and she has been working at the gym for longer than that. Jasmine knows that I don't get wasted. Jasmine knows I am in excellent health and physical condition.

I try to walk straighter so that she doesn't notice how high I am, but I don't have the energy. I continue to stumble toward her. My face feels expressionless, and, unfortunately, I know my face is easy to read, so this can't look good. I can tell by the look on Jasmine's face that it doesn't. "Ang, are you okay?"

Just play it cool and then go upstairs and take the pills.

I can't even pretend to play it cool. I burst into tears and Jasmine gives me a huge hug. "Talk to me. What's wrong?"

Jasmine and I have never had this intimate of a conversation, but I feel so hopeless right now, and it feels so good to have someone to talk to, so I tell her everything, including why I am so high right now. I expect her to judge me. I expect her to berate me for being an idiot and going home with Marc. I expect to scare her off with how psycho I am right now. But Jasmine offers me a gift that I have received very few times— unconditional love.

She is completely compassionate and empathetic. We talk, we hug, and we talk some more. In the back of my mind, I still want to take the pills when I go upstairs until Jasmine mentions something. "You know, I was upstairs, and I needed to get something out of my car. I wasn't going to do it until later, but something kept telling me to come down now. When I saw you stumbling down the street, I knew something wasn't right. This happened for a reason. Do you understand?"

"Yes." And I do. I will not go upstairs and take the pills, but that also means white-knuckling life for the unknown future. The only thing that keeps me going is feeling there is a reason I am still here.

IT was creepy how calm and collected Marc was while blatantly cheating on Julia with me. How ironic to be on the other side of his scandalousness. I wonder if he ever told any of the other women about me, as he did me about Julia. If they knew, did they care? Because I don't know Julia very well, but from what I do know about her, I know that she would be pissed. If he did tell the other women, why didn't they ever reach out to me with the truth?

Wait, why don't I tell Julia the truth?

The truth hurts, but I would want to know if I were her. Isn't that Girl Code? I don't think it would be good for my image since I look like the villain. I don't want to embarrass myself. I don't want to admit to someone other than Joe and Jasmine what happened. But if I were her, I would want to know the truth.

I'm not brave enough to speak the truth.

I pause, and a total sense of peace overflows my body. Marc treated me like shit for many years, and I never stood up for myself. I mean, sometimes I tried, but it never lasted long. What he did to me the night of the rooftop party was not okay. Yes, part of the reason I want Julia to know is Girl Code, but another part of me that wants to speak up for myself in a way that I never have before. I start typing an email to Kimberly Parke, the only way I know how to contact Julia.

I'll write it, and if I change my mind, I don't have to send it.

Because Marc moved to his new condo after we broke up, there is no reason I should know anything about it. I type what happened and a super detailed description about his condo— the outside of the building, where to park, the elevator, the hallway, the number on his door, the paint on the wall of his bedroom, the all-night traffic sounds outside of his bedroom window, and the arrangement of the toiletries in his bathroom. I attach the picture Shawn Dolla took with Marc and me, dancing with his hands all over me. The image is a screenshot of my text thread that shows Shawn is the sender, and it has the time and date stamp from the text thread. I am so content that this is coming from a place of speaking the truth and not vindictiveness that I do not hesitate to hit send. I have no idea what Kimberly is going to think of this or if she will even send it to Julia, but I don't give a shit. I spoke up for myself and Julia and whatever happens, happens.

About an hour later, Kimberly responds. I can hear my heart thumping through my chest as I open the email.

Oh wow, this is big. Can I call you later?

Kimberly calls me a few hours later. "I wasn't expecting this. I mean, it's my birthday weekend and all, and I don't want to have to deal with this."

At first, I feel bad for ruining her birthday, but then I appreciate the beauty of poetic justice. "Oh, sorry, I didn't realize it was your birthday."

"Okay, well, I was thinking that I will call Julia and have her call you, and you can tell her."

Why is she weaseling out of telling Julia? Julia doesn't want to hear something like this from me. She wants to hear it from her friend. Is Kimberly this socially inept?

But upon reflection, I take accountability for my part in this mess, so I agree to woman up and tell Julia myself. I have nothing to lose. Kimberly and I devise a plan for her to call Julia and then Julia to call me. Around the time I am expecting the call from Julia, Kimberly calls me. As I thought, Julia was not interested in talking to me, so Kimberly told her. Julia demanded the email, presumably to confront Marc. About an hour later, my phone buzzes with a text notification. I rush to my phone to read the text from Kimberly, except it's from Marc.

> So you had to get your revenge on me. You win. You are a miserable person.

That wasn't what this was about. I know he would never believe me, but the last thing I want to do is hurt him and Julia. I, of all people, know how bad it hurts. But I had to stick up for myself and Girl Code, even though Julia probably doesn't see it that way. I thought standing up for myself would feel good, but now I feel shitty because I hurt two people, three if I include ruining Kimberly's birthday, even though I know in my heart that I did the right thing. I call Joe.

"You shouldn't have done that."

"Why?"

"It's none of your business."

"What do you mean it's none of my business? I was *there*. She deserved to know the truth."

"You shouldn't have done it."

Maybe he's right.

How am I ever going to get through the rest of my life?

I don't know what the hell I am doing.

I wake up early and walk through the resort to the beach to self-practice yoga and meditate before the beach gets busy. I normally don't like staying at resorts, but in the Dominican Republic, this is the practical option. The beach is pleasantly deserted, like I hoped it would be. I lay down my towel and follow a self-guided yoga practice for about forty-five minutes, facing the peaceful ocean. After I finish, there is calm and love overflowing my heart. I sit in my mind's silence to meditate, as the onshore wind blows the scents of the ocean directly into my face. The smell of a cigarette stings my nostril.

What the hell? I'm trying to meditate, damn it!

I didn't think there was anybody else on the beach other than people occasionally walking by. I turn around, and the only other person within smelling distance is the security guard at the resort.

Being on duty, it doesn't seem likely that he would be smoking. I look at his hands. Empty.

Who the hell is smoking?

Then, I realize because the wind is onshore, the only way I would be able to smell someone smoking is if they were in the ocean in front of me. The smell is gone just as fast as it arrived.

"Thank you, Dad."

CHAPTER 9

GETTING accepted into levels five and six of The Second City Chicago Sketch Writing Comedy Program has been the highlight of this past year. My class is writing and producing a show! But I know after our show finishes its one-month run at the end of March, this phase will be over, and I need to do something more permanently rewarding with my life. I am ready for a change. My finance job is draining the life out of me. I want to keep writing. The sketch comedy writing program has shown me that I am capable of writing and good at it, but I don't know what I want to do with it.

Dad was only sixty-three years old when he died. Life is too short not to do what you want to do. I want more out of life. It's February, and it's savagely cold and windy. I'm sick and tired of being cold all of the time, and I'm sick and tired of the negativity in Chicago. Everybody is so angry. Being an empath, I am like a sponge, soaking it all in. Something is missing. My mind keeps turning to Hawaii. I want to move there.

But how?

My friend Christi moved to Hawaii eleven years ago. Ever since visiting her for the first time in 2008, my heart has held a piece of Hawaii, and I have always wanted to move there. I can't immediately explain the allure. There is something about the magic in the atmosphere. Unlike Chicago, where I have to fight off the negative energy from infiltrating my aura, I welcome the Aloha spirit with open arms. Everyone seems happier. Plus, it's warm and sunny all year round. Then, of course, there's the fantasy element, and I know moving to a remote, tropical island will not solve my problems, but at least I can be somewhere warm and sunny while I deal with my shit. Christi moved off-island in 2013, but my heart still remembers. I miss Hawaii in the same heart-aching way that I would miss a person. There is still a part of me that regrets not moving there while Christi was there. My excuse has always been that I don't have enough money, but, at this point, I have saved quite a bit. My soul is slowly dying from the frigid cold and wind of February, but I am still too scared to move because of one last limiting belief.

I am thirty-seven years old. I am too old to make new friends.

But I know I have to make some more changes to my life. I keep thinking about it but don't do anything. I need to do something. I research motivational seminars in Chicago. I just need a kick in the butt to take some action. I find one that takes place in a few weeks. It's called 'Fear Not!' and is about overcoming your fears. The title sounds fierce, exactly what I need.

In the meantime, I will fake it until I make it. I Google Oahu real estate agents and email Agnes, regularly featured on HGTV's *Hawaii Life*. I confidently type out that I'm moving to Hawaii at the end of this year and give her a price range that is a terrifying amount over my actual budget. If I am going to fake it, I am going hard on all aspects. We arrange a time to have a conversation about the specifics.

I wonder if she can tell what an impostor I am.

After we talk, she sets me up on a weekly email alert for new listings. I feel like such a fraud. I need this motivational seminar, so I'm not scared about every single step toward moving to Hawaii. The day arrives, and I dress in a black sweater, distressed leggings, and bejeweled pearl and diamond black Steve Madden army boots.

I'm tired and don't feel like going, but I know this seminar will give me the boost I need to get my life in order. I am not too familiar with the neighborhood, River West. Therefore, I'm not sure about the parking situation. Because parking is either non-existent or costs a fortune in most neighborhoods, I take an Uber. The Uber pulls up in front of a residential condo building on a sketchy, poorly lit street. The driver sounds as unsure as I am. "Is this it?"

I look at the address. "Uhhhh, yeah, I guess." I get out of the car, wishing I had brought my pepper spray. I attempt to open the front door of the building, and it is locked. It's too cold for this shit. Luckily, there is a door person there to buzz me in. She greets me as I walk through the door. "Can I help you?"

"Yeah, I'm here for the seminar?"

This can't be the right place.

"Oh, yes! Sign in here."

Okay, maybe it is?

She hands me the guestbook, and I sign in. She instructs me to go to the twelfth floor. I get in the elevator, and the twelfth floor is the top floor. The elevator doors open, revealing the entertainment area of the building. To my right is a modern-looking living room area with couches, a big-screen TV, and a fireplace. And to my left is an equally modern kitchen area with stainless steel appliances and an island with chairs lined up facing the countertop and appliances. The space is designed with many windows, including a skylight, to receive natural lighting but it's 6 p.m. in the winter, so the natural light is pitch black. There is LED lighting, but the whole ambiance seems artificial because it's fighting mother nature's darkness. The seminar is set up so that the presenter will be standing in the kitchen with the attendees at the barstools on the island. Right now, there are only four people seated at the island and an elderly couple seated behind the island, in the living room area. The elderly man is in a wheelchair and is sleeping but looks dead considering his pale pallor. I cannot see his chest move when he breathes. However, there is fresh drool oozing out the side of his mouth, so that is a positive sign of life. The elderly woman with him doesn't seem to be alarmed, so I think it's safe to say that he is alive. As I quickly assess the scene with massive confusion, a woman standing in the kitchen, who seems to be part of the seminar, makes a beeline to me. "Hi! What's your name?"

"Hi, I'm Angie."

"Hi, Angie! I'm Sheila. What brings you to the event?

What? Why is she interrogating me before I've had a chance to take off my coat?

"I'm making some changes in my life and need some motivation to implement them."

"Great! What kind of changes?"

Why is she putting me on the spot right now?

"I think I want to start a writing project, but I don't know if I have the courage to do it."

I also want to move to Hawaii, but I'm way too embarrassed to admit that to you right now.

"Awesome! How did you hear about the event?

Why are we doing this? Shouldn't this be part of group introductions?

"Um, I don't know. Google?"

There is an awkward pause. It's roasting in here with the fireplace blazing, and this conversation feels too forced. I am so socially and physically uncomfortable that I can't stand it. Before the sweat starts soaking through my clothes, I need to take off my eight hundred and fifty-fill goose-down, ankle-length coat.

"Let me take your coat."

Finally!

Sheila hangs up my coat and finally accepts me into the kitchen island audience. There are two young ladies at the far end, who seem to be about my age, two ladies in the middle, who seem to be my mother's age, and then me. Oh, and of course, the two elderly people sitting behind us. And there is a really good-looking, muscular guy in the kitchen, who seems to be one of the speakers. And that's it. This is the motivational seminar. Five attendees, two mystery, elderly attendees, and two speakers. And everyone else is in pairs, so I feel like a third wheel for all four pairs. I would love to get the hell out of here right now, but with such a small crowd, I would feel awkward getting up and leaving. It might offend Sheila.

The seminar begins. Sheila and Shane, the good-looking, fit guy, introduce themselves, and then we start going around the room to make introductions. There are hors d'oeuvres on the island, and the two ladies sitting next to me crunch away the entire time, which is audibly offensive. The two young ladies on the end start speaking. There is Lori, a spinning and yoga instructor, and her friend Jenny, an esthetician. Lori is cute with short, curly, brown hair and bright pink lipstick, and Jenny is blonde with a much more Plain Jane look. Lori tells us that she is going to a motivational seminar in Denver in May with Tony Robbins and Gary Vee. I don't want to interrupt her, but I can't help myself. "Wait, Tony Robbins and Gary Vee are going to be at the *same* event?"

"Yeah!" She gives me the details. After Jenny introduces herself, we move down to the two ladies sitting beside me, still stuffing their faces with crunchy food. It turns out these guests are Sheila's mom and her friend.

Are you kidding me? She couldn't fill enough seats and had to get pity attendees?

Even worse, the elderly couple behind us are Sheila's grandparents. This means that there are only three real attendees, including myself.

What did I get myself into?

Then, they get to me. With outward confidence and inward shame, I explain that I am trying to get over my fears and figure out what I want to do with my life. The huge entertainment room is quiet, except for the fireplace's crackling and me talking about how I want to be a writer, but I don't know how to start. I don't feel comfortable talking in front of people, even in this small of a crowd.

Can we please just start the event so I can get motivated already?

Finally, Shane starts the presentation. He talks about non-GMO and organic food, the evils of Monsanto, how he drives two hours to the suburbs to get specially filtered water and range-free eggs, and doesn't have cable because he doesn't want radio waves emitted in his house. He also mentions, at least eight times, that he won a contest to get personally coached by a no-name motivational speaker. His attractiveness starts dwindling as he weaves in and out of the painfully boring details of the great lengths he goes to stay in an uncontaminated bubble. The last spark is extinguished when he says he meditates for a minimum of two hours a day.

How does he have this much time on his hands?

My interest slightly piques when Shane starts talking about probiotics, which I have recently started taking. I mention that I buy mine at Target, and he supplement-shames me by basically saying that a store for peasants such as Target couldn't possibly have the best quality strains of probiotics, and he recommends a brand that costs about the same as my monthly mortgage principal payment.

Needless to say, I am extremely confused about how any of this correlates with facing our fears (allegedly, if you don't expose your body to poison, you won't feel anxious and fearful). I am annoyed that they wasted my money and free time. The seminar lasts thirty minutes over the scheduled two hours, and it is the most painful two hours and thirty minutes of my life. All I want to do is leave, but Sheila has my coat hostage. I am not brave enough to get up and leave by getting my own damn coat to make a statement of "Screw you, this seminar sucks!" which is ironic at a 'Fear Not!' seminar, although Sheila's grandparents had the balls to leave an hour ago.

I escape after the seminar finally ends. Not so fast. Sheila accosts me after I put on my coat. "Hi, Angie! I am wondering if you have the availability to have lunch this coming week to talk about my coaching programs?"

I don't know how to say, "Hell to the motherfucking no!" politely. "Maybe! Send me an email!"

But there is one good thing that came out of this event. The visions of the Denver Lollapalooza of motivational speakers have me so excited that in the morning-after hangover from the organic food rant, I book a trip to Denver and buy my seminar ticket. The lowest tier ticket is fifty dollars. The mid-tier ticket is five hundred dollars and includes a Q&A lunch with Gary Vee and close-to-the-front floor seating. The top tier ticket is an opportunity to meet Tony Robbins and first or second-row floor seating. This is a heftier one thousand five hundred dollars.

I don't deserve to meet Tony Robbins.

I don't even deserve to be at that event.

I am not worthy of spending that much money on myself.

Despite the barrage of my critical inner voice, I click on the lunch with Gary Vee option, which is terrifying and not something I feel deserving of. But I am determined to make changes in my life. From now on, I'm playing at a higher level.

CHAPTER 10

THE calendar turns to March. My mind turns to Luna. I would love to connect with Dad again since it's been a year since our last session. Maybe he has advice about what I should do with my life, most importantly, how to move to Hawaii and be a writer. I'm also concerned because I haven't been smelling Dad as much, and I don't know what that means.

Is he mad at me?

When I walk in the door, Luna already has a message from Dad. "He's telling me to look at your nails." I show Luna my fingernails. My favorite hobby is nail art, and I tried a more advanced design this week. It warms my heart that he noticed. We situate ourselves in her back room for the reading. When Luna connects with him this time, he seems happier, making me happy. I feel more connected to him, which is a relief since I haven't been smelling him as much. I have been writing him letters, and Luna tells me he loves my letters. I vow to write him a letter every single day going forward.

"Why doesn't he visit me anymore?"

She closes her eyes. "I see coins. Does that mean anything to you?"

"Yes! He would always empty the change from his pocket and put it in a jar on his dresser. And when Mom and I cleaned out his house, they were everywhere."

"Look for coins. When you see coins, they are from him. He wants you to pick them up."

"Okay."

I tell Luna about my dream to move to Hawaii.

Don't admit this dream to anybody! I'll never go. I'm too old to make new friends, and Rick will never let me work remotely.

Luna agrees that I belong there, but for some reason, I feel that is her own opinion and not a message from her Spirit Guides. She then asks an unexpected question. "What's happening in May?"

"Um...I don't know."

"Something is happening in May."

May... May... May... Oh yeah, I can't believe I forgot!

"I am going to an event in Denver with Tony Robbins and Gary Vee."

She closes her eyes and taps her pen on her notebook as she receives the message. Then, she opens her eyes and looks at me with an intensity that gives me chills. "That event. Go to that event."

Um, duh, it's Tony Robbins and Gary Vee. Of course, it's going to be amazing.

But is it my answer to being a writer and moving to Hawaii?

Luna has one last message for me. "Thirty-eight is going to be your year."

I turn thirty-eight in June.

But it could take all year, which means I may not be happy again for over a year. I want to be happy now.

$\mathcal{D}$ENVER is still over a month away. My class's sketch comedy show just wrapped up, and the cold weather in Chicago is killing my soul. Hawaii is on my mind more than ever. I am mostly clueless about how I could pull off a move four thousand miles away with my job, but I have an idea for a first step. My friend Beth and her husband own a rental condo in Destin, Florida. I am staying there for the entire month of April to get away from the cold and the agitation of the city. I pitched my one-month stay in Florida to my manager, Rick, on the angle of how the cold weather negatively affects my autoimmune disorder, which is true and part of the reason I am going, but not the entire story. There is an ulterior motive for Florida. Right now, I work from home most of the time anyway. Being in Florida for a month will prove that I can handle working remotely outside of Chicago so that I can set myself up to ask Rick if I can work remotely in Hawaii. I don't know what the second step is, but I will figure it out when I get there. I have been with the company for five years now and have successfully created finance operations within global IT and get shit done like nobody's business. Despite this, it still seems like a long shot that he will allow me to work off mainland America and it is solely hinged on coming out of the Denver event so delirious with motivation that I will ask with zero fear.

The month in Florida is a much-needed escape from the real world. Unfortunately, it rains every weekend, which are my only days off from work, and I wanted to spend the weekends at the beach. But I believe this is a blessing in disguise. Being indoors all weekend gives me the time and opportunity to set up the website for my blog. The idea for my creative writing blog came about a year ago. One morning, I was running through Lincoln Park and I saw a single, unscathed Louboutin high heel, lying on its side, red bottom blazing, right next to a huge pile of half-frozen, dog poop.

What happened here?

I immediately went home and wrote a fictional short story about what happened there. This further inspired me to take more pictures of random street findings and write backstories on how the scene came about. I wanted to turn it into a blog, but I was terrified to put myself out there.

People won't read my stories.

I'm a horrible writer.

I don't know what I am doing.

Taking The Second City Sketch Writing Program over the past year has boosted my writing confidence and I know writing this blog and putting myself out there is part of becoming the person I need to be to move to Hawaii. Every weekend in Florida, as it is raining, I write more stories, set up my website, www.sowhathappenedhere.com, and build my Instagram page, @sowhathappenedhere, to promote the website. I want to do more with writing than this blog, but I don't know what I want to do yet. I will keep plugging away at *So...What Happened Here?* until I figure it out.

J wake up in Destin with an intuition hit.
Upgrade your seminar ticket to the meet and greet with Tony Robbins.

I email customer support and ask for assistance in upgrading my ticket. They respond the same day with instructions to call a phone number.

I don't deserve to meet Tony.

The critical inner voice is awake. I delete the email. About a week later, my intuition hits me over the head.

Upgrade your seminar ticket to the meet and greet with Tony Robbins.

I am now my intuition's bitch. I retrieve the email from Trash and call the number.

What am I doing?

I don't even belong at this seminar.

I wonder if the lady on the other end can tell what a fraud I am and how undeserving I am to be in the VIP tier.

I am terrified at the thought of spending this much money on myself and being in the VIP section, but I am ready to uplevel. I am ready to make some changes in my life. I am ready to move to Hawaii and be a writer, no matter how terrifying.

CHAPTER 11

MAY 2018

$\mathcal{I}$ return from Destin and the cold, Chicago wind is a punch in the face. It's May and still frigid, cloudy, and windy as shit. The city's negative energy immediately barges in on the door of my soul. But there is one glimmer of hope. I have proven that I can successfully work remotely outside of Chicago. Visions of Hawaii life are stronger than ever, and I now have the means. But my brain is still stuck on the fact that I am too old to make new friends, and Rick will laugh in my face if I ask him if I can move to Hawaii. But I can't ask Rick until I get the courage from the seminar. The Denver trip is less than two weeks away. I mark my calendar for the Monday after the Denver weekend to have the conversation with Rick. I am scared to death.

Despite spending over two thousand dollars between the ticket, airfare, and Airbnb for the Denver trip, I almost don't go because I am terrified of going alone. If I had stayed at the five hundred dollar ticket, I truly believe that I would have bailed out on the entire trip. But the sunk cost of the upgraded, non-refundable ticket is too high for me to stomach, so I go.

I land in Denver on Wednesday afternoon and take a shuttle bus to pick up my rental car. On the tightly packed shuttle, there is an attractive couple who seem to be business associates. They are next to me, so I can't help but overhear their conversation. Or maybe I am rationalizing being nosy.

"Yeah, I got it at that store. I can't think of what it's called. It's kind of like Target, except less organized."

The lady isn't able to guess, so they start talking about something else. As we pull up to the rental car area, he remembers. "T.J. Maxx!"

I wonder where they are from that he couldn't immediately recall T.J. Maxx. I get in my rental car and drive to my Airbnb. Denver is drab, but I am not here to sightsee. My host, Matt, sends me a text as I am driving to the unit.

> Hey! Will you be at the house around 5? I want to swing by on my way home from work and meet you.

Being from Chicago, this sounds like a huge red flag.

What kind of psychopath Airbnb host wants to meet their guests? Is he going to rape and kill me?

I comply because I have zero boundaries around things that make me uncomfortable.

> I'm on my way now.

> Great! See you soon!

After getting off the highway, I drive on the local streets. I see a few flags that look like a flag that I saw at the airport. As one is flapping in the wind, I see the bright yellow 'C.'

Is that for a sports team?

I get to the house, and Matt arrives a few minutes later. It turns out he doesn't want to rape and kill me. He is cool! He shows me around the house, and we shoot the shit for about forty-five minutes before he leaves. "Too bad you aren't staying for longer than the seminar, or I would invite you to hang out with my friends and me."

Wait, did I just make a friend?

You're too old to make new friends. That's why you can't move to Hawaii.

I just made a new friend, didn't you see?

I make a run to the grocery store to get food for dinner. On the way, I see more yellow 'C' flags. I can't figure out what the 'C' stands for. I am in Denver with a 'D.' I get enough food for two nights because I probably won't feel like going out to eat after the seminar tomorrow. It's an all-day event, and I am going to be tired.

I wake up with butterflies in my stomach. I haven't been this scared to do something in a long time.

It's not too late to back out. You can call Matt and hang out with him and his friends.

No! I need this motivation to ask Rick to move to Hawaii.

I strut out to my rental car in the brisk Denver air. I am wearing a black business casual top and pants because I want to look classy. I didn't want to wear heels because I know my feet would be killing me by the end of the day, so I am wearing blue knit, bedazzled sneakers that I got at Saks OFF 5TH that are sporty yet classy, but most of all, comfortable. I am ready to uplevel. I arrive at the event and head to the VIP line because, well, that's what I am today. After I get my wristband and VIP badge, I go down to floor level with total impostor syndrome. The arena is usually used for rodeos, and they have covered the dirt with flooring. The first two rows are reserved for VIPs.

I don't belong in the first row.

I don't even belong at this event.

I eye the second row. I usually like to sit in the aisle for claustrophobia reasons.

I am too visible in the aisle.

I need to hide.

Because the shame is bombarding me, and I feel I have no other choice, I sit on the third chair, in the second row. As the seats fill in, I feel uncomfortable being by myself because it seems that most people came in groups or at least pairs. Fortunately, the two girls sitting in front of me are super friendly and turn around to talk to me. Aubrey is from Denver and is a motivational speaker herself. Carrie recently got out of the military and is getting ready to move to North Carolina. Aubrey asks what I do for a living.

"I work in finance, but I want to be a writer."

Why am I telling people this? I am never going to be a writer.

I tell them about my blog. Aubrey instantly follows my blog Instagram account! The second row starts to fill up. A female approaches me and asks if the two seats to my left are taken. When I tell her they are not, she and her business partner sit down next to me. Eventually, most seats are filled, but not the seat on my right. Since I have brought my snakeskin purse in an attempt to appear high class and don't want it on the ground, I put it on the empty chair to my right, and if anyone needs a seat later, I will move it.

There are many more speakers than Gary Vee and Tony Robbins. Gary Vee is not until lunchtime, and Tony Robbins is the last speaker of the day. Robert Herjavec is here, and he is entertaining and informative, as are many of the other speakers. At one of the mid-morning breaks, I go to the bathroom and then back to my seat to check Instagram because I am too full of shame to meet new people and talk, and Aubrey and Carrie are not yet back in their seats. As I am on my phone, the guy who has been sitting to my left comes back and sits down. I don't look up from my phone, but out of my peripheral vision, I can see that the person next to me is wearing jeans. The guy who was sitting next to me all morning was wearing shorts.

Who is this?

I look up at him, and he turns to me. "Hi! I'm Mike!"

He holds out his hand, and I shake it. "Hi! I'm Angie!"

"What do you do?"

Not again! This is so embarrassing!

"I work in finance, but I want to be a writer."

He seems to be about my age, and he has amazing energy. He has dark hair, shaved in a fresh fade, and a goatee. We start talking, and it feels natural as if we are old friends meeting up for the first time in a long time. He is kind of cocky, which I usually dislike, but it doesn't interfere with our rapport. For whatever reason, I am drawn to him. He sat down because he knows the lady in the aisle seat, two seats down from me. When her business partner comes back to reclaim his seat, I don't want Mike to leave because I am enjoying our conversation so much.

"Where are you sitting?" I ask.

"Up there." He points to the cheap seats.

"If you want, nobody is sitting here. I can move my purse if you want to sit here."

"Sure!"

I have a seminar buddy!

Mike and I talk between speaker breaks, and then it is time for lunch. He doesn't have a Gary Vee pass, so we have to part ways for now.

Gary Vee is, of course, amazing. I love his no-nonsense, direct manner. Because he is so successful, I assume he flies private jets, but he has to rush out of the lunch because he went over time and is afraid he will miss his commercial flight. I love him even more. I can't wait to get back to the other building and tell Mike all about Gary Vee.

"How was it?" Mike immediately asks.

"It was so amazing! He gave a lot of really great advice on boosting your business through social media and basically not to give one shit about what anyone else thinks."

"Oh, cool! I asked someone else how the lunch went, and he told me all about the food."

We laugh. I continue, "Are you from Denver?"

"No, I'm from Columbus, Ohio. I moved here about a year and a half ago. I came to visit my friend, Jessica, and I loved it so much that I decided to stay here forever."

"Why do you love it so much?"

"The people are so nice here. Back in Ohio, everybody was a hater. But here, everybody is so nice and friendly."

What a cool perspective. I was hating on Denver because it's boring, but he's right. There are a lot of cool people here, including Matt, Aubrey, Carrie, and Mike. I like Mike's energy. He is positive, and I can tell he is a go-getter. The one thing about him that I don't like is that he comes off as a player. At some points, I can't tell if he is hitting on me or if he simply has a Rico Suave personality. He also tries to talk to me during the speakers. I find this slightly annoying because I paid a lot for my seat and want to absorb every single word. But I don't have the boundaries to tell him so.

Then comes Tony Robbins, who is, of course, amazing and a very captivating speaker. Mike is *still* trying to talk to me during the Tony Robbins portion. This is Tony Robbins. One does not talk while Tony is talking. I start to brush off Mike because he seems immature. At one point, Tony mentions Robin Williams and *Mork and Mindy*. Mike turns to me. "What's *Mork and Mindy*?"

I thought he was my age.

"How old are you?" I ask in a playful, yet challenging manner.

He sheepishly turns back to Tony.

Oh, now he wants to pay attention.

But it is good that we are now paying attention. Tony's point about Robin Williams is that success without fulfillment is the ultimate failure. Mike tries to show me something on this phone.

Um, Tony.

Then, Mike starts freaking out because his phone battery is on one percent, and he doesn't have a charger.

Who doesn't bring a fully charged phone to a Tony Robbins event?

At one point, Tony asks the crowd who is single. I half-raise my hand, embarrassed of my relationship status. Mike doesn't raise his hand and then whispers in my ear while motioning to the seats where he was originally sitting. "I don't want my girlfriends to get in a fight over me."

I don't know if he is serious, and Mike definitely seems immature, but he is still fun to talk to, especially when we have breakout exercises with partners. Unlike the beginning of the event, I feel more connected and am having fun. There are also moments where Tony commands us to run around and hug everyone in sight. On the one hand, it's fun. On the other hand, I feel like we might have drank some Kool-Aid at lunch. There is a girl with huge boobs and a skimpy top, and Mike and I make it a game to make sure we hug her during these moments. He probably enjoys it way more than I do, but I am having fun.

At the end of Tony's session, he directs us to close our eyes and physically reach for something that we want for the future and bring it to our hearts. I reach for Hawaii. This is the sole reason I am here, and I will not rest until I find a way to get there.

But you're too old to make friends in Hawaii.

Bitch, do you not see how much fun I am having with Mike, who I met within twenty-four hours of arriving in Denver?

At the end of the event, I part ways with Mike to stand in line for pictures with Tony Robbins. Before he leaves, he hands me his business card. And just like that, my seminar buddy is gone. Even though he kind of annoyed me, I miss him already. Especially since there is a line for Tony, and it would be fun to talk and laugh while we wait. I look at his business card. The last four digits of his phone number are 1444. Luna's address is 1444.

"That event. Go to that event."

Is this a sign?

Maybe it's the high of Tony Robbins, maybe it's the inexplicable pull to Mike, or maybe it's the vague Luna prophecy, but I text him, for no other reason than for him to have my number too.

> Mike! It's Angie.

> Heeeyyyyyy. What are you up to?

> Waiting in line for Tony. What are you up to?

> I went home.

> Boo.

> Want to grab a bite to eat?

A part of me doesn't. It's 7 p.m., and I have been in this arena since 9 a.m. I am tired, and my flight leaves at 6:30 a.m. Plus, I have food at the Airbnb that I bought at the grocery store yesterday. Old Me, who was inflexible and didn't like to lose sleep or deviate from certainty, wants to eat the food I bought at the grocery store and go to bed early. Besides, Mike is immature, so there can't be a connection between him and Luna's message. But I do feel a pull to him. New Me, who is flexible and more comfortable with uncertainty, wants to hang out with him. I want to continue the fun connection.

> Sure!

> I live at Fifth and Watson.

I have no idea what that means since this is my first visit to Denver. As I wait in line, my eyes scan the arena. In the middle, hanging from the ceiling right under the American flag, is that damn yellow 'C' flag.

What the hell does the 'C' stand for?

I start to turn to the guy behind me in line to ask when it hits me.

Colorado!

Thank goodness I didn't make an ass of myself and ask. At first, I feel silly, but then I realize that I have no idea what the Illinois flag looks like because we fly the Chicago flag in Chicago, not the state flag. I'm next in line for Tony Robbins. This was marketed as a "meet and greet," but we aren't even allowed to initiate a conversation with Tony. We have to give our name to the usher standing outside the curtained booth, who introduces Tony to us by our name. We get our picture taken, and are immediately ushered out of the booth. I'm on deck.

"What's your name?"

"Angie."

The curtain opens. "Hi, Tony, this is Angie."

"Hi, Angie! Nice to meet you!"

"Hi!"

His hands are massive, and his handshake is super firm— exactly how I like handshakes. I have no idea what to say or if I am even allowed to say anything. Luckily, he speaks first to relieve the awkwardness. "I love your hair! What do you call that color?"

I shrug and laugh nervously. "Red."

Oh my God, I just sounded like a total smart-ass to Tony Robbins.

We quickly smile for the picture, and all I can think about is how sweaty I am with all of that jumping around we did during his event and I didn't even do a hair and makeup check because

I was texting with Mike. After the camera flash, Tony and I go in for another firm handshake, and I leave. And that's it. It's over.

That's what I paid an extra grand for?

But it was worth playing at a higher level because now my confidence is sky high, and I made a new friend! I run into Aubrey and Carrie in the line to pick up our Tony photos.

"We are going to grab a bite to eat. Do you want to join us?"

"Thank you for the offer, but I have plans with Mike, the guy who was sitting next to me."

"Oooooh, he was *hot*!"

Carrie has interesting taste. I wouldn't necessarily use the word—wait, did I just make more friends here?

I call Mike as I walk to my rental car. I am starving. I may be hangry by the time I meet up with him. He reiterates that he lives at Fifth and Watson and that I can meet him by his place. That intersection still means nothing to me. I don't feel comfortable driving in this city because I don't know my way around. I have GPS, but I don't like driving. Matt told me about a place near the house called Linger. I suggest it to Mike, and he agrees.

Linger used to be a mortuary called O'Linger. I'm not sure why they went out of business, but when they did, they left the huge neon sign on the roof of the building. The restaurant took over, named it Linger, and uses the same sign, except they do not light up the O' section. I thought it might be creepy, but it has a trendy vibe.

Mike is not here yet, and the hostess tells me there is no wait for the rooftop seating. When I get upstairs, they clear off a table for us, and Mike arrives as if on cue. A waitress leads us to our table. He walks ahead of me. I am used to men letting me walk first. It's respectful. Plus, you would think he would at least want to be a pervert and look at my butt.

We sit down at our table with a clear view of Coors Field. Our dynamic is much different on the rooftop than at the seminar. At the seminar, he was kind of annoying and immature. At Linger, he is outgoing and funny. What I love most about Mike is how passionate and motivated he is. He has goals. This is the kind of person I need in my life. We laugh and eat until it gets dark and cold. I don't know if it is the endorphins from laughing, the deliciousness of our tacos after barely eating all day, or the glow of the neon sign, but I am starting to dig Mike. A lot. Like, I want to make out with him. I am horny and want to do more, but I would settle for a wet kiss. He seems interested too, but I can't tell for sure.

"When are you leaving?"

"My flight leaves at 6:30 tomorrow morning."

"You should change your flight and stay for the weekend. We can hang out. I can show you around Denver. You can sleep on my couch."

I'm not sure about that.

"I'm not sure about that."

"I have a comfortable couch."

Is he joking? If I stay at his house, then I am sleeping in his bed, preferably with him in it.

I have doubts, but I start looking up flights that depart on Sunday. As I do this, Mike looks at his calendar. His beautiful brown eyes are glimmering in the glow of the Linger pink, neon sign. "Shit, I have plans tomorrow night. I am going to a charity event and then my friend's birthday party. But I can hang out with you all day on Saturday."

Cue the needle scratching a record sound effect.

He is offering to let me stay with him for the weekend, but isn't inviting me to the event or at least his friend's birthday tomorrow?

I deserve to be accompanied all weekend, not only selectively when it fits his schedule. Who wouldn't want to take a beautiful girl from Chicago and flaunt her all over Denver? Something is up. I don't know if it's the high of Tony Robbins or the laughing, but I generally don't have this much self-respect. I can't spend the weekend at his place if he ditches me Friday night. I don't deserve to be alone in Denver on a Friday night. Nobody puts Angie in a corner.

"I'm sorry. I can't stay if we can't hang out tomorrow."

"It's just one night."

"Sorry, I can't."

This may be the first time I have stood up for what I deserve. It feels weird because it means missing out on hanging out with Mike for the rest of the weekend, but a big part of me feels proud. Even though I am not staying all weekend, I want to stay as long as possible tonight. Maybe even invite him back to my Airbnb. But what I didn't realize about Denver is how much the temperature swings throughout the day. During the day, it was eighty degrees, but now, it's about fifty degrees, and sitting on the rooftop is freezing. I am wearing a sleeveless shirt. I don't want to end my time with Mike, but I am freezing my ass off. We step outside the restaurant, and there is an ice cream place next door. Mike's eyes light up. "Do you want to get ice cream?"

I don't because I am already so cold, but I am not turning down ice cream with Mike. "Sure, but let me get my jacket out of the car."

We walk to my rental car. It's only about three blocks away, but we have to walk up a hill to get there. Chicago is flat as a pancake, and I'm not used to these elevation grade changes. "It feels like we are walking in San Francisco."

Mike laughs. "Let me help you." He puts his hand on the small of my back to give me a boost. His hand touching me is electrifying. I can't wait to make out with him tonight. I grab my jacket out of the car, and we head back down the hill to get ice cream. There is a line, but Mike assures me the line goes fast, so we fall behind the couple at the end of the line. The guy of the couple holds up a gigantic wooden spoon. "Sorry, this is the end of the line."

That is an efficient closing system to give the last customers of the day a conspicuous wooden spoon. I pull out my Chicago moves. "But if you let us in front of you, you will still be at the end of the line."

Unlike Chicago, he surprisingly and immediately agrees to let us cut in front of them. Mike and I continue our talking and laughing. We get ice cream cones, and Mike pays. He also paid for dinner. This is starting to feel like a date. We find a bench and continue talking and laughing. I'm giddy from being around him. By the way he is looking at me, I can tell he is into me too. I wonder when he is going to make his move.

We finish eating the ice cream, and between eating something cold and the temperature dropping even more since dinner, I need to get in the car and turn on the heat. Mike had taken an Uber to Linger, so he follows me to my car, to sit in the heat, while ordering an Uber home.

Wait, are we not hooking up? Why are we not making out yet?

I feel like the chemistry is here, but he is ordering an Uber. Either he can come to my Airbnb or invite me to his place. I can drive to either one. I get the feeling that something is up, and I tense up. "I can take you home. How far away do you live?"

Does that sound too desperate?

"About forty minutes away."

Wow, that is a long drive, and I hate driving. I especially hate driving when I am unfamiliar, which I will be on the way back.

It doesn't matter anyway because he doesn't take the bait. We chat until the Uber pulls up. He turns to me, gives me a big hug, exits the car, and walks across the street to his ride. No kiss. After all of that sexual chemistry, not even a kiss.

Did I do something wrong?

Something is wrong with me.

Plus, he didn't even want to hang out with me tomorrow. I feel a lump in my stomach. Luckily, I am still riding high and equally exhausted from the seminar, so I go back to my Airbnb to shower and get to sleep. As soon as I get back, Mike starts texting me.

> I had a great time. Have a safe flight tomorrow.

We text some more flirty banter back and forth.

Wait, why are we texting if he didn't want to kiss me?

WAITING at the gate at 6 a.m., Mike starts texting me again.

> I wish you didn't have to leave. We could have had fun this weekend.

A part of me is filled with regret, but another part of me doesn't want to be treated like leftovers tonight if he is going out and leaving me on my own. Landing in Chicago, I discover it's a dreary forty degrees.

Maybe I should have stayed in Denver.

The good news is that I now know that I can make friends anywhere, regardless of my age. The second hurdle is asking Rick if I can work remotely in Hawaii. I have an in-person meeting with him on Monday morning.

ACCORDING to plan, my motivation endured the weekend and is still strong today. I am super nervous, but if Rick says no, then I will look for another job that would let me remote. Even though keeping this job is the ideal outcome, I am not dependent on my job offering me this benefit. It's only a minor setback if it doesn't work out that way. I still have visions of Rick laughing in my face, but my Tony Robbins delirium can handle it. Plus, I have experience with awkward moments with Rick. On my first day five years ago, as he was giving me a tour of the office, I slipped and fell in the copy room because I thought it was a good idea to wear five-inch espadrilles to work and they didn't play well with the slick, although very clean, floor. He awkwardly asked if I was okay, but, internally, was probably horrified that I might file a workman's comp claim the first day on the job.

Rick and I walk to the conference room and spark up some small talk. The small talk continues as we sit down. Then, I start in on my rehearsed pitch. "As you know, I have an autoimmune disorder, and I went to Florida to work for a month. When I got there, all of my symptoms went away. When I got back, they all came back."

This is all true, but I am leaving out all of the other reasons I want to move. I take a breath and chicken out on my rehearsed pitch. Instead of going in for the direct ask, I go indirect. "So, what I wanted to talk to you about today was, if I move away from Chicago to somewhere warmer, can I keep my job?"

He doesn't even flinch. "I don't care where you are, as long as you get your job done."

"What about Hawaii?" I say as I inwardly cringe and hold my breath.

He's going to fire me on the spot for being such a dumb-ass.

Without batting an eye he says, "I don't care where you are as long as you get your job done."

It's that easy?!? I've been worried about this for months! And it was nothing!

"Thank you!"

CHAPTER 12

JUNE 2018

FOR the first week after Rick says yes, I don't do anything. I am frozen by fear. Then, I realize that I have no idea how much my condo is worth, when is a good time to sell, or anything about selling a home. I want to contact a real estate agent, but I only know Kimberly Parke, and I will be damned if I give her my business again. Out of fear, I continue with my life, thinking about finding a real estate agent but not doing anything about it because I am too scared to take any forward action into the unknown.

As I rush to my front door after running errands, I run into my neighbor, Stacey, in the hallway. As we are talking, I put myself out there and mention that I am going to move to Hawaii and need to sell my condo.

"My best friend's mom is a real estate agent! Do you want me to text you her info?"

Um, yes!

Stacey connects me to Michelle, who visits me in my unit. We look up comps in the neighborhood. My condo's market value is at least forty thousand dollars more than I bought four years ago.

"When is a good time to sell?

"Summer is always good. When do you want to move?"

Um, NOW!

"I don't know… I should probably stay through budget kick-off at work in October, so I guess November? I could always stay with a friend if it sells sooner."

I know Joe would take me in, but that might be a logistical nightmare. I haven't even thought about shipping my stuff or finding a place to live in Hawaii. I kind of start freaking out, and Michelle can sense that I am overwhelmed. "How about we put it on the market the first week of August? That will give you time to figure everything else out, and we can always adjust the date if necessary."

I like the way Michelle thinks. We shoot for a listing date of early August. In the meantime, I make a long list of everything that needs to be done.

I don't know what I am doing, but I'm doing this!

I set up estimates for moving quotes, research car shipping, and email Agnes. I am no longer an impostor because I really am moving to Hawaii at the end of this year, and with the money that I am making off the sale of my condo, plus the nice raise and bonus I got a few months ago at work, I am getting closer to my dream budget.

This 'Act As If' shit works!

> Hi, Agnes! Good news! I am getting ready to move to Hawaii. I still want to buy a condo, but I need help finding a short-term rental to have a place to live before I start looking to buy.

My heart drops as I read her response.

> Oh, that's great news! Unfortunately, I don't do rentals. I am sure you can do a Google search to find someone to help you. But once you are settled in, let me know when you are ready to buy!

I know real estate agents don't make money off rentals, but I am buying a condo later, so I would think it would be worth her time to help me. I feel discouraged. I am not interested in working with her anymore.

But how in the hell am I going to find another real estate agent in Hawaii?

A few days later, I am dissociating from the stress in my life by scrolling through my Instagram Explore page. I stumble across a picture of a guy surfing in a business suit in Hawaii. He looks like an Asian model. His name is Kyle, and he is a real estate agent on Oahu.

Ask, and you shall receive! That shit works too!

I send Kyle a DM and explain the situation. I don't think I have ever sent anyone a DM before. I thought that was for thirsty dudes. I feel like an idiot but then realize that I will have to get used to being uncomfortable this entire process. I don't know what the hell I am doing with any of this, so this will be happening a lot over the next five months. It's scary as shit, but this is the price of admission of leveling up and moving to Hawaii.

Kyle responds! He is happy to help. We set up a time to talk on the phone. I like Kyle immediately. His calm demeanor radiates the Aloha spirit. Also, he is interested in accommodating my short-term rental idea while we look for a condo. He has an even better idea: stay in a fully furnished vacation rental for a month while we look for a short-term rental, and stay in the short-term rental while we look for a condo. This will require extra logistics with shipping my belongings, but I feel more comfortable about this arrangement. I am sold on being Kyle's client when he immediately emails a list of vacation rentals to choose from. I pick one out and reserve it for November. The more steps I take, the more Hawaii is becoming a reality. But, yet, it still seems unreal. And terrifying.

Do I have the courage to go through with this?

What if I get scared and back out?

I am slow to announce my moving plans to family and friends. I feel like an impostor. I gradually start telling people because I know that if I announce the news, not following through would be a failure.

I am finishing up my workday and my friend, Estelle, is in my neighborhood getting the tire changed on her bike. Estelle and I worked together for over four years, and we were pretty tight, to the point that we had regular therapy sessions crying in each other's offices. Our company was bought by another company, and we were all laid off. I found a new job quickly, thanks to Estelle's husband, Chris, helping me get a job at his employer, while Estelle took some time off to take care of her kids. When I started my new job, the void of not having Estelle as a co-worker was like grieving a breakup. I missed her so much. One time I went to the bathroom to cry because I didn't have Estelle's office to go to, and then that thought exacerbated my existing sadness, and I started to cry harder. Once I got over Estelle, she went back to the workforce and started calling me crying about not having me around at work.

I meet Estelle at a dive bar next to the bike shop. It's us and a bunch of construction workers who love the idea of being in a bar with two cute girls. We are not as thrilled, so we hole up in the corner, chatting away. I break the news of my move.

"Oh my God! I'm so happy for you! You know what? This guy, Greg, that I went to college with, lives in Honolulu. Let me connect you with him." She pulls up his Facebook account, and there are tons of pictures of him in Hawaii, but he is always with a blonde girl, presumably his girlfriend.

"If he has a girlfriend, he probably won't be interested in hanging out. And I don't want to be a third wheel."

"I don't think that is his girlfriend. I'll connect you with him."

I am doubtful, but Estelle starts a group text with the three of us, and, girlfriend or not, Greg is excited to add me to his friend group. Since I am allowing myself to be seen by actually telling people that I am moving, the next step is to tell Mom. I know she isn't going to be happy. Whenever I have even casually talked about moving to Hawaii, she has tried to put me on a guilt trip because it's too far away from her, even though Amy has lived in both Orlando and L.A., which are both much further away than Chicago. Mom is planning to visit next weekend. I will tell her then, in person.

Entire weekends with Mom are hard for me. My parents divorced when I was in college, and Mom never remarried. I feel that she relies on me for the happiness and emotional support that she should be getting from a significant other. This conversation will be tricky because I feel tied to her happiness, and moving further away will cause her to be unhappy. The guilt is already squeezing my heart.

Mom arrives around noon on Saturday, and we go out to lunch. Sitting at an outdoor table, the ambiance is nice, but it feels like there is a brick in my stomach. There is no good way to break this, so I start talking to ease into it. "So, because I was able to successfully work remotely in Florida for a month, I asked my manager if I could keep my job if I move away from Chicago—"

"Where would you go?"

This is so typical of Mom to interrupt me while I am talking. Because her interruptions are rude and trigger the shit out of me, I immediately change directions from easing into it to slapping her in the face. "Hawaii."

Her face turns stone-cold and she turns away from me. She can't even look at me. "What about your condo?"

"I already talked to a real estate agent. I'm going to put it on the market this summer."

"What if you lose money on it?"

"I won't. The market value is at least forty thousand dollars more than when I bought it."

"You don't have anywhere to live there."

"I'm talking to a real estate agent to figure it out."

"You don't have any friends there."

"I'll make friends. I would think that you would be excited that you have a free place to stay in Hawaii."

"Well, Hawaii isn't really a place I want to visit. It's too far away and too expensive."

She never has anything positive to say to me. Why can't she be happy for me for once in her life?

This is the hardest decision of my life, and she is raining negativity all over something that is already extremely terrifying. The guilt quickly transforms to shame. I have a flashback to the conversation with Dad about moving to Chicago.

"Chicago is expensive. You're not going to be able to afford it."

"It's the armpit of the nation."

"There's too much traffic. I'm not visiting you."

"You're going to hate it there."

"I'm not helping you move."

A huge part of me never wants to talk to Mom again after I move. That strategy didn't work out so well with Dad. The pain of retching guilt I felt after he died was too unbearable. I know not talking to her is not the answer, but I can't deal with her negativity. I need supportive people right now, and sadly, it can't be Mom.

Nobody supports me.

Ω**AD's** brother, Ron, has been battling cancer, and I just found out through my cousin, Aaron, that he has passed. I didn't know Ron very well, and seeing him at Dad's funeral was the first time I had seen him in a long time. I send my condolences to Aaron and order flowers to be delivered for the funeral. At the risk of sounding cheesy, I let Aaron in on a secret.

> I know this sounds weird, but Dad still visits me. It's subtle, but I know it's him. And he's changed a lot in the past year in the signs that he shows me, so I know that he's happier now and in a better place. Just know that you didn't lose your dad, the relationship is just different now, as long as you pay attention to how he shows up for you.

Ω am working from home on my kitchen island. The scent hits me like a slap in the face. Even though she follows the Tollhouse recipe on the chocolate chip bag, Mom's chocolate chip cookies have a distinct scent: the scent that I smell right now. I feel a cold breeze at my ankles. "Dad?"

The smell and breeze are gone. I smile.

Dad is showing Ron the ropes.

Chapter 13

J need to get something important out of the way before I move to Hawaii— visit my family. Mom plans a family gathering at Grandma's house in Indiana, making it more convenient to say goodbye to everyone at once. As always, with them, I feel disconnected. It's as if we are mechanically going through the motions of what a family should do when someone moves away.

My uncle Dan surprises me by addressing me in front of the entire family. "You're the bravest one out of all of us." This is the most positive thing anybody in my family has ever said to me.

As Mom and I leave, Grandma doesn't even stand up to hug me goodbye but leaves parting words. "This is the last time I am going to see you."

For the past five or so years, at any family gathering, Grandma likes to passive-aggressively remind us of her age. Her remarks are met with groans because we all know she will be around the following year. I feel confident that I will see her again. "I'll see you again when I visit!"

As Mom and I leave, Grandma stands up to pour herself a cup of coffee.

But she didn't stand up to hug me.

G REG and I have been casually texting, and a few weeks before I move, he sends me a text.

> Hey Ang! I'm at a cool party with
> my friends at the Art Museum. It
> will be fun when you are here and
> can come with us next time.

I like that he calls me Ang because that is what my close friends and family call me. I am excited that I already have a friend lined up!

Shit is starting to get real. Luckily, the buyers of my condo bought it for their son, and they are not in a hurry for him to move in. They are accommodating me staying in the unit until the end of October, and I will live with Joe for a few days before my flight. But, to accommodate the estimated travel times for truck and boat logistics for the shipping of my car, I ship it four weeks early. It is much easier to go without a car in Chicago than in Hawaii.

The day my car is to be picked up, the truck driver, Atlan, calls me and asks me to meet him in an industrial complex about five miles away from my home. As I am driving there, I realize that I have no way to get home. Atlan is a middle-aged, heavy-set Asian man, and he is super nice, but I am still apprehensive about shipping my baby in a truck from Chicago to Long Beach, California. Ever since I was six years old and had a Barbie Ferrari, my dream car has always been a red convertible. I bought this bright red Volkswagen Eos two years ago, and it's paid in full and totally mine. I love this car, but more than that, it's a symbol that I can achieve my heart's desires, even though haters told me that convertibles are too expensive, too dangerous, the insurance costs too much, and red cars get more speeding tickets. I call it The Fly Trapper because when I told my friend Nenad I was buying it, he foreshadowed my experience driving around Chicago in a red convertible.

"You are going to attract all of the flies."

After I pay Atlan the required one thousand dollars in cash that he stashes in a compartment in his clipboard, he offers to drive me home in my car. I drive and have questions because I am nervous about trusting him with The Fly Trapper. "So... how long have you been doing this?"

"Eight years now."

Oh, thank God.

"Where do you live?"

"I am based in Chicago and make the drive to Long Beach twice each month, picking up cars along the way. I know the people at the Matson dock pretty well because at least one car each shipment is on its way to Hawaii."

"Oh really? That is surprising."

"Yeah, but it's fun because I have gotten to know the Matson staff so well that they wave and open up the gate when they see me coming!"

I abandon the interrogation about his car transportation skills because I seem to be in good hands. "Do you have a family?"

He tells me about his family that lives in Chicago and his struggles being a Mongolian immigrant, especially learning to speak English.

"Well, you speak English very well, considering how many exceptions there are to the rules." I have so much respect for non-native English speakers who learn to speak English coherently, and Atlan's skills are impressive. When we arrive at my building, I have no reservations about handing over the key to my car. As I go upstairs, my chest tightens as terror strikes. There is no turning back now. My condo is under contract, my car is officially in transit, my non-refundable vacation rental is reserved and paid for, my one-way airfare is purchased, and my movers are scheduled to come in a few weeks.

What if this is the worst mistake of my life?

What if this is the most magical thing to ever happen to me?

As part of my final plans, I energetically let go of Mike. It's been fun flirty texting with him all summer, but I am entering a new phase of my life and don't need that kind of player energy. I want to meet my soulmate, and I can't do that while flirting with someone in Denver. But the universe has an amazing sense of humor.

Mike texts that he wants to talk on the phone to catch up. It's strange because we have only talked on the phone a few times, but it's kind of like a death row inmate requesting the last meal. I know I will leave him in the dust when I move to Hawaii, so why not talk to him one last time? As we talk, he tells me that he wants to write a book, but he is not a writer. And he knows I am because I courageously told him at the seminar. "Would you be interested in writing my book?"

I am not bold enough to write my own book, so I love the idea of writing for someone else. Also, I feel thirsty for this connection with Mike because it is scary as shit moving to Hawaii by myself. Working on the book will be a good distraction. "Sure!"

"That's not weird if you write it for me under my name?"

"No, it's called ghostwriting. Have you ever heard of Neil Strauss? That's what he does."

We make plans to have weekly calls to work on the book project, which means this cancels out my plan to write off Mike. But I am stoked about writing a book!

Speaking of Neil Strauss, I wonder if he has written anything lately?

I look him up, and it turns out that three years ago, he wrote a book called *The Truth*. And now, he is married with a son. I read the summary of *The Truth*. Apparently, after writing *The Game*, which is about his stint as a pick up artist, he went to sex addiction rehab and turned his life around. I download *The Truth* immediately to my Kindle, and even though I am swamped with moving and work, I make the time to read it each night. The book is long, but so amazing that I read it in three days. I start following Neil on Instagram and sign up for his email newsletter. His transformation inspires me.

THE next big steps of the move are the movers picking up my stuff, closing on my condo, and then moving to Joe's for my final days in Chicago.

Plot twist! The closing of my condo is delayed because the City of Chicago suspiciously, I mean randomly, inspected our building last month. There were many small things like light bulbs out, a bicycle in the parking garage, etc., that needed to be resolved, or we would get fined. No big deal. Except the buyer's lender did not approve the loan on the condition that the issues get resolved. The property manager fixed everything for our court hearing today, but the judge did not show up, and the case is delayed until January. I freak out on Michelle because the buyers are her clients. I told her a month ago to get a new lender, but the lender is "her guy," and she wanted to see how the court hearing played out. Now, we are in a snafu because this condo needs to close before I leave in two weeks. Michelle finally agrees to get a new lender, but now the closing date is not until November 5th, which is three days after I move. It's not ideal, but it's not a show-stopper. Big brother Joe is my lawyer, so he comes over with the documents to sign him over as power of attorney so he can close without me.

"How is your packing going?"

"Well, the movers are packing everything I am shipping, because they have to sign off on the boxes. Everything else is going in these three huge suitcases." I gesture to the enormous suitcases that I bought at T.J. Maxx— you know, the store that's kind of like an unorganized Target. Despite being ridiculously huge, I am nervous about all of the stuff I need for my first month fitting in all three of them.

"Don't forget to roll your clothes." He is like a dad, too, with unsolicited but usually helpful advice.

I N my last week in Chicago, I say my final goodbyes to friends. During this time, I realize that I have outgrown many friendships here. One of the people I make a point to say goodbye to is Jasmine. We meet at Starbucks. We chit-chat for a while, but, finally, I say what I have wanted to say every time I have seen her over the past year.

"Before I leave, I want to say thank you for saving me that day." I choke on my tears mid-sentence, and Jasmine reaches for my hand. Even though we still don't know each other very well, I feel so connected to her at this moment.

"There was a reason I am the one who found you. Promise me you will never harm yourself like that again."

"Okay."

$\mathcal{I}$ meet Estelle at Broken English, a modern Mexican restaurant in my neighborhood. It's the only Mexican restaurant I have ever been to that plays hip-hop.

"So, where are you going to live?"

"I have a vacation rental booked for the first month and, during that time, my real estate agent and I are going to look for a shorter-term rental, maybe six months or so, while I look for a condo to buy."

"What is the housing market like right now?"

I have been so busy with moving arrangements, that I haven't even looked. Even though I no longer use Agnes as a real estate agent, I am still on her weekly email updates but have been deleting them. The next day, I browse some of her emails. There is a condo in Ala Moana, one of my preferred neighborhoods, in my price range, with all of my must-haves! On a whim, I text Kyle. I am scheduled to land in Honolulu on Friday afternoon, and we are planning to look at short-term rentals on Saturday morning.

> Hey, Kyle! I know this is a last-minute change, but I was wondering if instead of looking for a rental on Saturday we can take a look at this condo.

I send him the link. He is down! He sets up an appointment with the seller's real estate agent at 9 a.m. on Saturday.

I'm doing this!

THE movers take my stuff from my condo, and all I am left with is an air mattress, so I can spend my final days in Chicago in my own home with everything that I am going to take in three oversized suitcases on the airplane. The realization that almost everything I own, including my car, is currently in transit on multi-modal logistics and out of my control hits me upside the head. Talk about taking the plunge.

What if this doesn't work out?

The night before my flight, I start to pack my suitcases without any real strategy because I am too distracted by inwardly cringing at how much this is going to cost in luggage fees. I still have more stuff to pack, but now, all three are full and can't fit anything else.

This can't be happening! I need this stuff!

I panic and start trying to stuff things in, even though it's clear nothing else will fit. Joe's words echo in my brain.

"Don't forget to roll your clothes."

I didn't roll my clothes, but I don't want to undo all of the work I have done. I have been packing for almost an hour now. My phone rings. It's my friend Beth, who rented me the Florida condo. Beth and I met in college and were roommates in Indianapolis on September 11, 2001. After I moved to Chicago, we didn't stay in touch much but always texted each other on September 11th. Last year, Beth picked up the phone to call me on September 11th. We hadn't talked in almost ten years. It was long overdue. We have been talking on the phone more, and she knows I am moving to Hawaii tomorrow. Part of me doesn't want to waste time talking on the phone, but my intuition is guiding me to answer.

"Hey, Beth!"

"Hey, Angie! How's it going?"

"Ugh, I am freaking out. I am packing my suitcases, and not everything fits."

"Did you roll your clothes?"

I knew there was a reason I answered the phone. After we finish our conversation, I take everything out of all three suitcases and re-pack, this time rolling my clothes. It all fits!

Chapter 14

It still doesn't seem real that I am moving to Hawaii today. I wake up, and it is still dark and cold, but I go outside on my balcony to breathe the crisp, cold air and look at the lit-up Chicago skyline one last time. There are things I love about Chicago, but it's time for the next chapter.

Big brother Joe picks me up. He helps me load the three over-sized suitcases into his truck. I can feel the tears creeping up.

I am so scared. What if this is the worst mistake of my entire life?

Joe is talking away, so it helps me repress the emotions, but it is kind of triggering because I feel like he is sweeping the gravity that I am getting ready to move four thousand miles away under the rug. As we pull up to O'Hare, I can't hold it back any longer. I start tearing up. I am scared about this life decision and I am freaking out about my three suitcases. "I have you here to help me, but what am I going to do in Honolulu?"

"Don't worry about it until you get there. You'll figure it out. Relax and enjoy your flight."

He gives me a big bear hug, and I am on my own. I check in my two hundred and twenty pounds worth of suitcases, and it costs seven hundred dollars. I swipe my credit card like a boss because I am moving to Hawaii and don't give a shit about luggage fees. Joe gave me a guest pass to the United Club, so after I pass through security, that is where I head.

I don't belong here. I only have a guest pass.

But I feel more confident because I am moving to Hawaii by myself, so I make my way around and grab some food for breakfast and find a table by the window so I can hook up to Wi-Fi and work a little bit to ease my nerves. The United Club is fun! I don't even feel like I am in the airport because it's so much nicer than the rest of the terminal. The wait isn't long until I board United Flight 219, the one-way flight launching me into my new chapter.

I'm doing this!

*D*URING the almost nine-hour flight, I do as Joe instructed— relax. I have time to think and reflect on my time in Chicago and a warm feeling overflows my heart. I now truly understand that everything is always working in our favor, even though we may not understand it at the time. In 2012, when I was laid off from my job due to an acquisition, I found a new job immediately and banked my six-month severance package, which I used on the down payment on my condo. Dad dying and Marc dropping me on my ass put me through the worst grief ever, but that led me to decide to make changes in my life, which led me to the lame motivational seminar, which led me to the Tony Robbins/ Gary Vee seminar, which gave me the motivation to ask Rick to work remotely from Hawaii and meet Mike, with whom I am now working on a book. Then, I sold my condo for a profit. And even though Dad didn't have much, I did inherit a modest amount from the sale of his house after paying off the balance of the mortgage. The six months severance, my inheritance, the profit from my condo sale, and the rest of my home equity all led me to be able to afford a condo in my desired price range in Hawaii. Through all of the struggles, I thought the world was against me, but everything was working out in my favor and leading me to this moment. I now know why I couldn't have moved to Hawaii before. I had to go through the experiences for the growth to become the person I am now to finally get past the limiting beliefs and be brave enough to take the risk. And this sets me up even more once I start making moves in Hawaii.

"Ladies and gentlemen, as we start our descent, please make sure your seat backs and tray tables are in their full upright position. Make sure your seatbelt is securely fastened, and all carry-on luggage is stowed underneath the seat in front of you or overhead bins. Thank you."

A big part of me wants to start freaking out about handling my suitcases alone, but I am not going to worry about it until I get to the luggage carousel.

"Ladies and Gentlemen, welcome to Honolulu. Local time is 1:30 p.m. and the temperature is seventy-nine degrees."

Seventy-nine degrees in November! What the hell was I so worried about?

I deplane and head to the outdoor walkway at HNL to go to baggage claim. The fresh breeze blows through my hair. I can feel the warmth of the sun on my skin. The view of the mountains is beautiful.

This is my home!

My heart is overflowing with so much joy that the fear I was feeling in Chicago has been replaced with courage. I know this is not going to be an easy transition, but I am willing to do whatever it takes to settle into my new home and new life. I swagger to baggage claim and am so excited to be here that I don't care about how I am going to handle my three suitcases. I will figure it out just like I figured out how to sell my condo and ship my stuff.

I wrangle all three oversized suitcases off the luggage carousel my own damn self, and I see people gaping at the massive size of my luggage. I wheel all three, two in one hand, one in the other, outside to the cab stand. I feel like such a badass. I see people looking at me, and I assume they are impressed by my unparalleled suitcase handling agility. At this moment, I resolve that I will no longer be afraid of every damn thing anymore because I can solve all of my problems intelligently and courageously. If I can move to Hawaii by myself, I can do anything.

The excitement is exploding out of my heart as I look out the window of my Uber to my vacation rental on Piikoi Street. I don't know much about the Makiki neighborhood other than it has a grocery store and everything I need within walking distance. Luckily, the unit is just as nice as it looked on the listing. It has a big shower, washer/dryer, nice appliances, a desk for working, and a lanai overlooking the Ko'olau mountain range, which is everything I need and want for the next month while my furniture is in transit. My car is already here, but the dock has closed for the weekend and will not open until Monday. I unpack all three suitcases immediately because I want this to feel like home for next month, because well, it is. Luckily, the bed is comfortable, and I fall asleep as soon as my head hits the soft pillows.

BEFORE meeting up with Kyle Saturday morning, I go for a run along the beachfront in Ala Moana Park.

I can't believe I live here!

There is a slight drizzle, but it feels refreshing. Then, in typical Hawaiian style, there is a rainbow after the rain. My heart warms. I know this transition isn't going to be easy, but I know in my heart I have made the right decision.

Kyle seems to be about my age and looks even more like an Asian model in person than he did on his Instagram. I quickly learn that is because he and his wife are models. I would normally be intimidated by this, but he is so cool that his aesthetically flawless appearance doesn't even faze me. He picks me up at my rental since I don't have my car yet. I am kind of freaking out about looking at a condo right away, but his calm Aloha demeanor puts me in check. My Chicago personality is going to need a lot of adjusting here. We meet the seller's real estate agent, Maggie, who has a flower tucked in her ear. The unit is everything I want! This is a big deal considering my price range is on the cusp of a lot of major fixer-uppers. My intuition tells me to put an offer in on this condo. As Kyle and I leave, he asks the inevitable. "What do you think?"

"I love it."

I describe my situation with the Chicago condo. It starts raining. He suggests going to a café to chat. I am freaking out because I haven't even been here for twenty-four hours, and I am already thinking about putting an offer in on a condo when my condo in Chicago hasn't even officially closed. This is happening too fast.

Kyle can sense that I am overwhelmed and calmly talks to me with no pressure. He gives me a sense of comfort and connection that eases the tightness in my chest. After a while, we aren't even talking about the condo. We are shooting the shit as if we are old friends. Because of this, I calm down even more and start to think more clearly. I have bought a condo before, and I have been looking for Hawaii listings for a year. I know my price range, and I know what I want. I want to put in an offer on that condo. Because my Chicago condo is closing on Tuesday, Kyle wisely suggests that we wait until Tuesday to put in our offer.

IT's 4 a.m. on Monday, and I just got up to work on Chicago time. It is strange but not too bad, especially since my internal clock has not adjusted to local time. I log off at 1 p.m. Hawaii time and order an Uber to pick up my car. My Uber driver is nice and likes to talk, which is a good distraction from the long drive. As we pull up to the Matson dock, I see my bright red Fly Trapper in the front row. I can't believe how excited I am to see my car. When I pull away, the first thing I do is put the top down, of course.

Top down in November! And I don't even need to turn on the heat!

Tuesday rolls around. Joe texts me. The Chicago condo is closed! I text Kyle. He submits the offer! But it's not all good news. In the meantime, there was a cash offer on the condo. Maggie told Kyle that she liked me better, but they obviously can't turn down a cash buyer. I understand, but am also disappointed. But now, my heart is set on buying a condo. I talk to Kyle, and we decide to continue with the direction change of skipping a short-term rental and looking to buy a condo. This may take longer than a month, so we have a backup plan to rent another vacation rental if needed. Like everything else, I will figure it out and make it happen. Old Me would have been in a total panic right now, but New Me will relax and go with the flow.

AFTER a few days of getting settled in Hawaii, I text Greg to see if he wants to hang out.

> I've been feeling under the weather plus I'm training for the marathon, maybe next week.

Next week arrives, and I text him again.

> My friend who is an event coordinator got tickets to the Bruno Mars concert, maybe next week.

Next week arrives, and I text him again. I don't have any friends yet, so I have no shame in seeming desperate.

> I am going to be spending the weekend at my gf's house in Kailua, maybe next week.

Got it. All he had to do was say so. I suspected he had a girlfriend anyway, so it wouldn't have been a surprise. I am going to forget about Greg and focus on making new friends. The problem is, it's harder than I thought it would be to make friends in Hawaii. I made friends everywhere I went in Chicago— the gym, yoga, and even places like Trader Joe's. I can't figure out why it is so difficult in Hawaii, especially after the Denver experience.

MIKE and I have been having weekly calls to work on the book project, except that we mostly get sidetracked by catching up that we haven't been talking about the book much. I am excited to get started on the book, but since I have been struggling to make friends, I enjoy my weekly calls with Mike for the sake of human interaction, even though it's over Zoom. The banter is less flirtatious, and we are growing closer as friends. Growing closer to him brings a few new challenges to the dynamic. Mike seems to have a mindset that one should always have a positive attitude no matter what. I understand the importance of a positive attitude, but I also understand that it's okay to have negative emotions, like anger and sadness, as long as you don't stay in that state. I am also bothered by how he glorifies all of his other female friends and hardly says anything complimentary or supportive toward me.

"Diana is such a go-getter."

"Melody has been top in sales for the past two years."

"I love Ashley's mind."

I know I shouldn't be taking any of this personally, but I am. I feel less-than his other female friends. I wonder why he intentionally says these things to me.

Is he trying to provoke me?

I wish I could find a way to make more local friends. I struggle for a few more weeks, and then, out of the blue, I get a text from Greg.

> Hey, I know it's short notice, but do you want to meet me at happy hour this afternoon?

I am so lonely and desperate for human connection that I respond immediately, even though he has been dodging me since I landed here.

> Sounds good!

I meet Greg at a restaurant called Moku. He had texted that he would be sitting at the bar with an Aloha shirt and hat. Even with such a firm description, I am afraid I won't be able to find him.

What if every dude at the bar is wearing an Aloha shirt and hat?

Wearing a false sense of confidence, I walk into Moku and immediately spot Greg at the bar, mostly because not only is he dressed exactly how he said he would be, but he is looking directly at me. He stands up and gives me a big bear hug, which feels good because this is the only person I have interacted with in person in almost a month, except Kyle.

We sit down and start chatting like old friends. Greg is extremely easy to talk to, and we develop immediate rapport. Greg goes deep into his trauma about how his mom died when he was in high school and the fallout with his dad. He even changed his last name to his mom's last name to disassociate with his dad. Sharing such personal information creates a sense of closeness with Greg. I feel like he is my best friend, even though we just met. He also confides in me about his girlfriend, Tessa. She is a cocaine addict and has a host of other issues, so they are the on-and-off type of couple. She is extremely wealthy because her extremely wealthy former husband committed suicide, and she inherited his fortune. Greg seems codependent on her for money and confidence. I get the sense that is why he has been so flaky since I arrived here.

I am getting ready to sign up for an improv class to meet people, and since Greg is cool and funny, I think he might like it too. "Hey, do you want to take an improv class with me?"

"Maybe."

Maybe he doesn't want to do an activity with me.

"Why, what's wrong?"

"I don't know. I don't like to commit to things."

I don't know how I feel about this. It makes me think he is waiting for a better offer to do something more fun with someone else. Nevertheless, at the end of the night, I am ecstatic because I finally have a new friend here! About a week after Moku's, Greg calls me.

"Hey Ang! I am going to sign up for that improv class that you told me about."

"Really?"

"Why do you act surprised?"

"I don't know, you didn't seem excited about it, but I am glad you are joining!"

$\mathcal{K}$YLE and I resume condo searching, which is manageable with my new work schedule of logging off at 1 p.m. On the days that I am not looking for a home or running errands, I go to the beach after work to take a nap. To the beach. After work. On weekdays. In November.

What the hell was I so afraid of? Living here is amazing!

In late November, I start to get a little panicked about not finding a condo yet. Kyle starts to send me listings out of the higher end of my price range. I mostly turn them down, but there is one that I like with an ocean view. When we arrive at the showing, I am appalled at how small it is. But that is not the worst part. The carpet in the bedroom is filthy, and in the kitchen, two counter panels form an 'L' to close off the kitchen from the living room. The kitchen counter materials and colors are mismatched.

Is this a joke? At this list price?

I am ready to ask Kyle to pause the search so that I can find another monthly vacation rental, but then I get an email from Agnes' automated listing. There is a condo in an off-the-beaten-path neighborhood, but it's near Diamond Head, an iconic inactive volcano on South Oahu, and it fits all my requirements. Best yet, it's in my price range! I send it to Kyle. He texts me back.

> I don't know. There are some sketchy areas on that street. Let me check it out and I will get back to you.

He gets back to me, and it's in a good section! The day we visit, we meet there. As I am driving down Date Street, there is a beautiful view of Diamond Head. I have a good feeling in my heart about this. The unit is empty, except for a few staged items. I love it! It was completely remodeled four years ago, so everything is new, including the appliances.

"So, what do you think?"

"It's small. But I like it. A lot."

"Do you want to put in an offer?"

"Yes."

Someone else has already put in an offer, but they have a sketchy loan deal. The seller accepts our offer! It's mid-November, and because I am applying for a mortgage, the closing won't happen for another month. To save us the trouble of looking for another vacation rental, Kyle negotiates with the seller to let me rent from him until the sale closes. There is only one problem. My furniture shipment has been delayed. Hopefully, it gets here by the time I move in.

It doesn't, but everything else is going smoothly, so I don't care. One of my friends from Chicago bought me a gift certificate to Bed Bath & Beyond as a going away gift, so I use it to buy a nice air mattress. And the seller's real estate agent gives me the bar stools that she had used for staging.

This won't be so bad!

Until it is. Sleeping on an air mattress for two weeks is too uncomfortable. But finally, my furniture arrives! I unpack everything immediately because I am anxious for my newly closed home to feel like home.

CHAPTER 15

*G*REG is running the Honolulu Marathon. I synched up with him on his bib number so I can track him on the mobile app and cheer him on at the finish line. I have run sixteen marathons due to my former excessive exercising tendencies, so I know how motivational it is to have someone cheering you on, especially during the homestretch. Joe would always wait for me at the one-mile-to-go marker on the Chicago Marathon course, which was one of my favorite parts of the race. Greg told me his projected finish time, and I dutifully line up thirty minutes before that. But the app keeps predicting a slower and slower finish time. I think he started walking. I am worried.

I hope he is okay.

After waiting for almost an hour and a half, finally, I see him wearily jogging down the street. "Yeah!!! Go, Greg!!!"

He gives me the kind of exhausted, half-hearted smile you would expect to receive at mile twenty-six of a marathon. I text him to ask where to meet him. He doesn't respond.

Okay, he's probably getting his medal and Gatorade or whatever.

He still doesn't respond. I start walking home, and I feel my phone vibrate with a text notification.

We're by the tree.

It's a park. There are hundreds of trees.

Which tree?

No response.

We? He must be with Tessa. Is that why he doesn't want to meet up with me? I want to meet her.

(The trees by the tent.)

There are at least fifty tents set up all over the park. At this point, I understand that he is not interested in meeting up, probably because he is with Tessa, but why should that matter? He didn't mention that she is jealous. I feel hurt that I wasted my Sunday morning cheering him on when it wasn't even appreciated.

I am working from home and go to the bathroom. The sink is quickly filling up with water.

Oh my God! What the hell?!

I run to the kitchen and get a pot to scoop the water out of the sink and into the shower. It keeps coming. And it's not clean, so I am desperate not to get this dirty water on anything but the sink or shower. In between scoops, I run to get my phone to call an emergency plumber. Unfortunately, when you live on an island, it takes two hours for an emergency plumber to arrive. For the two hours I am waiting, I scoop the water from the sink to the shower in pure adrenaline mode.

The plumber, Micah, is young, probably in his early to mid-twenties, and seems to know what he is doing until he is finished. I have some questions. "What caused this?"

"Oh, it's hard to say. It happens sometimes."

"So...how do I prevent this from happening again?"

"You can't."

What? Is this a joke?

I am afraid to leave the house now, and when I do, my heart skips a beat every time I open the front door upon my return because I am afraid to see a flood.

I don't even feel comfortable in my new home.

I have been getting Neil Strauss' newsletter. He is hosting an event in January in L.A. It's about healing your core wounds instead of putting Band-Aids on all your problems. Usually, his events are for his all-male private society members, but this is open to everybody to apply. I have leveled-up my life so much by moving here, but I am already reaching for the next level. There is still an anxious, fearful version of me hiding behind the badass-mover-to-Hawaii version of me. I'm accepted for Neil's intensive.

J arrive at LAX, and it's freezing. Okay, it's like fifty degrees, but I live in Hawaii now, so it might as well be ten degrees. I've never been to L.A. before and, unfortunately, I won't have time to explore because the seminar is all day for three days straight.

The Neil intensive is, well, intense. We do a lot of deep inner work that brings up a lot of emotional shit. A lot. I feel disconnected from the group because it is mostly men. The most notable part of the entire experience is when we do this crazy breathing exercise where we are lying on the ground, breathing a specific way, and listening to a specific kind of music at a specific volume. I have never heard so many grown men hysterically crying before. I think it's weird that I am not crying until I realize that I am. I touch my face, and it's wet from the waterfall of tears running out of my eyes, but my entire body is numb, so I didn't even realize I was crying. Before this crazy breathing exercise, most of my childhood memories are from six years old or older, and all I remember is Dad being emotionally unavailable. But during this exercise, I have flashbacks of when I was younger than six years old, and Dad is laughing and playing with us. I remember how he used to kiss us all goodbye before he left for work. I remember him taking me on the Dumbo ride at Disney World. I remember how after he withdrew from us emotionally, I would intentionally try to make him mad for no other reason than to get an emotional reaction from him because even anger felt better than nothing.

J come back to Hawaii from L.A. as a whole new person. I am ready to conquer my life and respond as a functional adult and no longer react like a teenager or child. I finally feel like I deserve to be loved.

Because I didn't get a lot of sleep the weekend of the seminar, by Thursday, I am exhausted. I go to the beach after work to take a nap. When I get home from the beach, I open the front door. A pool of water has crept out of my bedroom and into my living room.

Oh. My. Fucking. God.

I run to the bathroom and see that the bathroom sink is overflowing with water. I have only owned this condo for a month. I have only lived in Hawaii for a little over two months. I do not know anyone who can help me. I don't trust the plumber that came last time because whatever he did, didn't work. I call the resident manager of the building, Mickey. He is on the other side of the island and cannot get back and unlock the dry vac for at least another hour. In the meantime, he gives me a few phone numbers for emergency plumbers. Hysterically sobbing, I start calling the plumbers. One lady tells me that they can't come today, but they can come tomorrow.

"What the fuck do you mean you can't come today? I thought you were a fucking emergency service!"

I'm being an asshole. I need to get a grip.

I finally find a plumber who can come soon. While I wait, I alternate between scooping the water filling in the sink with a kitchen pot, dumping it in the shower, and mopping the existing water off the floor with my Betsey Johnson bath towels. I don't have any junk towels because I just moved here and got rid of all my extra stuff. I knew the transition here would not be easy, but this exceeded my worst-case scenarios.

The wood floor in most of my new condo is ruined. My condo association files an insurance claim, but it only covers "as-built," so I have to file another claim with my homeowner's insurance if I want wood flooring, which I do. I know nothing about buying wood floors. One of the reasons I bought this condo is because it had already been remodeled, and I didn't want to do anything else for several more years. More shit I don't know anything about and don't want to deal with.

I fucked up. Moving to Hawaii was a mistake.

CHAPTER 16

*G*REG and I are having a blast and making new friends in improv class. Most of our class goes on weekly social outings. I am finally starting to feel like part of a community here, but there is still a sense of disconnect. In Chicago, there is a mob ties mentality. Your friend tribe is composed of your ride or dies. In Hawaii, everybody is so flaky that it's hard to know who you can depend on. We just finished a class, and are at a local bar. I am sitting across from Greg. He refers to his girlfriend, Tessa, as his lover.

"Why did you call her that?"

"She doesn't want a boyfriend, so we agreed that we are lovers."

Why does he put up with that?

Through hanging out with Greg more, I start to pick up that he puts up with it because he has severe codependency issues. This is when I realize that Greg and Tessa mirror what Marc and I were. Greg is so afraid of abandonment that he is willing to put up with Tessa's disrespect and non-commitment, even when she goes on drug binges and tells him how much she hates him and how horrible he is. To him, that is less painful than the loss of love. And because he lacks self-love, he takes her back every time because his cup is empty, and he uses her breadcrumbs to fill it up. Greg and I get along so well because we are a lot alike. That is exactly why he gets on my nerves sometimes too. He is cool, funny, and could date just about anybody he wants, but only craves love from Tessa, who is incapable of giving it to him.

I am starting to have a weird issue with my tongue. It will randomly get all red and swollen as if I burnt it eating something hot. At first, I brush it off as stress related to the flood, but it is starting to concern me, so I go to a doctor, who prescribes anti-fungal medication, which works for only a few weeks. He refers me to an infection specialist, who prescribes another anti-fungal, which does not work. That doctor refers me to, allegedly, the best ENT doctor on the island, who has a waiting list of two months to get in to see him unless I want to see his physician's assistant instead, which I do. All of this time, I am tired and stressed out about my tongue and not going out on the weekends much, if at all. Greg and Tessa have been "off," so Greg needs a going out buddy, and I am not in the mood. I explain to him my tongue issues, but finally, one night, I agree to go out. Around 11 p.m., I call it a night.

"It's only 11. You never hang out anymore. You're no fun."

"Greg, I have issues with my tongue. I need to take care of my health."

"Okay, well, whatever."

THE ENT physician's assistant wants to do a biopsy of my tongue.

"It might be Lupus."

Why is he saying this without even investigating?!

For over a week, while waiting for the biopsy result, I assume I have Lupus. Greg has no sympathy. "Do you want to come out with Jacob and me this weekend?"

"I can't. I'm still having issues with my tongue. I had to get a biopsy. The doctor thinks it's Lupus."

"You never come out with us anymore."

"Greg, I had a piece of my tongue cut off. I may have the mother of all autoimmune diseases. I am exhausted from waking up at 4 a.m. all week for work. I want to stay in tonight."

"Well, hopefully, you are ready to come out next weekend."

WHEN I arrive at the follow-up appointment for the biopsy, I am expecting the worst.

"Your results are inconclusive. Come back in six months, and maybe it will be gone by then."

Is this a joke?

GOOGLE recommends an article to me.

You May Have a Vitamin B12 Deficiency if Your Tongue Looks Like This.

Right in my face is a picture of a tongue that looks exactly like mine. I went to three doctors and had a piece of my tongue cut off, and all I needed to do was take more vitamin B12. I start taking daily B12 supplements, and after only a few days, my tongue is back to normal.

MY nice neighbors referred me to a flooring store. I start asking around and researching wood floors. Everybody I talk to says to get luxury vinyl.

Ew, gross! I am NOT getting a vinyl floor.

I walk into the store and am instantly attracted to a Koa wood floor on display. It's beautiful. I read the description.

Luxury Vinyl.

Oh really? I guess it's not that bad....

I talk to the sales guy, Billy, and explain the flood and that I need new wood flooring. Billy is kind of an airhead but cool. "Well, if you are concerned about water damage, you should get our luxury vinyl. It's waterproof."

Sold!

In the meantime, State Farm has sent me my reimbursement check for my homeowner's insurance, but the condo association has not reimbursed me. It's been two months. I call the property manager, Dave, several times each week, and each time, he promises me the check will be cut "soon," but it never is. Adding to my frustrations, the contractors are coming next week to replace the floor. They will be working from 8 a.m. to 4 p.m., Monday through Friday. There are two problems with this. I will need another place to work from 8 a.m. until I log off work, and I won't be able to take the daily afternoon nap that I need from waking up at 4 a.m. The good news is because I can't come home until 4 p.m., I can kill time by going to the beach after work all week. Hopefully, I can nap at the beach.

What I didn't consider about working in coffee shops is the noise. Not only is this bad for my concentration, but I also cannot do conference calls during the time I am working outside of my home. Luckily, this is not a problem for most of the week. But there is another issue. My phone rings. It's my project manager who's installing the floor. "Where is your trim?"

"My what?" I yell over the espresso machine.

"Floor trim."

"What's that?"

"It's the baseboard where the flooring ends."

"I didn't buy that. I didn't know that I needed it."

"You need it with any wood floor. Didn't the sales guy tell you that?"

"No."

"Well, if you order it today, we can pick it up later."

"Okay."

I call Billy. I decide not to be petty and not voice my irritation that he didn't tell me that I needed trim, even though I had told him I had never bought flooring before. I want to make this phone call quick and get back to work.

"Hi, Billy! It's Angie Hawkins. I need to order some trim. My contractor will pick it up this afternoon."

"Oh, you didn't tell me you needed trim."

Breathe.

"I didn't know I needed it."

"Yeah, all wood floors need trim."

Breathe. Breathe. Breathe.

THE floor is finally replaced, but I am still waiting on my five thousand dollar insurance reimbursement from the condo association. Dave has started avoiding me completely. Finally, one day he answers my call.

"Hi, Dave! It's Angie Hawkins. I'm calling on the status of my check."

"Yeah, I talked to the Board, and the insurance deductible was five thousand dollars, and since your check is only five thousand dollars, paying for the deductible absorbs your payout."

"Wait, why am I responsible for the deductible? You filed the claim on my behalf because it was a building issue."

"Well, we charge the homeowner the deductible so that they have the incentive to file a claim with their homeowner's insurance instead."

Breathe. Breathe. Breathe.

"This is a building issue, which is why you filed a claim on my behalf in the first place. If you wanted me to file the entire claim with my homeowner's insurance, all you had to do was say so. Nobody ever mentioned this to me. But my homeowner's insurance shouldn't pay for something that was a building issue."

"So you think that every time there is a building issue, and we file a claim on a homeowner's behalf, that we should use the reserves to pay it?"

"Yes! That is what the reserves are for! That's what our monthly association fees are for!"

"I'm sorry. We can't reimburse you."

When I moved here, I knew the Aloha spirit was very different from the Chicago spirit, and I have been doing a really good job not being Chicago in Hawaii. But Chicago Angie is about to go HAM, and I cannot stop her.

"This was a known building issue! I had a backflow issue at the beginning of January and had an emergency plumber come, for which I spent four hundred dollars of my OWN money to fix a building issue. THEN, my plumber snaked the plug to another unit in the stack. I heard from my neighbors later that each unit in my stack was hiring a different plumber to snake their clog.

All this time, Mickey was aware of this happening and didn't do anything to fix the main issue, which eventually flooded my unit. THEN, Mickey initiated the building insurance claim on my behalf because he admitted it was a building issue. THEN, I had to pay a thousand dollar deductible to my homeowner's insurance to get an upgraded floor. If you wanted me to use my homeowner's insurance for the entire repair, all you had to do was say so, but nobody told me! But that's beside the point because the condo association insurance should be paying for it because it was a KNOWN BUILDING ISSUE! I'm calling a lawyer! I'm NOT paying the deductible!"

I end the call, disappointed in myself for losing control. All of the shit I learned at the Neil intensive feels so irrelevant right now because I am not practicing any of it. I feel so defeated.

I hate dealing with everything by myself.

I'm in the middle of work, so I will wait until later to research lawyers. About an hour later, my phone rings. It's Dave. I have only partially cooled off and don't want to talk to him again, but I want to catch him while he is calling me because he is so hard to get a hold of.

"Hi, Dave."

"Hi Angie, I talked to the Board, and they will pay the deductible. I'll have Accounts Payable cut a check to you this week."

Why did that have to be so complicated?

MY health issues are better, I am getting more into the swing of my work routine of waking up at 4 a.m., and Greg has invited me to Art after Dark, a monthly event at the Art Museum with some improv friends. I have not hung out with Greg and my improv friends for several months due to my tongue issues, and I quit taking classes because the late weekday class schedule wasn't working out with my early morning work schedule. It is fun catching up with everyone until Greg starts laying into me.

"You never hang out with us anymore."

"You never come out."

"You need to come out more."

"Greg, I am here right now, and you aren't even appreciating it because you are too busy complaining about how I haven't been hanging out, even though I told you a gazillion times that I have been having health issues and exhausted from dealing with the flood aftermath! Plus, I am not a partier like you are. Even if I were going out, I wouldn't be raging until 4 a.m. like you like to do."

"Wow, you're mad about this."

"Yes, I'm mad! I'm not even having a good time because you have been nagging me all night."

"I just wish you would come out more."

I go home. My chest feels like it's in a vice grip. Greg is my best friend right now. I don't want to stop hanging out with him, but I have to. He wants me to be someone I am not, and his lack of boundaries is suffocating.

No wonder Marc dropped me on my ass. I was exactly like Greg.

MIKE and I have been having our weekly Zoom calls to work on the book project but we are still getting side-tracked and end up chatting for hours on end. He's so easy to talk to, and I love laughing with him, but I still feel like he pits me against his other female friends. And his toxic positivity mindset makes me feel like I'm wrong to feel anything other than good. We aren't working on the book, and he isn't good for my self-esteem.

Why am I still talking to him?

Maybe I'm lonely because I still don't have a lot of friends here and have only been on a few dates. I don't know why, but I feel ready to meet The One.

Where is my person?

CHAPTER 17

MARCH 2019

I don't remember how I found Jess's post. I think I was dissociating by scrolling through Instagram and got caught up in the rabbit hole of Instagram Explore. Her post was an advertisement for a Twerkshop. Twerking is something I have never done, or even tried to do, although I love to dance. But twerking? That is way too risqué for me. Although...I would love to learn.

Am I crazy? I am going to make a fool of myself dancing with a bunch of young, sexy girls.

I close the app. But damn it, my intuition is knocking me upside the head.

Do it.

Intuition, please! I don't want to make an ass of myself. Please don't make me do this!

DO IT!

I do not dare ignore my intuition assaulting me. I go back to the post and sign up for the Twerkshop, which is happening next weekend. It's two hours long. I assume there is a break halfway. I make a deal with myself that if I am making an ass of myself, I can leave halfway through.

I arrive five minutes before the class, and there is already a full room. The room is small. I would guess that the capacity is about twenty-five people. There is a full wall mirror at the front of the room and a disco ball. I love disco balls, so this seems like a good omen. The only open spots are in the front. But wait! I see a space I can squeeze into at the back of the room, so that is exactly where I go. Some of the other girls came with friends, so they are already engaged in conversation. I sit in silence on my mat and wait for class to start.

We start the class with a guided meditation. Jess is a yoga teacher who doesn't give a shit about traditional yoga practice, thus, she incorporates twerking and hip-hop music into her class. I love everything about her, from her hippie attitude and long, blonde, beachy hair down to the boldness of her full-body tattoos. In the guided meditation, she asks us to recall the last time we felt free. I know the point of the exercise is to recall something from when we were like four years old and ran through the sprinkler naked, but I can't think of anything. For as long as I can remember, I was always forced to conform to Mom's controlling, confining standards. If I didn't comply, I had to bear her wrath or judgment. It didn't feel safe to be me. Masking my true self continued into adulthood. I don't think I have ever felt free.

I can do some of the moves for the first half of the dance portion, but I can't figure out how most of the other girls are moving with the ease of a Nicki Minaj backup dancer. Embarrassed and glad I am in the back of the room, I resign that my body doesn't move that way. But it turns out someone else, who is much braver than me, is having the same problem, and she boldly asks Jess the exact question in my head. "What am I doing wrong?"

"You're not letting your body move."

"I don't think I can move my body that way."

"I went to my first twerk class ten years ago, and I almost walked out because I was so frustrated and resigned that my body couldn't move that way."

This is shocking news considering how sexually Jess is dancing in this class. She continues, "Then, I realized that my body *can* move that way, but wasn't because I was raised to not be sexually open. In our society, women are labeled as hoes or sluts if they move their bodies sexually. Forget all of that right now. We are in a safe space, so move how you would if you were having sex."

A-ha!

In the safe environment that Jess created, I tell myself that my body *can* move that way and permit myself to be as sexual as possible in the middle of this studio of much younger and thinner, scantily clad girls with the light refractions of the disco ball and hip-hop music blaring so loud I can feel the bass in my chest. I shit you not, I go straight from hardly being able to move my body to twerking so aggressively that I could be an extra in a rap video. I can't believe what I see in the mirror! All it took was a change in a limiting belief.

Oh, I get it now. Thank you, Intuition.

I love this feeling of freedom. I don't care if I look awkward grinding on the floor. I don't care that I have camel toe in my hot pink booty shorts. I don't care that Mom would be embarrassed to call me her daughter right now. I don't care. I don't care. I don't care. I feel like the child I was never allowed to be. My inner child is so overjoyed that I could cry. I feel connected here. Jess has a weekly class for Shakti, a.k.a. twerk yoga, and I am going to be her new regular. Plus, this will be a good way to meet people.

Next level here I come!

I'M talking to Mom on the phone, except she is the only one talking, and I am listening. "I was talking to one of my co-workers about you the other day." My ears perk up as I continue to listen. "I told her that I am visiting my daughter in Hawaii in a few weeks, and she said, 'Oh, you must be so proud of your daughter for living out her dream!' and I said, 'I never thought of it that way.'"

The shame feels like an explosion in my chest.

Why is she telling me this?

She never thought of it that way because she never thought about how happy Hawaii could make me, only how miserable it would make her. I can't believe she is saying this out loud to me. She continues talking about work, sweeping the can of worms she just opened right back under the rug. I don't even know how to respond. So I don't and let the resentment silently build inside me.

J am at my Grandma Mary's funeral, except she is standing next to me, totally alive and well. I am telling her that I am extremely anxious about Mom's visit, and overall angry and resentful about how I was raised by her judgmental and emotionally controlling hand. Grandma delivers wise advice. "Don't make drama about the past."

I wake up. Mom's mom, Mary, is my last living grandparent. She is ninety-two years old and still in relatively good health, but this dream leaves a bad taste in my mouth. The next day, my Aunt Cynthia calls me. Cynthia rarely calls me.

Oh shit! The dream! Grandma died!

I answer the phone. We chit-chat for a few minutes, and everything seems to be fine, but I am still worried. "Is Grandma okay? I had a dream that she died."

"Yes, she's fine. I wouldn't worry about it. I have dreams sometimes that people die."

She's right. It was just a dream.

But what an amazing message.

*J*T'S 5 a.m. on Saturday. Because I get up so early during the week for work, I tend to also get up early on the weekends. After eating a light breakfast, I go to the gym to work out. The gym is about a mile and a half away. I usually run there as part of my workout, but I am not feeling up to running, so I ride my bike.

When I bought this bike, I had a stress fracture in my sacrum and couldn't run for several months. I bought the bike to fill the void of running. I didn't care what I bought because I simply wanted something to satisfy my over-exercise compulsion. The salesperson showed me this bike, and I immediately loved it. It wasn't until I was paying for it that I realized the make and model was a Kona Lanai. Even in 2009, I felt it was a sign that I would be moving with it to Hawaii one day. I shipped the bike here, and there was some damage to it. Luckily, a bike store down the street could fix it, and the moving company reimbursed me for the damages. The Kona and I have been through a lot, and I have always been protective of it. In Chicago, I would always use the front tire cable with my lock to lock up the front tire.

This is Hawaii, no need for things like that. People are so nice here!

Well, some people. After my workout, I walk to my bike, and both wheels are missing. I'm not surprised. The tires were made out of Kevlar. I haven't had a flat tire in nine years.

It will be okay. I'll get new wheels.

But as I unlock the frame from the post, I notice how old and beat up it is.

This bike is ten years old. Maybe it's time for a whole new bike.

Then, I see one of the local bike share stations, Biki, about twenty yards away.

Maybe I can Biki now. I don't have enough storage space, and it's kind of a hassle to store my bike in my bedroom closet anyway.

I stand on the sidewalk for a minute and calmly assess the situation.

Yes, I will Biki now.

I feel relieved. Now, I will have more room for storage in my bedroom closet, and I don't have to worry about it getting stolen. After unlocking my bike, I gift the thief, or someone else, the rest of the bike. I leave the frame and take the lock with me as I casually stroll to the Biki station. Then, I stop dead in my tracks.

What the hell just happened?

The beloved bike I paid to ship here just had its wheels stripped, and I had zero emotional reaction whatsoever.

Is this what growth looks like?

Old Me would have still been standing near the naked frame, sobbing uncontrollably about how helpless I am in this unfair world and spent who knows how much time and money buying new wheels or a new bike to restore my version of normal so that I didn't feel any discomfort. New Me, comfortable with uncertainty and solving my problems intelligently and courageously, barely batted my eyes at unexpectedly pivoting on my transportation options.

J logged off work, and I am walking out the door to grab a Biki to ride to my friend Kahea's house. My phone rings. It's Mom. She never calls me. And it's Monday during the day. This seems like an odd time for her to call anyway. I don't have time to talk on the phone because I don't want to be late, but my intuition tells me to answer.

"Hi, Mom!"

"Hi Ang! Are you finished working?"

"Yeah, I just logged off and am on my way to a friend's house."

"I need to tell you something."

Oh shit.

"Grandma died."

My stomach drops as my eyes laser focus on a license plate of a car parked on the street. As I gasp, my free hand flies to cover my mouth. "Oh my God!" My voice cracks as the tears start to form. "What happened?"

She died in her sleep, which is the best way to go. I know she has been depressed lately. Being ninety-two years old, a lot of her family and friends have passed, and she isn't pleased with how the world has turned out during her lifespan. I remember her last words.

"This is the last time I am going to see you."

She was right. And I have a feeling the dream I had last month meant something more. Mom offers to pay for my flight for the funeral.

"I appreciate the offer, but I don't want to see Grandma dead. I would rather do a lei ceremony here."

Also, I'm not ready to see my family again yet. I arrive at Kahea's, and as soon as I walk through the door, I burst into tears. "My grandma died."

She hugs me, walks to her closet, and pulls out a notebook. "I know this sounds weird, but my Spirit Guides are telling me to give you a notebook."

I am slightly surprised because I know Kahea from pole dancing class, and I know she is an energy healer, but I didn't know she was a medium.

"No, that's not weird at all. I love notebooks. I have at least five different journals going at any given time."

"Do you want to connect to your Grandma?"

"Sure."

She sits on the floor across from her couch and closes her eyes. I plop down on the couch. Her eyes pop back open. "Sit up straight!"

I jerk out of my slouched position and sit up with perfect posture with my feet on the floor.

"Sorry, I don't know why I just said that."

"It's exactly something my grandma would say to me if she saw me sitting like that. Did you see how fast I reacted?"

We both laugh, and I find it comforting that Grandma is with us right now. I cry tears of joy.

She connects to Grandma and has a message for me. "You're too pretty to think that you're not."

Warm tears run down my cheeks onto my neck. Grandma was always critical of my appearance. It warms my heart to hear her say this. Like Dad, it makes me happy that she seems happier on the other side, without the ego running the show.

I buy a lei and have a lei ceremony in the ocean. Before releasing the flowers to the sea, I spell Gma with the flowers, hoping she can see them from Heaven.

On the day of the funeral, Mom sends me a text. It's a picture of Grandma in her casket. I am insanely triggered.

> I told you I didn't want to see her dead!

> Sorry, I didn't mean to upset you.

Really? Because you didn't even consider my feelings.

I suppress the anger and don't respond because if I told her it hurt my feelings that she sent a picture of Grandma when I specifically told her I didn't want to see her dead, I don't think she would care. I envision her usual response of dismissing my emotions as being too sensitive instead of exploring why she didn't respect my boundaries. I don't have the courage to speak up to her. The resentment continues to pile up. I am tired of holding it in but I don't think she would be open to listening if I told her that she hurt my feelings.

I'm not important.

Chapter 18

WITH my thirty-ninth birthday coming up, I start to feel a sense of dread about turning forty. I feel old. I had the courage to move to Hawaii, but I still feel that there is so much missing from my life. I still have a feeling of being disconnected from everyone and everything. And it doesn't help that I haven't found my person yet.

Am I meant to wander around single for the rest of my life?

I want to go into my forties on fire. I set a goal of developing the capacity to feel the fear while growing outside my comfort zone. I create three milestones to accomplish for the rest of this year:

1. Take a surfing lesson because I am a city person and not comfortable in the ocean.

2. Go to a networking event to meet new people because I feel awkward trying to make new friends here.

3. Plan a trip to New Zealand and Australia because traveling to two countries by myself feels terrifying, yet badass.

As part of my first milestone, I schedule a surfing lesson with Ozzy, the guy an Australian blogger in a cooking class last month told me about. I have no idea what to expect. I am athletic, but I am not a water person and have never done anything like surfing. In the days leading up to the lesson, I am terrified.

I am going to look like an idiot.

I'm too old to learn how to surf.

The lesson is on a Sunday morning, and I walk the mile to Waikiki to burn off some of my nervous energy. Waikiki is to

Oahu as the Magnificent Mile, or Navy Pier is to Chicago— full of
tourists. If you are a tourist, it's the place to be. If you live here, you
avoid it at all costs. For this reason, I think this is only the second
time I have been to Waikiki since I have lived here. Walking down
Kalakaua brings nostalgia from all of the times I visited Hawaii
and wanted so badly to live here. Suddenly, my heart is overflowing
with love and positive expectation.

I am exactly where I need to be.

When I was texting with Ozzy, he told me to meet him at the
Duke statue in Waikiki. I did not tell him what I look like, nor do
I know what he looks like. As I approach the Duke statue, I see
an older man with a tanned, weathered face with shoulder-length,
wavy, brown/salt and pepper hair. He is intriguing to me, and I
instantly hope this is Ozzy. A huge, captivating smile spreads
across his face as we lock eyes. I return the smile. "Are you Ozzy?"

"Hi, Angie!"

He embraces me in a huge hug, and at this moment, I know I
am in good hands. We walk to his umbrella that is already set up
on the beach.

"Have you ever surfed before?"

"No."

"What made you take a lesson?"

"I just turned thirty-nine, and I want to go into my forties on
fire."

Why am I telling him how old I am??

"You look great for thirty-nine. Do you know how to swim?"

"Yes."

"Where are you from?"

Oh great, I must look like a tourist.

"I live here."

"Where are you *originally* from?"

"Chicago."

He is totally easy to talk to, which makes me feel more comfortable about the lesson. He is older, maybe late fifties, but he is
attractive for an older man. He is skinny, with no butt, which I
usually don't find attractive, but I think his smile and laugh make

him attractive. His aura radiates the Aloha spirit, and I know I will enjoy his company, even if I hate surfing. We start with a land demonstration, then we hit the water and paddle out to the waves. I am scared, but Ozzy distracts me by asking, "Where do you live?"

"Kapahulu."

"How long have you lived here?"

"Eight months."

Why is it so embarrassing to admit what a newcomer I am?

We immediately start with the water demonstration, which differs from the land demonstration because the water is moving and the land wasn't. I get off to a rocky start, but Ozzy is positive and offers helpful feedback each time I try to stand up on a wave. Every time I paddle back out to him, he is watching with his captivating smile. I learn that there is a lot of waiting involved in surfing, which is fine because I enjoy talking to Ozzy as we wait for the next set of waves.

"What do you do to work out?"

Because I have an athletic physique, I get this question a lot. Usually, it's annoying because it's like going through the formality of someone casually asking how you are doing when they don't care, but for some reason, I don't mind that Ozzy asked.

"Run, lift weights, dance…"

Should I tell him that by dance, I mean twerk yoga? Should I tell him about pole dancing?

Part of me is embarrassed to tell someone I just met about pole dancing, but talking to Ozzy is like talking to an old friend. What the hell.

"….pole dance."

"Where do you pole dance?"

"In my living room. I also take classes."

Ozzy laughs. "You have a pole in your living room?"

I laugh. "Yes."

"Being fit will help you with surfing."

"I know, but I wish I would have started when I was younger and more fearless."

"That's what my girlfriend said when she started surfing."

Of course, a man this charismatic has a girlfriend. She's probably just as cool as he is.

I am not great at surfing and only manage to stand up one time, but I have an absolute blast! Being immersed in the ocean is fun and oddly refreshing. And surfing is so interesting to me because it feels like you are walking on water. Ozzy is extremely generous with his time, and we end up staying out longer than an hour. I am sad when the lesson ends. I want more. "Can I take another lesson with you sometime?"

"Absolutely!"

I surprise myself by asking, but I would like to learn more about this extremely difficult yet fun sport. Ozzy seems to have enjoyed my company as much as I enjoyed his because he is pleased that I would like to come back. We schedule another lesson for when I get back from my mainland trip to Chicago and Denver.

I'm going into my forties on fire!

CHAPTER 19

MY trip to the mainland feels overwhelming because there is so much packed into a small time frame. I am looking forward to Chicago the most because, even though it's primarily for work, I miss my friends and the city itself. Then, Denver. Mike has been acting distant lately, and we have been more sporadic with the book meetings, mostly because we have both been busier. But he seems excited about me coming, and I am excited about seeing him in person for the second time, even though I know him so much better now. I'm excited to talk more about the book project.

Landing in O'Hare feels strange as a non-resident. I step outside to catch my Uber, and even though it's June, it's evening, and it's chilly. But it's Chicago, and I am so happy to be back that the chilly air feels welcoming. My Uber driver flies down the Expressway at about ninety miles per hour, swerving in and out of traffic on the way to Joe's house in the South Loop. At first, I am terrified because I have been submerged in turtle-slow island driving for the past eight months, but then I feel the rush of the speed of the car, and it feels amazing. As we approach the Armitage exit, I see the huge red State Farm digital billboard with the skyline in the background.

I'm home!

But do I still consider Chicago home?

I arrive at Joe's, and it feels good to hug someone I know. I am glad I am staying with him instead of at a hotel. It feels homier this way. Plus, I can tell he likes to have a guest to accommodate.

"You look tan!"

"Thank you? Nice to see you too?"

The dynamics are different with Joe, but I think it's because I am a different person now. One evening, I spill some of my drink on the kitchen island. Calm and collected, I start wiping it up.

"There you go, freaking out like you always do about everything."

"What are you talking about? I'm not even freaking out."

"Yes, you are."

Is he for real? Oh wait, he is viewing me through his old lens of Old Me, who used to freak out about everything.

I shake my head, suppressing a smile, and finish cleaning up.

M IKE picks me up at the Denver airport. He walks up to me and gives me a huge bear hug. We laugh and talk just like old friends catching up. I mean, we are, except this is only the second time we have seen each other in person. We first stop at my Airbnb so I can drop off my luggage and change into a cute yellow dress. I brought him an Aloha shirt as a gift, and he puts it on immediately, even though it is wrinkled as shit, but I smile inside because he likes it enough to wear it like that. Then, we head to a restaurant. Mike has chosen it based on me telling him that I love ribs, and nowhere in Hawaii has good ribs.

When we arrive, the hostess asks if we would like to sit in-side or outside. "Outside." It flies out of my mouth without even thinking because I love being outside. They seat us at a table in the outdoor courtyard, and the waiter asks for our drink order. Mike orders two shots of limoncello. For whatever reason, the server attendant initially brings out only one shot. Mike grabs it and dumps it down his throat.

Okay, I thought we could have a toast, but whatever, you can drink the first one without me.

She then brings my shot which I take by myself, which doesn't feel as fun. We order some appetizers. I feel sweat dripping down my back.

It's so hot out here.

We just started eating this hot food, and it's only going to get worse. I turn to Mike. "Should we ask to get a table inside? I'm sweating."

"Wow, you're more high maintenance than me."

Since when is switching tables if you are uncomfortable high maintenance?

The waiter doesn't mind at all and moves us indoors. Mike walks ahead of me, and the waiter leads us to one of those tables where one side is a comfy booth seat and faces the restaurant, and the other side is an uncomfortable chair and only faces the other person at the booth. Mike immediately takes the comfy booth seat with a view.

Okay, since I've never been to the restaurant before and you can go anytime you want, I guess I'll face the wall.

Mike orders another round of shots, and we order food. Some cute girls walk into the dining area. Mike pauses our conversation and stares them down. I mean, we aren't on a date, but it feels disrespectful— to them and me.

"Are they cute?" I ask teasingly to point out that I notice him looking, but he takes the question very seriously.

He scrunches his face. "They're okay."

I think I have had too many shots. I have only had two, but they were strong. I am done drinking and eating. Mike and I are laughing, talking, and discussing our plans for tomorrow, including hot springs and massages. As we leave the restaurant, Mike wants to show me his place. We took an Uber to the restaurant, so it doesn't seem like a big deal to Uber to his place, and I can get another one back to my Airbnb later.

We get back to his apartment, and on the one hand, it looks familiar because I have seen it on Zoom so many times, but, on the other hand, Zoom misrepresented the dimensions. It looks a lot smaller and more college dorm-like with basic furniture and minimal decor. He wants to watch a movie. I hate watching movies, but I agree with the intention that I will watch the first twenty to thirty minutes, then bounce. Even though Evan, his roommate, is not home, he wants to watch it in his bedroom in case Evan comes home in the middle of the movie. We lay on his bed, which feels comfortable because this is something that I have done with my guy friends before. Mike turns on a movie that looks hideously boring, so I am not sure if I can even be polite about wanting to leave. As I am deciding my escape method, Mike turns over, grabs my ass under my dress, and then roughly moves his hand to the front side, which is not stimulating because of its aggressiveness. However, he did grab my ass, and no matter who touches my ass in any way, it always turns me on. I am slightly aroused, but confused. The ensuing events feature an extremely aggressive and mechanical act of intercourse that only concentrates on him getting off. And then he thinks he is done.

Oh hell no. If we are having sex, I am not leaving until I get mine.

I mount him and take care of business, but he throws me off and starts texting with someone. I haven't had a worse sexual experience since college. I get up and start getting dressed. In doing so, I start crying.

Mike gets pissed by my emotional display. "You need to leave now."

Wow, what a sensitive guy.

"And put on your glasses. You look different without your glasses. I don't like it."

The shame explodes in my chest.

I'm ugly if my glasses aren't covering up my face.

After this, I am not paying for my ride home. "Are you going to order my Uber?"

"What? Oh, yeah, sure." He starts texting again, clearly not ordering an Uber for me.

"Forget it," I snap as I order my own and leave. I'm mostly stunned on the ride back, and then I get back to my Airbnb and bawl my eyes out. I feel so used and violated.

DENVER is so boring, and I am alone all day now. The feelings of disconnection and worthlessness are overwhelming. I am making Mike's behavior about me. I wander around the city all day with a raw heart. I valued the friendship so much, probably too much, and I am placing my worth in his hands. I am craving the external validation that I am worth making love to and not being treated like a thing to stick a dick in. I am also grieving the loss of the book project.

What am I going to write about now?

The next few weeks in Hawaii, I go through the motions with a rawness in my heart. I have not heard from Mike and am unsure if we will ever talk again.

STARTING July is rough. I have lost Mike as a friend and feel aimless without the book project, but I am still determined to go into my forties on fire. I start looking for a new job that isn't so draining with IT-dominated alpha male energy and plan my New Zealand and Australia trip for December. I need to find a networking event to meet more friends and connections for a new job. I also want to take more lessons with Ozzy.

As we paddle out for our second lesson, he references his girlfriend again. Then, he corrects himself. "I don't know why I keep calling her my girlfriend. We have been married for three years."

Wow, that's strange. I could understand if they had only been married for three months.

He goes on to tell me that his wife is from New Zealand. I am extremely curious about how they met and how this relationship came about, but I don't pry, and he doesn't offer up too much information about her. He doesn't directly bad-mouth her, but he never says anything positive about her either. I get a strong feeling that he feels trapped by the marriage. I assume it's because Ozzy is a free spirit and would feel trapped being married to anybody. Then, he tells me that he has a photographer that takes pictures for lessons. This sounds like a good opportunity for getting out of my comfort zone.

"Can I hire your photographer for my next lesson?"

"You really don't want pictures, do you?"

Why is he trying to talk me out of this?

When we get back onshore, we schedule my next lesson with him and his photographer.

"Listen, you only need pictures this one time. You won't need to get them every time you have a lesson."

I know. I only want them once and never mentioned that I wanted them every time. Why would I? And why is he acting so weird and resistant about this?

O n the morning of the lesson, he introduces me to his photographer, Sarah. She is very plain looking and seems young. She has an accent, but I can't figure it out. It doesn't sound British, but it doesn't sound Australian either. We only chat for a few minutes before Ozzy and I paddle out while she sets up the camera onshore.

Wait, was that a New Zealand accent? Is that his wife? Surely he would have introduced her as his wife if it was his wife.

It's not like we are friends or anything, but I feel that we have built up a good enough rapport that he would feel comfortable introducing his wife to me, especially if she is his photographer.

"Was that your wife?"

"Huh? Oh, yeah." His response is short and sharp. He almost seems embarrassed. He didn't even look at me when he said it. He quickly changes the topic.

Well, the sex must be good if he doesn't like her but is still married to her.

Although I'm not sure how the sex works with him being so skinny. Once on shore after the lesson, he introduces her to his next lesson as his photographer, not his wife.

How weird.

Something is definitely up with them. She is clearly at least twenty years younger than him, and I am dying to know the back-story of how she is living here and married to him, but again, it's none of my business.

The pictures turn out good! They are edited because I don't remember the water being this blue, but my abs look good, so these are perfect for Instagram. I immediately post them. Mike is the first person to like my post within a few minutes of posting it. My heart skips a beat, and my brain runs into overdrive, overanalyzing everything as always.

Does this mean we are friends now?

Probably not, but at least he doesn't hate me. I have been feeling a huge void from the book project and miss our Zoom calls. But with the book project void, I have been putting my energy into planning my New Zealand and Australia trip in December. Because Ozzy's wife is from New Zealand and he has been there, I asked him about travel tips. He recommended Christchurch because that is where his wife is from. Ozzy is a fun guy who seems well-traveled, so I trust his opinion. I book my legs as follows: Honolulu–Christchurch, NZ–Queenstown, NZ–Melbourne, Australia–Honolulu. In researching Queenstown, I discover that it is quite an adventure town. Allegedly, bungee jumping was invented there, which is the most popular activity to book. This trip *is* about enduring the fear while growing outside of my comfort zone. It's only July, but my stomach drops as I hit the 'Book' button on the bungee website.

What am I getting myself into?

Even though there is a twenty-four-hour cancellation policy for refunds, I will not cancel no matter what. To take it a step further, I set a goal to not hesitate on the countdown.

I am doing this!

I book another lesson with Ozzy. I am so excited to take another lesson! I show up on the beach at our scheduled time, and he isn't here. Another surf instructor, Joey, recognizes me. "Are you looking for Ozzy?"

"Yeah, I have a lesson with him."

"Are you sure? He just took another lesson out. He won't be back for another hour."

He forgot about me.

The shame tightens up my chest.

I'm not important.

I feel awkward. Part of me wants to walk away and never take a lesson again. On the other hand, I recognize that this could be an honest mistake, and I want to play it off cool, even though I am freaking out inside. I send him a text acknowledging that I showed up because I am not sure if he expects me to show up at another time or truly forgot about me completely.

After about an hour, I feel the vibrating of a phone call in my bag. It's Ozzy. I don't want to answer. I hate talking on the phone, and I don't want to rehash that he forgot about me, especially since I thought we had a well-developed rapport. I answer. "Hi, Ozzy."

"Hi, Angie! Listen, I am so sorry about earlier. I thought I had you in my calendar, but I guess I forgot to put you in. The next lesson is on me, young lady. I am so sorry."

I appreciate the offer of a free lesson, but I feel like I am accepting scraps.

Okay, one more lesson with Ozzy.

CHAPTER 20

AUGUST 2019

WHEN I announced at work last year that I was moving to Hawaii, I found out about another employee, Hilary, who also works remotely in Hawaii on the island of Kauai. My work buddy, Sofia, is friends with Hilary and has gone on group vacations with her and some other girls from work. Sofia told me I would love Hilary and put us in contact. Hilary and I immediately started texting and did get along great! Hilary invited me to stay with her over the first weekend in August. Old Me would have shied away and got a hotel, but New Me, with the goal of developing the capacity to endure the fear while growing outside my comfort zone, is going in headfirst after only talking to Hilary on the phone one time.

EVERYBODY at work speaks highly of Hilary, but that is the problem. During this visit, all Hilary has been talking about is how everybody loves her, even non-work-related stories. It's nauseating. Surely this is not the side she shows to everybody else. We are talking in the living room right now, and I feel like we are bonding, which is a relief from Hilary patting herself on the back. The topic has turned to beauty, and I ask, "What kind of moisturizer do you use? Your skin looks great."

"It's not a moisturizer. It's Botox."

"Oh really? Aren't we too young for Botox?"

"Not at all. You could use some right here." She points to the spot on her forehead right above the bridge of her nose as the shame explodes in my chest.

What kind of female tells another female that she needs Botox?

At this moment, I realize that my instant connection to Hilary was naive and only based on the fact that she was friends with Sofia. I should have gotten to know her better before spending a weekend with her.

TODAY is my last full day in Kauai, and I am heading to the beach by myself to take a break from Hilary. I am scrolling through my Instagram stories, and Mike has posted about a networking event that he is hosting later this month for his business clients. He usually only has events with his closest business associates, but since it's an open invitation, there will be a lot more people. His stories include something about a whole pig on the buffet. I reply jokingly.

I'll be there!

He replies instantly.

You should come!

Should I?

I want to prove that I can be cool and sweep everything that happened under the rug so that we can restart the book project.

"A sweep is as lucky as lucky can be!"

I am also seeking external validation after the shame explosion last visit. Plus, a networking event is the second milestone for my goal. This way, I don't have to find another event.

If you are serious, I can check my schedule.

Sure, I would love for you to meet my people.

This seems like an honest attempt to reconcile the friendship. I make a note in my calendar to check my schedule when I get home.

When I return from the beach, Hilary tells me about her vacation to Guam last year. She stayed at an Airbnb. The host, Vanessa, is from Japan and wanted to go on an extended trip to see family, but has five dogs. Hilary went back for a month to dog-sit while Vanessa and her husband went to Japan.

"If you are ever interested in dog-sitting for Vanessa, I can let her know."

"Five dogs seem like a lot."

"No, it's fine. They're totally cool."

"Okay, give Vanessa my number."

I say this, thinking I will do it sometime next year, but Vanessa texts me immediately after Hilary sends her my phone number, asking when I can come. I don't want to commit to a full month because I would miss too many pole dancing classes, and I don't want to fall back from my group, so I tell her I can come for three weeks starting at the end of September. She starts incessantly texting me instructions about the dogs and videos of them. She also has a cat now, and she is blowing up my phone with texts on how to take care of the cat. For whatever reason, she just sent me a video of the cat in action in the litter box. The constant texts are overwhelming.

> Can you please make a list and we can go through it when I get there?

KAUAI was beautiful, but I am so glad to be back home. I search for flights to Denver, and they are pretty affordable. Plus, I can work remotely in Denver, so I don't need to take time off work. I am on the fence. On the one hand, I want to prove that I am serious about reconciling our friendship by supporting him. I need to rekindle the book project because I still don't have a book project of my own. On the other hand, I don't want to face Mike again. The memories are too painful to ignore. And I can tell he has hesitations about seeing me. He has not yet committed to meeting up with me outside the event. Normally, this would be a deal-breaker for me to come, but I'm not sure I want to see him outside of the safety of the event either. But I have this nagging feeling that I need to take this trip to face my demons, to prove that I can do anything no matter how difficult, scary, or uncertain. I send a text to Mike that I am coming.

Awesome!

Is it? Why am I going back?

CHAPTER 21

$\mathcal{I}$ swore I would never go back. After the last trip, with a lump in my throat and my entire body exhausted and overwhelmed with grief, I journaled in large, loopy cursive with my pencil and notebook:.

What's good about this?
I never have to go back to Denver.

I never wanted to go back. Every plain, boring inch of that city is imprinted with the pain and shame my heart discharged on that emotionally raw day. Yesterday, I was on the brink of backing out, and I begged Grandma to show me a sign in the form of seeing the number 1444. I saw a tree-cutter truck with a phone number painted in big, bold numbers. The last four digits of the phone number were 1444. That's the number I always ask her to show me when I am on the right path. That damn phone number was in at least four different places on the truck. It was a barrage. Her sign was crystal clear, just how I always ask for it.

Even though every ounce of my logic is telling me, "Don't ever go back," my intuition is yelling, "Yes, bitch, pack that suitcase!" And I bought a personalized, engraved, luxury writing instrument for Mike as a gift. I only wanted to get him a little Hawaiian trinket from the ABC Store, like a dashboard hula dancer or tiki salt and pepper shakers, but one day I was meditating, and it came to me in a crystal clear message: Buy him a pen. Since I am my intuition's bitch, I obeyed. But now I feel embarrassed. I feel like I am rewarding bad behavior. I am waiting for my Uber with my Betsey Johnson flower print carry-on suitcase, and there is still time to turn back. But I don't turn back. I get my ass in the backseat of that Uber and dread every minute of the ride to the airport for my red-eye flight with what feels like lead in my heart. At least I packed my prescription Clonazepam to sleep on the plane. It's a nervous system suppressant that I use for emergency anxiety attacks. As if returning to Denver isn't bad enough, as I anxiously sit in the backseat of the Uber, I text Mike.

> If you're free at 7 a.m. tomor-
> row, I would love a ride from the
> airport to my Airbnb. No pressure
> if it doesn't work out with your
> schedule.

I chicken out by not asking a direct question for fear of rejection.

Why did I even text him at all?

He doesn't respond immediately, like he always does. The dynamics have changed so much between us. I arrive at the airport, and the bustle helps distract me from the mounting embarrassment of setting myself up for rejection. The renovations also help distract. The old décor of the Honolulu airport was so 1970's wood-everything-Hawaiian-retro. Now it's modern and takes away from the nostalgia of it all. My chest tightens with the anxiety of Mike not responding to my text. I remind myself that I am a functional adult, and I need to be willing to hear a "no" to my request. I respect other people's free will. But it's hard to accept no response at all. I take my Clonazepam.

As I am waiting to board the flight, a native Hawaiian-looking man with a ponytail and few teeth approaches me and asks about my hair. The Clonazepam is kicking in. My eyelids are heavy, and my brain is foggy. And I'm irritable because I am still upset that Mike hasn't texted back.

"What do you call that color?" the man asks.

"Red."

It's like the Tony Robbins conversation all over again.

"Is that your natural color?"

"No."

He doesn't get that I can't stand talking to him.

"What is it? Brown?"

"Dirty Blonde."

What difference does it make? Maybe he should be concerned about the fact that he is missing an alarming number of teeth.

"Does anybody ever call you Red?"

Why is this ass rubbing salt in my wounds?

Marc used to call me Red. I stop and realize that I am getting triggered, and it is nobody's responsibility but my own to handle it like an adult. I calm down and stop myself from taking my anger out on him.

"Sometimes." My jaw relaxes.

"What about Fireball?"

"No. Nobody has ever called me that."

I kind of like that I have a spunky, new nickname!

"I'm going to call you that."

"Okay."

I have warmed up to this man. Then, a woman, who seems to be his wife or girlfriend approaches, and they walk away without him saying goodbye. I wonder if she knows he talks to random girls and assigns them nicknames. Strangely, my mood is enhanced by this encounter. Nobody has given me a cute nickname since Marc called me Red. My heart feels at peace until my phone vibrates with a text notification.

> Shit, I have a few people staying with me, or I would! Ugh. Sorry!

I have a firm text value system that believes everybody deserves a response. But I can't do it. I am speechless. There is still time to turn around and go back home. Part of me is embarrassed that I asked. Part of me is hurt. I want to spend time with him outside the event to fix the friendship. I know from his text that will not happen. Grandma would never guide me wrong. There is a reason for this trip. The trip no longer has anything to do with repairing a broken friendship and has everything to do with me being stronger and more courageous than ever. This trip is now my starter mission to be the best version of myself possible, no matter how scary. I will fly from Hawaii to go to a social event in Denver of two hundred people where I only know one person and have an amazing time because it will help me grow outside of my comfort zone.

As I step into the aircraft, a passenger boarding at the gate next over waves excitedly at me. I do not recognize him, so I stare at him blankly. My clear lack of expression does not faze him.

"Hey! I know you!"

"From where?"

"Turtle Bay!" His confidence diminishes. "Right?"

"No." I keep walking.

Does he think I'm a tourist? Do I look like a tourist? How could he mistake me for anyone else?

I realize I'm being a bitch, and calm down. Everything is triggering me because my emotions are all over the place— sad, guilty, abandoned, rejected, tired, lonely, embarrassed, shameful, but oddly, slightly hopeful. I find my aisle seat next to two males. I love sitting next to men on airplanes. They never have to go to the bathroom. And I plan on sleeping on this flight, even though my heart is now sad. I miss the friendship that Mike and I used to have. I miss the idea of having a book project. I put on my Colorado sweatshirt that I bought after the last trip as a joke. I don't know what kind of joke it was or how it could've possibly been funny, but it made sense at the time when the Instagram ad popped up and I bought it. The Colorado sweatshirt is comfortable, but it's not warm. The cabin is freezing. The Clonazepam is in full force, so I put on my neck pillow and sleep. I wake up mid-flight and check the time. I have three hours to go and I am so cold that I can't stand it.

Have I really turned this soft since moving from Chicago?

It's probably room temperature, and I'm shivering like a Chihuahua on a mild spring day. I need to sleep more. I ask the passing flight attendant for a blanket, and he recites the rule that only one blanket is allowed per passenger. The guy sitting next to me is awake, playing a game on his phone, and isn't using his blanket. Old Me would have silently suffered knowing that there was a blanket not in use right next to me. New Me boldly asks him if I can have his blanket. He says yes! Two blankets aren't that much better than one, but it buys me a few more hours of sleep.

As soon as the plane lands at 7 a.m., I can feel the drab Denver atmosphere encroach on my Aloha aura. The Uber driver doesn't talk, so I stare out the window at the wide expanse of undeveloped land. On the way to my Airbnb, we pass the arena where I first met Mike at the Tony Robbins event. The memories are strong. That first time in Denver was so magical.

What the hell happened?

I arrive at the Airbnb, which is an actual bed and breakfast. It's the same address I stayed at last time, but a different room. This room has an entrance on the exterior of the building and seems less secure, which bothers me because this is such a weird neighborhood. It's in the mid-stages of gentrifying, so while this building and a few others are modern, a lot of the surrounding houses are old and run down. I hear a lady down the street yelling at a girl parked in the street because she is parked in her handicapped spot. She yells obscenities. It reminds me of a watered-down version of Chicago until the girl on the receiving end of the obscenities doesn't retaliate with her own anger, but apologizes profusely.

I go to my room and have a good cry on my bed. Because of the way I am interpreting Mike's actions, I feel like I am the only one putting an honest effort into rekindling the friendship, so I feel sad and abandoned, especially since I am hanging out alone in Denver right now just like last time. Then, I feel the familiar tightness and pain in my chest as shame and unworthiness rear their ugly, familiar heads. I have spent so much time and money on self-help and here I am crying like a child because I feel like I am not important.

Why do I feel everything so deeply?

I remember to breathe and hug myself. Hugging myself feels pathetic and comforting at the same time.

It's 8 a.m. and time to log into work. I am fortunate that I have a job that can be done from anywhere and be somewhat flexible

with the hours. For the first time in a long time, I enjoy work because it's a distraction from this horrible trip. I used to enjoy my
job, but the corporate culture is now toxic and draining. I work
with too many high-maintenance, energy vampires. And with all
of the management changes lately, I am afraid things may change
too much, and I will get laid off. I want to be a writer but I don't
have an idea for a book. That is why I wanted to work on the book
project with Mike. My phone vibrates with a text notification
from Mike.

> Are you at Air B&B?

> Yes

Why the hell does he care?

No response. My theory is that he feels guilty about not giving
me a ride, so he wants to text me to show that he is making some
effort. My brain always fills in the gaps when it doesn't have the answers. And there are a lot of gaps right now. The stories I weave can
get scary sometimes, but this one makes sense. And since he isn't
responding, it doesn't give me much to go off of, so I roll with it.

THE event starts in a few minutes. I want to be fashionably late.
I put on my BCBG bright orange dress and white Cecelia
New York hibiscus shoes, which both look amazingly Hawaiian
even though I bought them online. Then, I remember the personalized, luxury writing instrument.

Should I bring the gift to the event or mail it later?

I'm still embarrassed about it, plus it's not the type of event
where you would bring a gift. I text Mike to tell him I got him a
gift and ask if I should bring it. He doesn't respond immediately
like he always does. Or at least like he used to do. I order an Uber
and leave the pen in my room. The Uber driver doesn't talk. I don't
feel like talking either. Being in a car with someone other than
Mike reminds me of how he hasn't responded to my text, and I've
been here all day and haven't seen or talked to him yet. But my

anxiety is too much to handle, and I need to get used to talking to strangers because that is what I will be doing at the event.

"So…is this your full-time job?"

"No. I'm in a band, and we're on a break right now, so I do this in my downtime."

"What kind of band?"

"It's called Eminence Ensemble."

He describes their music, but I am not paying attention because I am Googling the name. The band comes right up before I finish typing the full word ensemble. We chat about the different venues they play, and then he pulls up at the restaurant. I want to keep talking to this guy, but it's time to walk boldly into the unknown.

I commit to staying for an hour, and then I can leave. The hostess crosses out my name on the VIP list and directs me downstairs. This restaurant has a hipster vibe, but in a way that seems forced, as if they are trying too hard to get the ambiance to the perfect level of trendiness with too many Edison bulbs and red leather seating. There are not a lot of people here yet. I see Mike. He's talking in a group of men, and I touch his shoulder. He turns around and gives me a big hug. It's rushed, so it doesn't feel as comforting as I had hoped. "Did you get your VIP wristband yet?" He points to the VIP area and tells me he will catch up with me later. I don't hold my breath. I know he doesn't want to catch up with me later.

A cute girl is working in VIP with long black hair and glitter eyeshadow. I compliment her eyeshadow because I know that it had to take forever to apply. I wonder how she sealed it in place because I don't see a trace of glitter anywhere else on her face. She gives me a wristband. Unfortunately, the liquor supply in VIP does not include tequila, so I go upstairs and purchase my own Don Julio on the rocks. I cannot remember the last time I had to buy myself a drink.

Have I ever bought myself a drink?

I go back downstairs to find someone to talk to. Everybody is already in cliques. I stand off to the side, awkwardly deciding on what to do. I contemplate leaving altogether. Then, a heavy-set, middle-aged woman with brown hair walks in and looks as awkward as I do. She speaks first. "Hi! I don't know anybody here, so I'm roaming around."

"I don't know anybody either." I try to say it in a relatable way, but I feel like I sound desperate. She introduces herself as Tracey, and we talk for a few minutes, but then she says she wants to mingle with other people. I want to scream, "No!" because I want someone to talk to, but that would definitely sound desperate. I accept her departure and head for the bathroom. Luckily, there is nobody else in here, so I have time to regroup. The bathroom is decorated in Mexican tile, which clashes with the dark interior of the rest of the restaurant and further adds to the forced hipster vibe. I come out and circle the crowd to find someone to talk to. Everybody is still in cliques. I turn to head upstairs and run into Tracey and a young girl with a lot of makeup and super long, thick, false eyelashes, who introduces herself as Rochelle. It turns out Rochelle is Mike's new, right-hand business developer. Since I haven't talked to him much since the last time I was here two months ago, I didn't know about her. She's cute, but I can't get past all the makeup, over-the-top eyelashes, and bright pink, long, fake fingernails. I think she would be a naturally pretty girl if she weren't trying so hard to be something else. Rochelle hasn't eaten yet, so she loads up a plate on the buffet behind us. She asks if I have eaten, and since I haven't and I'm desperate for conversation, I also grab a plate. The buffet is already picked over, and all that is left is a few shreds of pork and some rice. Rochelle is taking mostly what is left of the salad, which is iceberg lettuce. I take the leftover pork. Tracey joins us. She can't escape me now.

We head upstairs with our plates and find a booth to sit down. You could cut the awkward silence with a knife until a good-looking, younger man approaches and sits next to me. He introduces himself to each person at the table, ending with me. "Hi, my name is Mark." He hands me his business card. His name is spelled like Marc's. Of course, his name is Marc with a 'c.' The universe is hilarious. Marc proceeds to only talk to me, and I love it because he is the first interesting person to take an interest in me. As we talk, I cut my dry-ass shred of pork with a butter knife, and the knife slips from having zero grip on the meat, throwing the pork and rice from my plate all over the table. My neck and face warm instantly. Luckily, Marc is cool and helps me clean it up. Marc and I continue to chat excitedly and establish great rapport. The best part is, as Marc and I are engaged in a lively conversation, out of my peripheral vision, I see Mike pull up a chair and sit down at the table, where a few other people have joined Rochelle and Tracey. I don't want to break away from Marc, so I ignore Mike. He shouldn't mind considering he hasn't shown interest in talking to me since I arrived in Denver at 7 a.m. this morning. Anyway, I am digging this Marc dude. He looks young, but he talks maturely, and he's smooth with words. He tells me, "You give out such amazing energy. I can feel it."

Someone could tell me I am beautiful and sexy all day, but recognizing my energy is where it's at. But that's not all. Marc scores more points later in the conversation when I talk about something that happened ten years ago. He interrupts me. "You're about twenty-nine now, so you were like, what…nineteen?"

My heart melts. I want to give him a big hug for taking ten years off my actual age, but that would be too inappropriate. Thank God I have social skills, or I would have embarrassed myself with Tracey, who seems to have left the table. Marc and I talk about Hawaii for a bit, and he tells me that he has a crazy story to tell me about his only trip to Hawaii, but can't tell me now because he wants to mingle some more. What a tease. But he adds that the rush to get home is because he likes to go to bed early. I have a fondness for people who go to bed early because we are such a rare breed.

Before Marc leaves, we hit up the photo booth together. I call it a photo booth because that is what they used to be called when they were awkwardly small booths. This is one of those photo stations with props. As we approach, the girl of the girl/guy duo running the photo station looks directly at me. "We've been waiting for you to stop by since you arrived."

Me? They targeted me as a desirable photo station participant!

The pictures are fun and turn out well. Before leaving, Marc reminds me that I have his business card, so I should text him when I get him home, and he can call me to tell me the Hawaii story. I accept his departure without desperation because he left with good energy, and there are other people back at the table I can talk to, even though Mike has since left. This is how I meet HPeter. I don't understand his name.

"Is it 'H' period, Peter?"

"No, just HPeter."

"Is there a space between 'H' and Peter?"

I need to know how to visualize this name in my head. Otherwise, I won't be able to listen to anything else because I will be distracted by the spelling of his name. He shows me his Instagram account, which confirms 'H' no space, Peter. HPeter is a photographer and is hosting a fashion event in two months. I would come back for it, but I hate Denver and never intend to return here. Ever. After talking with HPeter, I gather the courage to mingle. People are less clique-y now. I meet Alden and Ethan. Ethan tells us about another bar called Back Porch. I want to leave because I feel like this event is triggering a lot of shame around Mike and our friendship, or lack thereof. I hate being here. Ethan wants to recruit a few more people, but it's like herding cats. A half an hour later, with no progress, Alden and I leave by ourselves. It feels good to be outside. It feels lonely to be with someone other than Mike in Denver.

Why do I feel lonely when there is someone right next to me?

Back Porch is packed, so we do not stay. We are both hungry because Alden didn't eat either. We pop into a sushi place and take seats at the bar. The female bartender is cute, with short brown hair and dark-rimmed glasses. She looks directly at me. "You look really pretty."

I want to hug her. It's 10:30 p.m., and she's the first person to say that to me tonight.

"Thank you! You're the first person to say that to me tonight."

She looks at Alden, and I realize we probably look like a couple, which makes him look like an asshole. I don't care. Her compliment means everything. I was starving, and it feels good to eat, but I'm disappointed that I'm eating sushi in Denver. I can eat sushi at home. I wanted pulled pork.

I don't understand why Grandma wanted me to come here.

I am not having a good time, and every damn thing is triggering me. Still, Alden is a nice guy. He doesn't have strong energy like Marc or Mike, but I enjoy our conversation. Then, I start getting anxious because I feel like we have been gone too long. I'm not sure why this is causing anxiety. I guarantee Mike has no idea that I am even gone. As we start walking back, I take the curbside of the sidewalk. Initially, not on purpose, but when I notice, instead of switching sides, I wait to see if Alden will switch. He doesn't. I am taking it personally instead of realizing that he has no idea how to treat a woman, which has nothing to do with me. Similarly, Mike has no idea how to treat an amazing friend who looks pretty, at least by the bartender's standards, and flew three thousand miles to be here, only to be ignored by him, which has nothing to do with my value as a person. When Alden and I get back to the venue, fewer people are there.

Thank God. I want to leave soon. As a matter of fact, I am going to leave now.

The universe says no. Mike appears and invites me to the outdoor seating area to get some fresh air. His arms are all around me, and I think this is to usher me outside, but once we get outside, his hands are still all over me. I think he is feeling to see if I have on underwear. I feel uncomfortable, but I don't set a boundary. The wounded inner child in me is getting high on his attention because he did nothing but ignore me earlier. I tell him he looks good tonight. He says thank you and continues talking about himself.

Then, people start taking pictures. It starts with group pictures, but then Mike wants a picture with the two of us. I don't have any pictures of us together. Our pictures don't turn out great. I need to learn how to correct my posture for photos. After our picture, the group pictures continue, and I sit down at a nearby booth. Once Mike is done with the pictures, I will say goodbye and leave. I am more than ready to go home.

But wait, the universe is on a roll. HPeter sits down next to me. He has the wandering mind of an artist but a deep intellect. He may have a touch of ADHD because it's hard to follow his train of thought. As we are talking, I see Mike talking to Melody, his ex-girlfriend. He conspicuously wipes something off the area of her blouse covering her boob, which looks more like he wants to touch her boob than concern about food crumbs. HPeter checks out my Instagram account and casually comments, "I like that you don't take yourself too seriously." I think this means that he likes that I don't give a shit about things that make pictures look good such as makeup, filters, or good posture. He also enjoys the video stories of me pole dancing in my living room.

Mike is standing next to the booth. Overhearing HPeter complimenting my pole dancing skills, he feels the need to chime in. "She tries."

Wow.

At this moment, I notice Mike's hand holding his drink. It's small, and his fingers are stubby. I look at his other hand. It's the same.

Why didn't I notice his small hands before?

HPeter asks when I am going back to Hawaii because he wants to do a photoshoot with me.

Me?!

I am so excited by this opportunity that I immediately set a time with him for tomorrow.

Okay, now I can leave.

But the universe is really turnt now. As I try to find Mike to say goodbye, I run into a group of guys I haven't met yet. They invite me to go to the strip club with them. I'm not tired yet, and nobody knows me here, so why not be ratchet? Plus, it's already 11:30 p.m. and I have a firm rule to not stay out after midnight because nothing good happens after midnight— case in point, Will's rooftop party. The fact that we are going to a strip club seems to foreshadow that prophecy. By the time we get there, I'll only have to stay for a few minutes.

Where the hell is Mike? I want to leave.

Finally, he appears, and I hug him to say goodbye. He does the thing where his hands are all over my body as we talk, and I am pretty sure he is still feeling for my underwear. I remind him that I have a gift for him, and he is free to stop by my Airbnb tomorrow to pick it up. I am still digging for those few minutes of one-on-one. But I don't ask him directly, like an adult. I passively say, "I have a gift for you if you want to stop by tomorrow and get it. I'm staying at the same place."

"I'll try. I have like four people visiting from out of town."

Um, I am one of those people.

"Okay, well, let me know."

I am such a doormat. Why am I letting him embarrass me?

I happily leave with the strip club crew. There is a guy named Alden, who is different from the Alden I ate sushi with. This is the first I have seen Alden #2, but this is not the first that Alden #2 has seen me. "I am glad you are coming with us. I have been eyeing you all night."

We pile in the Uber, and it's so tight that Alden #2 must sit in the front seat. The guy next to me puts his arm around me to fit in the backseat comfortably, but Alden #2 turns around from the front seat and eyes him like a lion protecting his lioness.

By this time, between Marc, the photo station girl, the sushi bartender, HPeter, and Alden #2, I should be happy with the amount of external validation I have received tonight. But I'm not. Mike didn't validate me. He did put his hands all over me. Okay, he didn't validate me respectfully. And he rejected my attempt to meet one-on-one.

We jump out of the Uber in front of the strip club at 11:52 p.m. I have eight minutes. It's crowded for a Wednesday night, and the girls are a higher caliber than I was expecting, which isn't saying much for a Wednesday night in Denver. The club has my favorite genre of music playing— hip-hop. As the boys get drinks, I dance by myself off to the side of the bar. At 11:59 p.m., I announce my departure. The boys thought I was joking about not staying out past midnight, but I need to get out of here. I order an Uber and go outside by myself to wait. I am disappointed that none of the boys, especially Alden #2, volunteer to wait with me to make sure I get in the Uber safely. I feel abandoned.

Maybe there is something wrong with me.

Or does no man in Denver know how to treat a woman?

The Uber pulls up, and I am embarrassed because I assume the driver is judging me for getting picked up at a strip club. The Uber driver doesn't talk. New Me is getting irritated that none of the damn Uber drivers in Denver talk. Plus, I want to prove to this guy that I am not drunk or a regular strip club goer. I make small talk. I hate small talk, but I am so eager for his validation that I happily initiate.

"So... is this your full-time job?"

"It is right now. I am going to school for my master's in IT. I used to be a mail carrier, but everybody who works for the postal service ends up going crazy."

I want to make a joke about going postal, but he sounds somber, so I bite my tongue. Plus, I think it's weird that he is getting a master's in "IT."

What does that mean? Is he talking down to me because I am a woman? I work in IT, too, damn it!

"I used to deliver mail where I am dropping you off. It used to be a drug rehab facility."

That makes a lot of sense to me, even more so now that I have an exterior room instead of an interior one like last time. It doesn't seem like it was set up for a B&B, especially since they don't even serve breakfast. I'm not sure how they have the credentials to call themselves a B&B. He drops me off at the side door, which used to be the main door, but isn't anymore, so I have to walk around from the side of the building to the main door in the dark in my heels, which are now hurting my feet. I should have asked him to turn around and drop me off appropriately.

Why didn't I ask? I am such a doormat.

I wake up around 6 a.m. to a text from Mike at 3:22 a.m.

> Strip club w me people? Lol I love of. It. Your safe?

I guess I should feel flattered, but I am so turned off by his clear non-interest in seeing me in person. I don't know why, but I reply. Then, he does something that doesn't happen often.

> Thank you soooooooo much for coming. It meant so much to me.

My heart melts. I have hope that I might be able to see him again before I leave tomorrow. I remind him about the gift.

> What is it!!!! I rarely get gifts, so I already love it.

I am hurt because I know this means I won't see him, so I tell him what it is. I get in the shower and take my time shaving my legs before responding that it's a personalized pen.

> Wow. That's amazing! I appreciate you!

I don't know if this means he likes it. I'll take whatever appreciation I can get from him because I know he doesn't express emotions well, if at all. It doesn't help that I overanalyze every single little thing to death.

I work eight to nine hours a day in Hawaii, but since I start at 4 a.m., I log off early in the afternoon. It's already noon Mountain time, and I want to log off, but the day is only halfway over. HPeter texts me. He wants to know if I can come earlier, around 2 p.m., so that we have more time for our photoshoot. I feel guilty about ditching work, but I can work when I return. Plus, I need to get out of this room. I am getting out of my comfort zone in a way I did not intend on this trip. Most of all, I feel special that HPeter thought I was pretty enough to do a photoshoot and special enough to make time in his busy schedule to do it. This overrides the shame and abandonment that I am feeling about Mike. I am happy that I have something to do this afternoon other than work.

Since I was working from my B&B room in a sports bra and booty shorts, and I know HPeter wanted to highlight my sporty physique, that's what I wear for the one-mile walk to his condo. This is something I would wear in public at home, so it seems acceptable. I also pack a bathing suit. I knew I had brought a bathing suit to Denver for something. As I walk down the street, I get a lot of stares.

Shit, my outfit.

I forgot that it's not acceptable here like it is in Hawaii. A dude, who seems to be about my age, but is homely and riding a BMX bike way too small for his build, rolls up and hits on me.

"Please leave me alone."

He doesn't leave me alone. He seems to think I might be interested in having sex with him, especially if he keeps acting thirsty.

"I am going to cross the street to get away from you."

I don't know why I felt the need to announce it. He starts yelling obscenities at me. He calls me a bitch.

I wasn't a bitch when you seemed to think you had a chance at getting these shorts off.

I don't know why, but I am absorbing his words. It stings. After a few blocks, I successfully ward it off.

I arrive at HPeter's and text him that I am in the lobby. My fear of abandonment thinks he is going to stand me up. He texts me immediately, like Mike used to do, that he is coming down. And he comes down immediately. Having someone so eager to spend the afternoon with me is comforting. It makes the six thousand mile round trip flight worth it. The lobby is fancy, and there are two door people, which I know from being the Treasurer on the Board of my condo association in Chicago, are expensive.

HPeter escorts me to his condo, where we will be doing the first part of the photoshoot. It's a studio. The interior design reflects his artsy, eclectic style. It's modern with a pop of a plum shade of purple, which a lot of men wouldn't have the courage or care to do. The mirrored wardrobe on the left side of the room is small but fits nicely in such a small studio. He must not have very many clothes. The dining table and purple chairs are the centerpieces of the unit.

There is no bed. I wonder where he sleeps. The purple couch is probably a pull-out. There is a stuffed gorilla on the pillow of the couch. I want to ask about the story behind the gorilla, but I am nervous about the photoshoot. He has bookcases full of books. I love bookcases. My dream one day is to have an entire library full of books.

HPeter and I talk for a little bit, and he tells me he wants to do some yoga pose pictures. He pulls out a blue yoga mat and puts it in the middle of his living room. He asks me to take off my glasses. I hesitate. I am so self-conscious without my glasses, especially after what happened with Mike. Initially, he takes some videos. I show him our sexy twerk yoga warm-up, which he likes better than the chaturanga flow. After about fifteen minutes, he sits down on the purple couch next to the stuffed gorilla and contemplates. "Your outfit is too gym-y."

Which is exactly what he said he wanted yesterday for our photo-shoot.

"I thought we could do some nudes and focus on your muscles, especially your back. I can get you a towel, and we would only expose the parts that I am taking pictures of."

Old Me would have felt uncomfortable and said no. New Me is uncomfortable yet open to new experiences and getting out of my comfort zone. I say yes. He's professional about it. He hands me a towel and goes to the bathroom. I undress how I do for my yearly OB-GYN exam or a massage: as fast as possible. When he comes back, I am draped in only a towel. We start in the living room, and he instructs me on how to position the towel so that I am covered in the discrete areas. Then, we relocate to the balcony. The last time I was naked on a balcony, it was in Chicago with Marc. It was cold, dark, and on the ninth floor. Coincidentally, this is also on the ninth floor. I pose away.

"Relax your face. Your forehead has too many wrinkles." He shows me a picture. My forehead is wrinkled.

Hilary was right. I need Botox.

He continues to instruct me on how to move the towel. But then, we start doing topless poses, and he wants me to do yoga poses without the towel. I agree because it sounds liberating. But it's not liberating. I feel uncomfortable with him taking pictures of me naked.

"You promise you won't do anything with these pictures, right?"

"I'll send them only to you, and I will destroy them on my end."

I am still uncomfortable. "Why don't we go out to the pool? I brought my bathing suit."

He hesitates.

"It's a Brazilian bikini bottom."

He likes the idea of that. He leaves the room and I change. But he can't settle for only a bikini. "When we do photoshoots, we use either glycerin or baby oil to make the skin look shiny."

"Do you have those things?"

"No, but let me see what I have."

He rummages in the kitchen. He finds avocado oil. I let him start rubbing avocado oil on my body, thinking he knows the proper technique, but he is smearing it on like I would have done to myself. Then, he seems to start getting too into it. I suggest we head to the pool. He hesitates but agrees.

We head down to the pool, which must be on top of the parking garage because it is on the fourth floor. We walk through an entertainment room with a row of toilets on display out in the middle of the room.

"What are those for?"

"The Condo Association is letting us vote on the new toilets."

"Wait, your Condo Association controls the inside of your unit?"

He continues to tell me about the strictness of the Association, especially when it comes to construction, because there is asbestos in the building.

Um, what?

We take some pictures by the pool. It's chilly. I'm glad I brought a towel. I get in the pool. I don't like it because I don't want to get chlorine in my hair. My hair is having enough problems on this trip with the dryness of the air, but I'm a team player, and I do it for the sake of art. We don't spend a lot of time taking photos by the pool because he is eager to go back upstairs.

We go back upstairs, and even though I still have a lot of oil on my skin, HPeter claims I need more because the water rinsed it off. As he goes to the kitchen to get the bottle of avocado oil, he tells me that his profession as a model photographer is lonely because he is constantly surrounded by beautiful girls but doesn't get to touch or date them. "I have to get massages instead."

"So, you get happy endings?"

"No, but the massages are different."

"You mean sensual?"

"Yes, it's the only way I get touched."

He sounds so lonely. And creepy.

Why did he just tell me this?

He positions me on the floor in a pose and starts to rub oil on me again. This time, I am even more uncomfortable. He stops on my stomach and closes his eyes, clearly fulfilling some sort of sexual fantasy on his end. "I can feel your energy."

Of course, you can. I have spent a lot of time and money working on my energy.

His body is trembling as if he is about to orgasm. His hand is no longer functionally rubbing avocado oil on me but lingers sexually. His tone changes. "I don't like the oak leaves on your bathing suit. You should take it off for the pictures."

"They're banana leaves."

"Tell me a secret about yourself."

"I don't have any secrets."

"What do you like sexually?"

I was hoping it wouldn't come to this and don't want to turn this sour. But...

"Look, I don't have sex with just anybody, and I'm cold and need to go back to work, so let's wrap this up." That took way too long for me to say. I should have said it when he asked me to take off my top.

Why do men interpret nice women as being sexually interested?

I'm scared that he will respond with anger or non-compliance, but luckily, he complies. Now that he knows I am not interested in sex, he is much less interested in the photoshoot and wraps things up. I honestly thought he was interested in a photoshoot with me, and now I am disappointed. And sad.

Doesn't he see there is more to me than sex?

I put on my booty shorts and start walking home. I have a text from Mike.

How long are you here for?

Tomorrow morning.

What difference does it make?

Going back home or you're doing a few places?

Back home.

Nowhere else, Asshole, I came to the mainland specifically to see you, and you won't even give me the time of day.

I'm interrupted by a text from HPeter. It's one of the topless pics from his balcony. Since my arm is covering my breasts, I send it to Mike and tell him I did a photoshoot with HPeter. It's one where I am not wearing glasses. Mike snapped at me the last time I didn't wear my glasses. I am acting out of my wound. The only reason I sent him the picture is to show him that somebody else was willing to spend time with me sans glasses and all. The text conversation dies off. Mike doesn't give a shit. I can't wait to leave in the morning. I haven't even been here two full days, and I hate it. I hate Denver. I hate that I did this to myself.

THE morning doesn't come fast enough. I pack up my stuff and order an Uber. Again, the Uber driver doesn't talk, but if he did, I might go on a rant about how much I hate Denver. We pass the Safeway distribution center that I remember from the last ride to the airport. So much has happened since then.

But has anything changed?

I'm never coming back here. I said that last time, but I mean it now. On the tram to my gate, I stand to subway surf as practice for my next lesson with Ozzy, but it's not as intense as the Chicago subway. I'm starting to get hungry. I spy a Chick-fil-A and get in line. An extremely rugged young man is paying for his food at the counter, dressed in full camping gear, including a ridiculously huge backpack. It's entirely possible that he hiked here from Argentina. He has a British accent. What strikes me the most about him is how happy he is. He is smiling and super friendly to the cashier—a real-life happy camper.

As I walk to my gate with lead in my heart, I notice my boarding pass is a center seat. I swore I chose an aisle seat. I always choose the aisle. Channeling New Me, I walk up to the gate attendant and ask if there are any available aisle seats. There are! I am issued a new boarding pass.

I wait for boarding to begin and feel the shame and sadness rise to the surface. I spent two days and a lot of money on Denver and only got to spend about five superficial minutes with Mike. My vision becomes blurry as the tears well up in my eyes. I need to find a remote corner to cry in.

Damn it! There are people everywhere. Where in the hell can I go to cry?

I am so angry with Mike and want to send him a shitty text, but I admit that I changed my intention for the trip to be about personal development, not re-kindling the friendship or book project. I challenge myself to send a text of love. Because of who he is, I have learned and grown so much. As much as I would love for him to be a blessing, I appreciate him for the bundle of lessons he is. And it's time to let him and the book project go, with love.

```
Mahalo for inviting me to your
event! I had such an amazing time.
Every person I met had genuine,
good energy. I am so incredibly
proud of you for everything you
have accomplished in the relative-
ly short time I have known you. And
```

> it's just as exciting to see the
> person you have grown into as a re-
> sult of that journey. It was great
> seeing you again and feeling your
> energy in person! Thanks for being
> you. Aloha.

I hit send and immediately turn off my phone out of fear. Fear that he won't respond. Fear that he will respond negatively. Fear that he won't respond immediately, like he used to, but doesn't anymore. On the plane, I bust out my notebook and pencil to journal about my weekend. I made many mistakes, but I also learned a lot from those mistakes. I start scribbling away at the list.

Lesson #1: I was not direct with Mike that I wanted to spend time with him outside the event. When Mike told me that he couldn't hang out because he had friends visiting from out of town, I wish I would have said, "I am one of those friends." I should have boldly spoken my truth with a direct request to spend time with him and been willing to hear a "no" to my request.

Lesson #2: The fact that I flew six thousand miles round trip and he made zero effort to spend even one minute with me outside of the event proves that he is not a friend of mine. From now on, I choose to be around friends who choose me.

Lesson #3: I did not set boundaries with HPeter. Even though I have come a long way in setting boundaries (something that was not even in my awareness until I was thirty-six years old), I still have a lot to keep learning and practicing.

Lesson #4: I have no regrets. I got out of my comfort zone, even though it was difficult and scary. I had the courage to go back to Denver. I had the courage to go to a social event where I didn't know anybody and met some cool people. I trusted my intuition to go to Denver, and I now

know the reason I needed to go was to see in person that it's time to let go of the friendship
and the book project. There was no other way for
me to see it.

After I finish journaling, my hand is cramped, and the lady across the aisle leans over. "Are you a writer or a school teacher?"

"Writer."

Even though I write, I don't identify with being a writer, but it seems too much to tell a stranger across the aisle of an airplane, where everyone in the section can hear, about my weak sense of self as a writer. We talk for a bit, and I learn she is stopping in Honolulu, but her final destination is Guam— the place I am going to in three weeks.

Chapter 22

I schedule another surfing lesson with Ozzy. I arrive at our scheduled time, and he is not there. Again.

I am not sure if he forgot about me. Again. Or got the time wrong. In case he got the time wrong and is expecting me at another time, I send him a text that I showed up. He calls me after about an hour. I don't want to answer.

I'm not important.

I answer. He forgot about me. Again. He apologizes profusely. Again. "Young lady, next lesson is on me."

I act nonchalantly, like it doesn't bother me, and tell him I will take him up on the lesson, but I internally vow that I won't. And I know he will probably forget about it because I am going to Guam for three weeks, and a few days after I get back, he and his wife are going surfing in the Philippines for three weeks. By the time we are both back on-island and available to have a lesson, it will be two months from now. I play the role of a polite client, but I am hurt by being forgotten twice. I want to continue to learn how to surf, but I am going to take a break. When I get back into it, I am going to find a different instructor.

I tell my pole dance instructor, Nicole, that I am going to miss three classes because I am going to Guam.

"Ew, why are you going to Guam? It's gross there."

I am hurt that she is hating on my adventure to expand my comfort zone. I tell her about how I am dog-sitting for Vanessa.

"Watch out for the snakes."

Wow, throwing more shade.

She adds, "Why doesn't she have anybody local to take care of the dogs?"

Great question. Why doesn't she?

I have more time to kill before my afternoon flight to Guam, so I write about my trip to Denver. Since I am not writing the book with Mike, maybe I can write a book about my travel experiences. Then, I head to the airport. Tony, my Uber driver, is talkative. He immediately asks, "Where are you going?"

"Guam."

"Watch out for the snakes."

Not again.

We change the subject. It turns out Tony was in Denver a few weeks ago.

"So was I!"

Fortunately, he has a lot to say about his trip, so I don't have to tell the embarrassing tale of how Mike dissed me. We arrive at the airport, and Tony lugs my heavy suitcase out of the back of the van. "This is going to cost you extra."

Why does everybody always have something negative to say?

I roll to the self-service kiosk. I brought my cheap pair of glasses to Guam because I didn't want to risk losing my Tom Ford frames to the dogs or snakes or whatever. As I am changing from my sunglasses to the cheap frames, one of the lenses pops out. Luckily, I have another pair of cheap glasses in my carry-on and put those on instead. I drop off my checked bag and head over to the security line, which is long. A scraggly man in front of me turns around and says, "This is a long line."

Shit, I don't want to get stuck in a conversation with him because the line is long, and it could be a painful experience.

I nod to his comment and don't say anything in response. I observe his appearance after he looks away. From the neck up, he looks homeless. He has unruly gray hair and snaggle teeth.

His skin is weathered, like an outdoorsman, which is confusing because he is extremely pale as if he never goes outside. From the neck down, he looks professional. He is well dressed in khakis and a button-down shirt, way overdressed for Hawaii. I pull out my phone. He won't talk to me if I am on my phone. But the line is long, and he is dying to talk to someone. In a very American accent, he tells me he is from Scotland. "I'm on my way to Vermont. We own a summer home there." He is alone. He must be using the royal "we." He overheard me tell the agriculture inspector that I am going to Guam. "What takes you to Guam?"

"Dog sitting."

He tells me that "we" need a dog sitter for three months each summer if I am interested. I am not. Next, I learn that he is a biologist. "They have a lot of brown tree snakes in Guam," he tells me.

I envision Guam to be one huge snake pit. He tells me that seeing a snake is a wonder because they like to hide and are afraid of people. Only the snakes in Australia are dangerous. Frogs, snails, and worms are what got him into biology. His snaggletooth is interesting. I can't tell if it is chipped or shorter and ragged-edged.

After we pass through security, we go opposite ways to our gates. As bitchy and critical as I was internally toward him, I enjoyed our conversation. I miss talking to him. The airport reminds me of being here three weeks ago, but I am happier this time. In this context, three weeks seems like a long time.

What if five dogs are too much?

I arrive in Guam at 6 p.m. on Saturday. Guam is twenty-one hours ahead of Hawaii. I see Vanessa's husband Alex holding a cardboard sign with simple, black Sharpie lettering:

Angie H.

Alex is kind of cute. He is young too. I envisioned Vanessa as older than me, but Alex seems younger than me, maybe late twenties or early thirties. We step outside, and the humidity is so thick you can cut it with a knife. I can hardly breathe. The sun has set, but it's still oppressively hot. It feels like Florida.

Alex drives slowly. Extremely slow. Even slower than Hawaiians. He also talks slowly, in a Forrest Gump kind of way, except with an Oklahoma drawl instead of a North Carolina drawl. I ask about how he met Vanessa. He was in the Air Force and met Vanessa when stationed in Guam. It was love at first sight, so he moved here and married her. We stop at the grocery store on the way back to the house. The produce is gross, and the store's selection is even worse than Hawaii.

Next stop is the house. It's dark, but from what I can see from the neighborhood, it looks run down. The homes are unkempt. There are abandoned cars and junk everywhere. There are stray animals, from roosters to cats to dogs roaming around the dirt road. We get to the end of the dirt road, and it's pitch black for lack of street lights. Alex drives just beyond where the dirt road ends to pull up to the house.

Stumpy, the dog, is outside, so I meet him first. As soon as we step inside, the other four, Dora, Alex, Spencer, and Sparkle, are jumping all over me. It's immediately clear that these dogs are not trained and have no dog manners whatsoever. The house is small so, with four dogs running around, it's a lot. I meet Vanessa, and she tells me I can keep them outside all of the time while they are gone, and I immediately know that is exactly what I am going to do.

For as small as the house is, it somehow has four bedrooms, two bathrooms, and an area for the kitchen, living room, and dining nook. Vanessa dabbles in art, so she has painted flowers and other designs all over the walls and ceiling. It looks childlike yet tasteful. Vanessa and Alex's flight is not until Sunday evening. It turns out they don't have jobs. Renting out the three extra bedrooms for Airbnb is how they earn income. I wonder what they do all day.

I learn on Sunday what they do all day. They sit around the house. Vanessa pets the dogs, and Alex watches YouTube videos. I ask what they normally do, hoping this is an anomaly. Alex says that is what they normally do. I go outside to hang with Vanessa and the dogs. This is how I learn that Alex the dog is named after

Alex the husband because Alex, the dog, is white, and Vanessa likes white boys. Vanessa lights up a cigarette and asks, "You smoke?"

"No, thank you."

"Of course, you don't smoke. Look at that body. Are you married?"

"No."

"Boyfriend?"

"No."

"Why not?"

"I'm just trying to work on myself and figure out what I want."

"Well, I can tell that someone as beautiful and independent as you deserves a high-caliber man and will not settle."

I laugh. "Thank you. I have settled in the past, but I am not settling anymore."

She is a heavy smoker and keeps repeating that she "can't" quit. It's not even noon, and I am bored out of my mind. I like connecting with Vanessa, but I need to get out of here. I text Hilary's local friend Zeke who she put me in touch with. He texts back immediately. He says that his parents need care and it will take time to find sitters, so it's not looking good. I borrow Vanessa and Alex's car and go to Tarzan Falls, a nearby hike. As I drive out of the neighborhood, I see that my nighttime suspicions are confirmed. The neighborhood is disgusting. Also, I notice that Guam, in general, has an institutional feel because for practical reasons, due to frequent typhoons, the homes are made out of concrete and have hurricane shutters.

How is it possible that Hilary stayed here as an Airbnb guest and agreed to come back for a month to dog sit?

There is only one other car here at Tarzan Falls, which is good because there is only room for about three cars in the dirt parking lot. I check my phone. Mom has emailed me to make sure I got here okay. I am triggered. She had asked me to let her know when I got here, and I told her to assume I made it safe unless she hears about a plane crash en route to Guam. I reply with a terse response. I feel suffocated by her lack of boundaries.

On the trail, I pass the girls from the other car. I see a lot of toads and salamanders, but no snakes. The waterfall is beautiful, and I take a moment to meditate, which is interrupted by Zeke blowing up my phone with texts. He found care for his parents and wants to hang out. Something seems weird about it, as if he's desperate for company. He texts that he can pick me up in forty-five minutes. I rush back to the house to shower and get ready. Island time is real. Two hours later, he picks me up. Vanessa is weird about not wanting him to know the address, so she drops me off at a nearby gas station to meet him. Zeke doesn't look anything like his Facebook picture. He is short, possibly shorter than me, and his teeth are equally as snaggly as the biologist from the airport. He has a bulging potbelly, but as we pull away from the gas station, tries to sell me the story that he jogs five miles a few times a week. I'm not buying it. I already have an uneasy feeling about this guy, so I set a boundary. "I can only hang out for a few hours because I want to take a nap before I take Vanessa and Alex to the airport."

Before we eat lunch, Zeke has a grill in the back of his pickup truck that he wants to drop off at a friend's house. The difficult part about this is that he doesn't know where his friend lives and, apparently, addresses are an afterthought in Guam because instead of texting him her address, she texted him a photo of a hand-drawn map that uses landmarks instead of street names. She is not answering her phone. Needless to say, it takes a long time to find her house. There are a few failed attempts. One of those attempts lands us in a yard with a huge sign that clearly reads: "No Trespassing. Owner will shoot." Zeke casually turns around in the driveway while I debate if I should duck. Twenty minutes later, we find out that this is his friend's house.

We eat lunch at a German restaurant that serves American food. The only thing German on the menu is a few German beers, of which Zeke has two during the course of lunch. The conversation is comfortable. He gloats about how much he loved Hilary when she was here. He tells me about how he lives his life around his elderly parents and kids. He has four kids. All of them are married with kids and all of them live in his house, basically because he doesn't have the boundaries to tell them to move out. His weak side reminds me of how passive Dad was. Zeke also reminds me of how I used to live my life for Mom, not understanding that I had the choice to live my own life however I wanted, as I do now. After lunch, he offers to drive me around to sightsee.

"Okay, but I can't stay out long because I want to take a nap before taking Vanessa and Alex to the airport."

We start driving. Zeke speaks up. "This will be a good spot for you to take pictures. Let's stop."

"Okay."

"Do you mind if I smoke?"

"Sure, as long as it's not blowing in my face."

I take a few pictures, even though it's not scenic. Zeke smokes. We get back into the car. Ten minutes later, we stop again. "This will be a good spot for you to take pictures."

We get out of the car. It's not scenic at all, so I don't take pictures. Zeke smokes. We get back into the car.

Okay, I get it now.

Ten minutes later, we stop again. "This will be a good spot for you to take pictures."

We get out of the car. It's not scenic at all, so I don't take pictures. Zeke smokes.

I need to break this cycle.

"I'm thirsty. Can we stop to get some water?"

We stop at a Mini Mart. I get water, and Zeke gets two beers.

"I need to get back to the house soon because I want to take a nap before I take Vanessa and Alex to the airport."

"Have you heard of Talofofo Falls? Let's go there."

He seems desperate for company. He doesn't want to drop me off. Someone with strong boundaries would tell him to take them home so they can take a nap. I agree to go to Talofofo Falls. I feel trapped. And I feel uncomfortable with him driving us around now that he has had four beers. When I was little, I remember Dad would drink beers while driving. When I was a young girl, it would scare me. When I was a teenager, it would make me angry.

Talofofo Falls is a tour of a waterfall, a cave where a Japanese Army Sergeant from WWII hid for over twenty-five years, and a bucket suspension ride. Zeke keeps taking pictures of me while we are on the bucket ride. Then, he demands we take a selfie. I am extremely confused as to why Hilary suggested Zeke would be someone fun for me to hang out with. Finally, he drops me off at the gas station, where Alex picks me up. Vanessa made dinner, and as we are eating, she talks about how much she loved Hilary.

Everybody loves Hilary. Why was she so catty to me?

They tell me the story about how when Hilary was dog-sitting, Stumpy and Alex got in a fight, and Hilary had to go to the ER because Stumpy bit her hand as she tried to break it up.

Why didn't Hilary tell me she was bit?!?

After dinner, I take a nap and get up at midnight to take them to the airport. I get lost in the neighborhood on the way home. I panic. Partially because I always panic when I am lost in a car, but this time because this is a bad neighborhood, and the people hanging out in the street have seen me circle several times. I don't want them to mess with me, and I'm getting scared. I think they smell my fear. Luckily, I find my way back to the house. The house feels creepy at night. It's not very secure. I lock the doors, but someone could easily crawl through one of the many windows.

On top of the gross house in the gross neighborhood, the dogs and cat are extremely needy of attention. I always put the dogs outside, but they bark their fool heads off if I am gone for more than ten minutes. They are used to Vanessa hanging out with them all of the time. I can't hang out with them all of the time. I need to work, plus I need to get out of the house at least for a few hours each day. The cat is the worst of them all. She's only two months old and needs her mother. She follows me everywhere and I can't sit down without her jumping all over me. I am used to living alone. I will not be alone these three weeks. Right now, three weeks seems like an eternity. I'm glad I will be working the entire time to help the time pass.

ODAY is my last day off before the work week, and I am hiking Mount Lam Lam, the world's tallest mountain, even though most of it is underwater. It is a moderate hike and very jungle-y. I brace myself for the snakes. No snakes yet, but I hear a wild animal skitter away. It sounds like a wild boar. There is not another soul around. If I get trampled by a wild boar, I'm screwed. I get to the top, and it starts sprinkling. I see a circular rainbow. It is so unique and beautiful. Whenever I see a rainbow, it makes me think of Grandma. I know she is with me right now.

I wish we could have been this close when she was alive.

Miraculously, I do not see one snake. I also do not see one other person. I slip on the way down, fall on my tailbone, and drive in the wrong direction on the way home, adding forty-five extra minutes to my drive. When I get back to the house, my shoes are muddy, so I clean them off with the hose in the front yard. I let Dora in the front yard with Stumpy and me, being extremely careful not to let any of the other dogs in the front yard because I don't want any biting or blood on them or me. As I clean off my shoes, I notice Stumpy and Dora run to the end of the driveway. I don't think anything of it and continue to wash off my shoes. Then, silence. None of these dogs are silent.

Shit!

I run to the end of the driveway. I see Stumpy, but not Dora. There is a guy next door at the house for sale, working on the lawn. I forget that I am wearing a sports bra and booty shorts.

"Did you see where the other dog went?"

He points to Vanessa's house as he stares at my body.

This dude is full of shit.

I run in the other direction down the street, yelling Dora's name like a madwoman. Finally, I see her come out of one of the neighbor's yards. All of the neighbors have dogs, and I know Dora is not fixed because Alex and Spencer came from one of her litters.

I hope she wasn't mating with one of the neighbor dogs and gets pregnant.

Y first night before work is exhausting. I try to sleep from 4 p.m. to 11 p.m. before working on Chicago time, but it's impossible because, despite my sleep mask, my body knows it is daylight. Not to mention, the dogs are howling like crazy. Not barking. Howling. It's like it's some *101 Dalmatians* shit. These dogs are so damn needy that I can't even sleep without them getting upset.

Only 2.9 more weeks.

I get up at 11 p.m. I slept with the door shut to keep out Lady and the sound of the dogs. The first thing I do is open the door and Lady is all over me. I can't even pee without her rubbing up against my legs and purring. I try to work at the kitchen table to get out of the bedroom, but Lady is all over my laptop. Plus, the neighbor's roosters are cock-a-doodle-doo-ing like crazy, and the four dogs in the backyard are barking at them, all at 11:30 p.m.

How in the hell am I supposed to have conference calls when it sounds like Old McDonald's farm?

I have to work in the bedroom, which is fine because the bedroom is air-conditioned and quiet. But it's so cramped. I feel claustrophobic.

notice that Lady doesn't quite know how to use the litter box. She does her duty there but doesn't cover it up. Whenever she poops, I have to clean it up immediately, or the whole hot and humid house smells like cat shit. Lady poops a lot, so I cut her food intake in half. That doesn't help matters, and I can't help but wonder if she is getting into the dog food that is stored in the laundry room.

Four days in, I get up at my usual 11 p.m. and work until 8 a.m. At 6 a.m., when the sun rises, I take a break to feed and hang out with the pets. I first take care of Lady, then go into the backyard where Alex, Spencer, Sparkle, and Dora are. Today, there is no Dora.

How could she disappear?!?

I run to the front of the house to make sure Stumpy is still there. Not only is Stumpy still there, but so is Dora.

Oh, thank God. She must have jumped the fence.

I miss Hawaii so much. On my fifth day, the three backyard dogs tear up the cushion on their wooden bed. Only three dogs because Dora jumped the fence again. I keep her in the front all of the time now because the fence is high, and I don't want her to get hurt jumping the fence. The cushion situation is how I realize how savage these dogs are. Most dogs have a sense of right and wrong and feel guilty when they do something bad. With most dogs, you know they did something bad before you even find what it is because they act so guilty. Not these dogs. They shredded the cushion up so bad that it took me almost an hour roaming around the yard to clean it up. They have been jumping all over me the entire time, bidding for my attention, with no clue that they did anything wrong. "Bad dogs" doesn't even register in their brains. Also, the dogs poop in the grass, but for whatever reason, they all pee on the cement area of the patio, which probably wouldn't be that big of a deal if it weren't ninety degrees and so damn humid. The patio reeks of dog piss. I scrub the cement down with soap and water, but the scent still lingers. There is a lot of significant information about this dog-sitting assignment that Hilary omitted.

I need to work out. I can't even take a walk because the neighborhood is sketchy, and it's too hot and humid. I Google gyms and find one of the only gyms on the entire island, which fortunately has five stars on Yelp. The gym is very state-of-the-art, unlike anything else in Guam. The girl at the counter tries to sell me a class pass for the classes, but I tell her I just want to work out. I look around. The only area to work out is where they are having the class. I pick up the class schedule so I know when not to come next time. I start my workout on the perimeter. The owner, Vinny, is teaching the class. He's young and extremely attractive with an amazing, chiseled body. I observe the class. His approach is extremely militant in the way he orders everybody around. And he shames one of the girls for not lining her bench up perfectly parallel to the seam on the floor. "And you still think you are a smart person?" Vinny snaps.

Even after the workout, when they are taking group photos for Instagram, Vinny barks at the group, "Two regular and one Boomerang!"

He casually approaches me and asks about my workouts. He tries to sell me on the classes. I don't want to do the classes. He is way too strict for me. But he sells me on the classes, probably because he is hot with a chiseled body. I go the next day.

I initiate a conversation with another class member, Tara. She doesn't know what is going on, so she follows Chris. Chris is half Korean, which he mentions at least three times throughout our first conversation. I also meet Ben, from the Philippines, and François, who is wearing huge, bling diamond earrings for this workout. It's a good workout but odd because the front desk girl is taking pictures like the paparazzi the entire time. I take it Vinny is big on pictures for social media. Since I had seen Vinny's militant style, I make sure to follow his every command, so I don't get shamed. We are doing squats today. Vinny asks me how much I can squat. I can't remember, but I don't want him to shame me for not knowing, so I confidently respond, "One fifty."

Oh shit, I hope I can squat one hundred and fifty pounds.

I can! And as I do, I hear Vinny shame Ben for not consolidating his weights. He is using ten-pound and thirty-five-pound plates instead of forty-five-pound plates. Vinny sneers, "Have you ever heard of math?"

THE dogs are starting to smell, so I give them baths. Giving five dogs baths is just as fun as it sounds. And Alex's jealousy is over the top. If I even think about the other dogs, especially Sparkle, he is all over me. I am starting to feel bad for Sparkle because I am starting to give her less attention in an attempt to keep Alex chill. I tried to let Dora socialize with the backyard dogs, but she keeps escaping to the front, and I am starting to wonder if it is because Alex is also blocking any attention that I try to give her. When she is in the front with Stumpy, I can give her plenty of attention.

I research things to do in Guam. I see that a group meets every Saturday to go hiking. I go to the meeting place, an open village with restaurants and such, but nothing is open until later, and there is no one around. I take it that the hiking group isn't meeting today. I get in my car to leave, but I see two Asians with hiking gear heading toward a covered shelter. I follow them. It's the hiking group! The Asians registered at a table in the back, so I approach the table. The grumpy man on the other side folds up the papers on the table that the Asians just signed and tells me registration starts in a few minutes. I take a seat and start checking Instagram. Meanwhile, other people continue to come in and are clearly registering with the grumpy old man at the table.

Fuck this shit.

I do something Old Me would have been too scared to do: get up and leave. I go to a beach on the north side instead. I can't wait to go home. Only two more weeks.

A FTER work one day, I go to the beach near the house. It's eerily deserted, as usual. I feel unsafe, as usual. And it's hot and humid, as usual. The sunscreen that I applied at the house is promptly sweated off. I want to take a dip in the ocean, but I can't get in more than up to my ankles because of the reef. I lay on the beach, stifling and sweating, when a guy in a Japanese-style van pulls up, basically right beside me, even though we are the only two people here. The sliding door is facing away from me. The Chicago in me thinks he is going to rape me. The van door is open for a long time.

I hope he is not jacking off.

After all of my worrying, it turns out he was putting on his snorkeling gear. He says hi to me before venturing off into the reef. I am so hot. I get in the ocean again to cool off. Snorkel Guy comes back and yells, "Are you barefoot?"

"Yes."

"It's not safe to have your feet unprotected on the reef!"

I don't need to be mansplained, Snorkel Guy. I am hot as shit and trying to cool off. Leave me alone.

"I know."

I have had enough. It's so hot and humid that I can't breathe. I walk back to the car. There is another car in the parking lot now. A man is sitting in the car listening to "Bette Davis Eyes" at an obscenely loud volume. He must be going through some shit. I see a rainbow on the way home. The second one I have seen in Guam.

Grandma, please save me from this hell hole.

Only a week and three days to go.

I can do this! Maybe. The dogs are so gross, and I don't want to give them baths again. Lady is still shitting like crazy. They are all so needy I can't stand it. I go to the beach again to escape. It's deserted except for some sketchy people in the parking lot. I will not be a victim. I can't take it anymore. The dogs are unruly. The cat is driving me nuts. The house is gross. The litter box is gross. The neighbor's roosters are gross. The neighborhood is gross. The beaches are gross. The weather is gross. I can't leave because of the pets, but something has to give. I text Vanessa and tell her that someone else needs to watch Lady. It's a start. Vanessa texts me back and says she will ask one of her friends.

I go to the gym, my safe haven. We start the workout with a two-minute jump rope warm-up. After the two minutes is up, Vinny goes on a rant. "Have you ever seen someone running with horrible form and you think to yourself, 'What the hell are they doing?' I just saw a dude last week at a 5k, and he looked like he was disabled and trying to run. I thought to myself, 'Dude, just stay home. You look stupid as fuck. Stop running. Go home.'" Vinny looks directly at me. "That's exactly how I felt when I saw you jump roping."

A fireball of shame explodes in my chest, but for the first time in my life, I don't absorb it and take it as the truth. The painful feeling is contained in my chest, but I simply observe it and let it peacefully pass through me. Then, I reflect.

Wow, he must be really emotionally fucked up to feel the need to embarrass me in front of this entire class, including Tara and Chris who are the only friends I have on this horrible dog sitting excursion.

I mean, this guy is the owner. He could have said, "Hey, I noticed you have an imbalance. I can help you fix it," or, "Here are some tips on jump roping form," or, "Maybe you can jog in place for the warm-up, so you don't get injured from having poor form." It's ironic because he is so beautiful on the outside, but all I see in this moment is how ugly he is. Old Me would start crying. Old Me would leave immediately, embarrassed and red-faced. Old Me would absorb every word of that rant and add it to her list of reasons why she doesn't deserve to be loved. But New Me takes the wheel and speaks up to this dude who clearly has small dick energy so bad that he feels the need to embarrass the fittest person in the class and the only person who actually lasted the whole two minutes jump roping, despite not having perfectly aligned feet. "I didn't realize my form was off. Thanks for pointing it out so I can work on it."

We finish the workout without further incident, but the gym, my former safe haven, now feels unsafe. I get in the car as I leave the gym, and Vanessa has texted me her friend Joanna's number. She is going to watch Lady! I text Joanna to get her address.

idk how to tell yu where I live/

Um, what?

I text Vanessa. In typical Vanessa fashion, she sends me a barrage of texts trying to explain where Joanna lives. I need an address. I don't understand why people don't use addresses here. I go back to the house to take a shower and figure out how to transport Lady. It's pouring down rain. I find a box in the laundry area. Vanessa has sent more texts about another topic. Her friend, whom she only refers to as "the Japanese man," is coming to take the car this evening after I drop off the cat because he needs it from now on to go to a class in the evenings. I still have another week here. I need the car.

> I'm sorry but I can't give him the car. I need it.

> I already promised him.

That car is my only escape from this hell hole house. I can't even go to the disgusting beach or get shamed by Vinny without a car. I need a car to buy food. I am speechless and try to form a response. In the meantime, Vanessa sends me a barrage of texts about where Joanna lives and The Japanese Man coming later. In these texts, she mentions that The Japanese Man has a key to the house.

Hell to the motherfucking no.

I felt unsafe before, and I now feel completely violated. I text Vanessa.

> I'm leaving.

She is pissed off and is understandably worried about the animals.

> If the Japanese man has the car and a key to the house, he can feed the pets.

> He's unreliable.

> Then why are you letting him take the car?

> Because he doesn't have insurance.

> It's not my problem that he doesn't have insurance and it's not my problem that he's not reliable. The car was part of the dog-sitting agreement.

Lightning strikes, and the boom of thunder is soon to follow. I need to get the hell out of here before The Japanese Man comes tonight. It's 3 p.m. I don't know what time she meant by "tonight," so I need to get out of here now. I fill up the pet's food and water to the brim. I pack in a frenzy. I change my flight. I book a hotel online for tonight. I grab my phone to call a cab.

Damn it! I don't know the address.

This street is not marked, probably because this isn't even a real street, and there are no numbers on the house. I run out to the car in the pouring rain. When Alex picked me up from the airport, he said insurance papers were in the glove compartment. There are none. There are a few documents, but they are not proof of insurance and are addressed to a P.O. box in the name Nathan B. Thomas. I am now unclear if this car even belongs to Vanessa and Alex, or if it's insured.

This is so fucked up.

I go into the house and rifle through some drawers. I find some papers with the same P.O. box and Nathan Thomas' name. Fortunately, I'm smart. The house next door is for sale. Because it's still monsoon raining, I get in the car and back down the driveway. I take a picture of the real estate agent sign, drive back up the driveway, and go into the house to look up the listing online. There's an address! I call a cab and give him the next door address. He gets here in thirty minutes. I feel guilty leaving the pets, but surely The Japanese Man can come at least every other day before Vanessa and Alex get back in a week.

The cab driver is friendly. "Do you live here?"

"No, I was visiting, but I'm leaving."

"Good thing you got me as a driver because most cabs wouldn't do a pickup in this neighborhood."

"Because it's sketchy?"

"Yeah."

"I know, I got conned into this dog sitting job, but there was a lot of information withheld from me, so I changed my flight and am trying to get the hell out of here."

"Oh, that sucks. I'm supposed to charge a thirty-dollar surcharge for picking up in this neighborhood, but I will waive it for you."

"Thank you!"

Although, I really don't care how much it costs to get out of here. He drops me off at the hotel as Hilary starts texting me. Vanessa is triangulating her. Hilary wants to help. I just want to take a nap. My phone vibrates with a text from Vanessa.

Have a nice life.

I don't respond. I feel betrayed by Hilary.

How could she intentionally put me in a totally shady and danger-ous situation?

Wait, why did I trust someone who told me I needed Botox?

J journal on the flight home.

Things I learned in Guam:

1. A little jealousy is cute; a lot of jealousy is ugly (Alex).

2. Beauty is an inside job (Vinny).

3. Love is unconditional (the dogs loved me even when I wasn't loving toward them when they chewed up the cushion or Lady every morning when she wanted attention and I wanted to wake up first).

4. Boredom leads to unproductive things (the dogs tearing up their bed cushion).

5. Ignore the haters (in over two weeks, I never saw even one snake).

I arrive in Honolulu on Thursday night, an entire week early. I hope The Japanese Man feeds the dogs.

M Y alarm is going off. It's 4 a.m. I worked on Chicago time in Guam, so I didn't think I would have bad jet lag, but I am exhausted. I can't wait to take a nap after work. My phone vibrates with a text notification.

So what do you think? Do you want to get started on the book again?

Chapter 23

I don't know how to respond to Mike's proposal to start working on the book again. Mostly, I want to tell him to fuck off. I can't believe he has the nerve to ask me to work on the book after he didn't even spare one second of personal time in Denver for me. I had texted him back that I needed a few days to think about it.

What is there to think about? He disrespected me.

This is a chance to work on a writing project.

Why don't I write a book about myself? I have been journaling about my trips. I even typed out the Denver saga while I was in Guam. And Guam is good writing material with the dogs and the jump roping incident.

No! You could never publish a book about yourself. Mom would never talk to you again and you would embarrass yourself by putting yourself out there like that. It's much safer to do the project with Mike because you can hide behind his story.

The shame wins. I send Mike a text with my decision.

I can work on the book project!

Despite the exclamation point, I am not excited at all. I feel like I am betraying myself by supporting someone who disrespected me. We set up a time to Zoom. Unlike before, when we would Zoom, I am filled with dread instead of looking forward to talking.

I adjust my laptop, so the camera is angled correctly for our Zoom call.

"Hey, Mike! How have you been?"

"Beautiful! Life is so perfect. I am so blessed to have such an amazing life."

Why do you put up this bullshit toxic positivity front every time we talk?

Then, he continues about himself and how everything is so perfect with him. Twenty minutes into Zoom-ing, he finally asks a question about me. Kind of. "Who did you like the most at my event?"

"I liked Marc the best. We had a really good conversation and he had a funny story about a trip he took to Hawaii."

"Marc likes to talk to all of the girls. He was hitting on some of my other female friends there. He has a girlfriend. I hope you aren't keeping in touch with him."

Why are you raining on my parade?

I don't give a shit if he talked to other girls at the event, and I don't care if he has a girlfriend. I enjoyed our connection because I flew three thousand miles to Denver, and he was one of the only people who treated me with the respect I deserve, and now Mike is trying to minimize it. Then, I tell Mike about my horrible experience in Guam.

"If you would have told me you were planning on going to Guam, I would have told you that was a bad idea."

Um, I told you while we were texting in Denver, but you were too busy hanging out with your other friends from out of town.

Then, I excitedly tell him about my upcoming trip to New Zealand and Australia. I add that I have bungee jumping already booked.

"Bungee jumping is for people who hate their lives."

"Excuse me?"

"I don't need adrenaline to get a rush. I get a rush from building my business."

You, you, you, blah, blah, blah.

Then, he tells me how I need to work on my confidence and how pretty and wonderful all of the girls who work for him are.

Maybe I wouldn't be so un-fucking-confident around you if you weren't always pitting me against the amazing, pretty girls that you know.

I explain to him that I am still struggling with the symptoms of my autoimmune disorder.

"It's all in your head. I wake up and tell myself how I want to feel."

Well, that's great that your body isn't attacking your thyroid.

Like our book calls before, we spend so much time on personal conversation that we don't even get to the book. We end the Zoom, and I feel a huge black hole in my stomach. Even though I do not feel love and connection with Mike, I feel it within myself, for myself, despite the critical inner voice.

I cannot do this book. There is no way I can have another Zoom call with him again. That was too painful.

But you have to do the book. You're too boring to write about yourself. You need to hide behind him.

No, I am not doing the book with him. I will write my own damn book. Better yet, I will tell him the reason why I don't want to do the book. I am going to speak my truth, no matter how scary.

Hahahahahaha, you are an idiot. Every time you have tried to speak up for yourself, it hasn't worked, and you end up embarrassed and on the receiving end of anger. He finally wants to be friends. If you speak your truth, he will hate you.

I have nothing to lose. I was already ready to let go of the friendship, and I am tired of doing shit I don't like and being in uncomfortable, painful situations because I am too afraid to speak up for myself.

Haha, good luck. You are going to regret this.

I have to protect myself in a way that nobody ever has before. With newfound confidence that has already been building up for my New Zealand and Australia trip that I am terrified about going alone, especially the bungee jumping part, I draft an email to Mike.

```
Hey Mike, I'm sending an email because this is
too long for a text, and I'm not a great texter.
Before I go into anything, I want to be clear
that I realize that a lot of this has to do with
```

issues that I need to work on (and I am), and
I take accountability for that. I love you as a
friend and think you are an amazing person, but
we got caught up in some dysfunctional dynamics.
I know a lot of this will sound like emotional
vomit because I feel things deeply. That's who I
am. And I'm tired of dimming that part of me to
please other people. I actually like that part
of me because having feelings is how I know my
soul is alive. The times in my life when I didn't
feel anything, I felt dead inside. This email is
me making an honest attempt to truly restore our
friendship, not just brushing shit under the rug
as I did before. You've been warned, so you can
stop reading here if you want.

After we talked on Monday, I went down a shame
spiral. I understand what you said about my mindset, and believe it or not, I have made a lot
of progress, but as valuable as our friendship
is in some ways, in other ways, it has really
chipped away at my self-esteem. In general, when
you frequently bring up how gorgeous and amazing all your young female friends are, I do feel
old and insecure. You are right. I have said out
loud that you make me feel old. And that is where
it stems from. I know that is my issue because
I am the only person making myself feel old and
insecure, but it's difficult for me when the comments are coming in faster than I can fend them
off. I'm not equipped with a strong enough shield
yet (I ordered one on Amazon, but shipping takes
forever here).

And then there's the Denver trip in June. I
thought I was over what happened this summer, but
talking to you brought it all back to the surface
like a putrid swamp monster. I know there were a

lot of misunderstandings that led to that point in your bedroom. I thought we were friends, so I was confused by your expectations for the night. When you didn't kiss me or touch me, I felt undesirable. When you weren't concerned about my sexual needs, I felt unworthy. And when you were texting with another girl while I was next to you, said mean things to me, and kicked me out, I felt used and disrespected. And when you ignored me the next day, I felt abandoned. I felt so embarrassed and ashamed. And that same disgusting shame came back up on Monday.

I reached out to you after the first Denver trip to restore the friendship without addressing any of the issues, which in hindsight, was not the best approach. When you invited me to your event in August, my acceptance was a sincere effort on my part to prove that I was serious about reconciling the book project by supporting you. When you told me at least twice at the event that you "would" hang out with me, but you had friends visiting from out of town, it felt like a punch in the stomach. Um, I was one of those friends from out of town. I flew six thousand miles/fourteen hours round trip to be there. After you said that, I felt embarrassed for showing up. I felt embarrassed for being so loyal and supportive of you. I felt embarrassed to call you my friend because you wouldn't even bring me around your friends that you always claim you hate because you hate everyone from Ohio. I felt so ashamed. My original text to you from the airport was going to be an angry rant about how disrespected I felt. But then I realized I was never upfront with you about wanting to hang out outside of the event, so I challenged myself to send you a text from a loving place and use the trip as a learning experience. Talking about your event with you on Monday brought back all the shame I felt after your event.

I never in a gazillion years thought you would ever reach out to me about our book. When you reached out to me, I didn't want to make the time because my plate was already full, but when I thought about it, I really wanted to do the book with you because I admire you so much and wanted to work with you. But that's the problem. I admire you from the place where our friendship used to be. We used to Zoom and talk and laugh, and you would give me great advice, and I have no idea what the hell happened. I have tried so hard to see things from your perspective, but you don't open up to me about anything. I don't know what goes on in your head. But I do know it was not your intention to hurt me. I know you are a good person with a good heart. But I can't have a shame spiral every Monday. My original draft of this was to end the friendship because I thought about what you said about my mindset and part of the issue is that I am still hanging around people who aren't good for me. I need to be ruth-less about cutting off people who are disempower-ing. Because you were adding to my insecurity, I thought I needed to cut you off. But I don't want to cut you off. I would love to work with you on the book, and I would actually love advice from you about how to change my mindset because you give great advice. Both of those things would be largely empowering and help with my journey.

If you are still reading, to make a very long story short, my point is that I want to have a mature, adult conversation about the dysfunction that happened. It's not a blame game because I'm not blaming you. I played an equal part in the chaos. I just want to understand your point of view. I want that but I don't need it. I can process through my shame and issues because I've spent so much damn time and money on self-help that I can heal my bullshit now. But if I do it by myself, then I have to separate from you, and I don't want to do that because I value you as a person and I want to be able to work on the book together. I know you are busy. I know you don't like talking about feelings. I know you don't care about the friendship as much as I do because you have many other people to replace me, and even if you didn't, you can just go out and find another writer. But airing it all out is what I need to be able to start the book. Just as important, I want to know what you need from me to feel supported. I want to know if I hurt you so I can make amends. I completely respect your decision if you are not comfortable having a conversation. And if that is the case, then I am not the right book partner for you anyway because we need that kind of openness to write a book together. I won't be offended if you don't respond to this and choose another writer.

I am not expecting him to respond. But the next day, he does.

This was incredibly taxing to read and unfortunate that I can not respond to soooooooooo much without analyzing every single sentence with a response that will take a litigation team and about two weeks. I am not a writer. I'll have to come back to this. Honestly, you have been supportive and equally inconsistent with me for whatever justified or unjustified reason.

You're not emotionally capable of conversing
w me. You love when I'm real, but if I'm too
real, then it hurts your feelings. Can't really
filter myself for you. You're ready to help me
then not, then you are, and now you're not. Up
and down. Upset, then happy. I'm an energy person. And this is just dark energy. Just because
things don't pan out the way you want them to,
you can't emotionally put that on someone who's
not responsible.

By the way, you became completely weird. And it
put me off. So I'm sorry we didn't cuddle and all
that other b*******, but again. Was it my responsibility to HAVE to be a certain way w you? No.

I really hope you do keep doing some soul
searching. And work on whatever problems you
think you have or whatever. But I'm not going
to invest my time doing a book with you. Even if
you're doing it for free. If it's going to waste
four hours of my day for the next 3 months before
you decide not to want to do it anymore. Sorry.
I wish you well.

My stomach drops.

I told you. You don't even know how to communicate.

I'm proud of myself for speaking my truth.

*Really? You made a fool of yourself. You showed who you really are,
and now he hates you. You don't deserve to be loved. You might as well
kill yourself. You have no purpose here.*

Okay, maybe you have a point.

THE next few weeks feel like a zombie trance. A lot has changed
since Marc and Dad, but in a way, nothing has. I'm still too
scared to speak my truth, and it's met with anger when I do. Anytime I show people who I am, they reject me. I don't know how to
communicate. I am too emotional. I'm having a hard time making

quality friends in Hawaii, which was my worst fear about moving here. Between two intensives and a personal coach, I spent almost ten thousand dollars this year on self-help.

For what? I am still a fearful, shameful child, and nothing will ever change.

I spent all of this time and money turning from codependent to strong and independent on the outside and only a little stronger and independent on the inside, and I hate it. I still feel so disconnected from love, and I have nobody to turn to when I am struggling.

I can't do this anymore. It's too emotionally painful.

I am on an airplane. Unlike most airplanes, this one is extremely spacious. It's so spacious that the luggage carousels are located on-board, and we pick up our luggage before deplaning. I can't find my suitcase. There are carousels on each side of the plane. I can feel the panic rise in my chest as I run back and forth between the two carousels, scanning every suitcase for mine. I see a suitcase that, from a distance, looks like my Betsey Johnson flower print carry-on, but as I reach for it, I can see that, even though it is similar, it's not mine.

I frantically keep searching, but all of the luggage has been unloaded, and I still can't find my suitcase. It's not here. I exit the plane, and Kahea is here at the airport to pick me up. I unleash my frustrations on her. "I can't find my suitcase! I need my stuff!"

"You don't need your baggage anymore. You have everything you need with you."

I wake up with a start.

Holy shit. She's right.

I have not been letting go of my old ways that aren't serving me anymore. I have changed, and it's time to step up and leave the old baggage behind.

Chapter 24

I am terrified about this trip to New Zealand and Australia, although that is the point. This is my last milestone goal to develop the capacity to endure the fear while expanding beyond my comfort zone. My biggest fear is that I will be bored out of my mind traveling so far away by myself. My second fear is that I am making a mistake by one-bagging. My friend Jacob went to Japan earlier this year for work. He went back for vacation with only a backpack. He swore it was the best experience of his life and claims that he will never use a suitcase again. I am going to three cities so my intuition is telling me this is a good idea, although my brain is telling me I may have taken the getting out of my comfort zone thing a little too far. But I am all in. I have already packed my Cotopaxi backpack, and I am ready.

My flight arrives in Auckland, New Zealand, at 8 p.m. local time, twenty-three hours ahead of Hawaii. It's still light out. That's because it's summer here, even though it's chilly. I have to transfer to the domestic terminal for my next flight, and luckily the walk is outdoors so I can get some fresh air. There is a green line painted on the street to lead the way.

The green line reminds me of when my family went on vacation to Boston around the time I was ten years old. There was a red line painted throughout the city that strategically led to various tourist attractions. I was wearing white Reebok Freestyle aerobic high-tops with the two Velcro straps at the top (Reeboks with the straps!). I took the red line seriously and walked directly on it the entire time. They had just touched it up somewhere along the line, and I didn't realize I was walking on wet, red paint until the end of the day when my parents smelled paint and traced it to my shoes. Those were my favorite shoes, and we had to throw them away.

The paint along the green line to the domestic terminal is dry and there is a sign that says the walk is fifteen minutes.

Ha! That's for slow walkers.

But I become a slow walker as I relish each breath of fresh air and enjoy the excitement that I am in New Zealand. By myself. With only a backpack. I can't see much from the confines of the airport, but the mountain scenery looks pretty. My skin feels dry from flying. I didn't bring lotion because of the limitations of a carry-on backpack, which is starting to feel heavy. I still have mixed feelings about this.

When my flight arrives in Christchurch, it's about 11 p.m. It's easy to grab an Uber to my hotel. I am staying at a bed and breakfast, which seems more fun than an Airbnb, especially since they actually serve breakfast, unlike the one in Denver. I buzz the front door, and a middle-aged woman in a bathrobe opens it. She is extremely nice. The B&B is an old mansion, and she sets me up in the maid's room which is huge and has two beds and two large, old-fashioned dressers. I am exhausted. I take a shower, brush my teeth and go to bed.

I wake up, and I can barely stand up because I am so nauseated. Thinking I am dehydrated, I try to drink some water, but my stomach isn't having it. I have signed up for a guided hike today. The tour guide, Nicole, is picking me up in two hours. That should be enough time to get something in my stomach and hopefully get over this wave of nausea. Unfortunately, it isn't. Because I can't get out of bed without getting dizzy, I lay in bed for two hours.

What should I do? Am I sick? Should I go to the hospital?

My anxiety doesn't help the situation and is compounding because I haven't eaten anything, and this hiking excursion is six hours long. I have snacks packed, but I need to eat breakfast. But I can't eat because I'm too nauseous. Nicole is supposed to arrive here in ten minutes. I need to pull myself together. I stand up and successfully fight through nausea as I get dressed, pack my bag, and head downstairs. Nicole is here already.

Nicole and I walk to her SUV, parked on the street. I am confused because Kiwis drive on the opposite side of the road, and the driver's side is reverse of U.S., so I start walking toward the wrong side of the car. I pull off my first foreign country obstacle and follow Nicole's lead to the proper side, and we head to a nearby hotel to pick up the other two hikers, Isha and Maha, an Indian newlywed couple from San Francisco.

The hike starts with Nicole taking us to a nearby café for coffee so that we can get to know each other and she can tell us about our day ahead. This café also has food, and Nicole has packed lunches for us. I have tea and a muffin at the café. I admit to Nicole that I had a slight headache and not feeling well, so she gives me some Tylenol. By the time we leave the café, I am feeling much less nauseous and more excited about the hike.

We explore the crater rim walkway along the Banks Peninsula, which has beautiful views of the ocean and mountains. We stop to eat lunch by the water. Nicole has packed frittatas and a healthy fruit salad. The hike is about six miles, but it goes by fast, even though it's sixty degrees Fahrenheit and gets really chilly when the clouds pass over the sun. At one point, I ask Nicole to take a picture of me. This is totally outside of my comfort zone because I hate pictures of myself, and I hate asking people favors. Nicole is an excellent guide and provides us with a lot of education about New Zealand. To complete the tour, she drops us back off at our hotels. I have never had this much white-glove service during a tourist activity.

I am starving. I only had a muffin for breakfast, and even though the packed lunch was tasty, it wasn't filling. My B&B is within walking distance to the Christchurch town center, so I check it out. It's a bunch of restaurants and stores, which is good because I need more clothes. I didn't realize it was going to be this cold in New Zealand. I buy a flannel shirt at Marmot that is fifty percent off because it is summer, even though it's perfect for this cold weather.

I grab a bite to eat and roam around. Christchurch is so boring. Like, really boring. It's one of the most boring places I have ever been. It's so plain and ordinary. I find this surprising because Ozzy specifically recommended coming here because this is where his wife is from.

Why did I take advice from someone who forgot about me twice?

Christchurch is odd too. There was a magnitude six earthquake in 2011 that destroyed much of the city. Half of the city was rebuilt, and the other half still hasn't been rebuilt, for whatever reason. The result is a mixed bag of modern and dilapidated construction. It's creepy that so many things haven't been rebuilt from almost ten years ago. It's like they want to preserve the horror.

I wake up early, with no nausea, and stroll around Christchurch again. It's still so boring that I can't stand it. My flight to Queenstown doesn't leave until this afternoon. I stroll around the botanic gardens to kill time. In the middle, there is a circular section with various rose bushes. I enter through the arched entrance, and the smell of roses immediately engulfs my nostrils. I walk around smelling and examining all of the colorful rose bushes. As I near the exit, I smell someone smoking.

Who the hell is smoking in this beautiful rose garden?

I look around, and the closest person is at the other end, and he is using both hands to hold a camera.

Dad!

I arrive in Queenstown, and it's even colder than Christchurch. I look at my phone. It's fifty degrees Fahrenheit. I catch an Uber to my hotel. The girl at check-in is nice and asks, "Would you like some milk?"

Um, what?

"No, thank you."

My room in Queenstown is nice, but it is freezing here. I crank up the heat. Because I have a kitchenette, I walk to the grocery store down the street to get food for the next few days. I buy a huge bag of groceries, including fresh produce, for thirty U.S. dollars. I am ballin' here with the currency conversion. Even more so when I go to Lululemon to buy more leggings and sweatshirts because I do not have enough cold-weather gear. When I looked at the weather before I left, I saw that the daily high was in the mid-sixties Fahrenheit. What I didn't look at was the hourly weather, which would have shown that it was in the thirties overnight, and most of the day only in the forties or fifties, until a two-hour time frame in the afternoon where it would reach the high.

First on the agenda on my first full day in Queenstown is canyoning, which is kind of like parkour because you do whatever you can to travel through the canyon. It's a four-hour guided tour, and I am scared because I am going alone. I am also scared about what kind of crazy things we will be doing because I am terrified of heights. I immediately make friends with Parish, who lives in Singapore. He is on vacation with his husband, but his husband, despite originally being from Minnesota, wants nothing to do with the cold water in the canyon. Because Parish and I are the only two solos, we bond and are canyoning buddies for the entire four-hour excursion. We also befriend a supermodel-looking German family, sans mom who is sick, of a dad, son, and daughter. They all have gorgeous faces and blonde hair and are super relatable despite having intimidatingly good looks.

The excursion starts by taking a bus to a remote location where they have the wetsuits and all of the equipment. Once we gear up, we head to the canyon, and they start us out easy with ziplining. Then, we rappel down a cliff, which I amazingly am not afraid of, and even smile for the picture. Then comes the hard stuff in the river of the canyon. First of all, the water is thirty-nine degrees Fahrenheit and feels freezing despite our wetsuits.

Our first maneuver is to do a backward somersault off a rock in the middle of the stream. One by one, we backward somersault until it is my turn, and I go without hesitation. The ice-cold water takes my breath away. Then, there is an optional jump off a forty-foot cliff.

There is no way I am jumping off that rock.

Wait, I am going bungee jumping tomorrow, so I need to stop being a little bitch. Plus, the entire reason I am here is to face my fears.

Despite the dread in my stomach, I start climbing the cliff. Now that I am at the top, I totally regret this, but the only way down is to jump. I know if I hesitate, I will be standing up here all day, so I jump. My stomach feels like it's in my throat. I think I am screaming. Plunging in the ice-cold water is so jarring that my brain freezes, and I forget what to do next. Thankfully, we are wearing life jackets, so by the time my brain realizes that I need to swim to the surface, I have already bobbed up.

I did it! I'm doing this!

After that, everything seems like child's play. We get to another crossing where we are standing on rocks, raised a few feet above the water. Parish is first in line, and I am second. The guide yells our next instruction. "You are going to Superman dive into the water!"

Parish doesn't even hesitate. He does a flying dive into the water. I turn to the guide. "Oh, you were being serious?"

"Yeah!"

I fearlessly follow Parish's lead. I was hoping I would adjust to the water temperature by now, but I am still freezing. But I am having so much damn fun! It's interesting how living life is like canyoning in freezing cold water: scary and shocking at first, but fun and easier the more you do it. Parish and I end up toward the middle of the line on the next leg, so we receive the instructions from the guide telephone style. The girl in front of me is from Spain and speaks English as a second language. After she receives her instructions from the person in front of her, she turns to me and relays the message. "We are swimming doggy style through the tunnel."

I laugh and relay the message to Parish exactly as I heard it.

When we get back to the equipment home base, we take hot showers in our bathing suits. My hands and feet are purple. Normally, I would be mad about being so cold, but I am having so much fun that I don't give a shit.

J wake up and have breakfast at a place called Joe's Diner. The waiter tells me I look lovely, and that sets my confidence for the day. Or so I think. I ride a gondola up the mountain with a familiar dread in my stomach.

What am I doing? What am I trying to prove?

When I sign in, I find out that I am the second person of the day to bungee jump, which means that I won't be seeing anybody jump ahead of me unless I get a chance to see the first person. I don't because they put on my harness and get me ready as the first jumper jumps. Callum, the guy with a handlebar mustache putting on my harness, asks in his sexy accent, "How are you planning on jumping today?"

"Um, I'm just trying not to die," I respond in my not-so-sexy, Midwest American accent.

"Well, you can either stand on the ledge and jump, or run and jump."

If I look over the ledge before I jump, it's definitely not happening.

"Run and jump."

The reality of the situation doesn't hit me until I am on deck. I'm lightheaded. I feel a panic attack coming on.

I can't do this. I need a minute.

Before I can open my mouth to tell the guy that I need a minute, he starts counting down.

"Five."

I'm not doing this.

"Four."

I'm not doing this.

"Three."

Wait, my goal is to not hesitate on the countdown.

"Two."

DOOOO EEEEEET!

I start running.

"One!"

I jump. I scream. Everything is silent. All I see are the pine trees beneath me becoming closer. The cord bounces me back up and I feel another breeze of crisp air.

Fuck! Shit!

I start falling again.

No, not again!

The cord bounces me back up. And I bounce up and down a few more times.

I want off! I want off!

The worst part is that there are trees below, so any malfunction would result in death, whereas there might be a chance with water. Also, I am wearing a waist harness, which I imagine is better than hanging upside down, but because of my jumping technique (or lack thereof), I got turned face down and am too afraid to make any kind of adjustment for fear of falling out. I finally stop and then I am dangling in mid-air, which is surprisingly way more terrifying than the bouncing. They throw me a ring that I have to clip to my harness for them to pull me up. Unfortunately, I now have to adjust myself in the harness, while hanging. My hands are shaking so badly that I can barely fasten the clip. As they reel me in, I don't look down. As I'm almost to the platform, the girl reeling me in becomes cheery and chatty, which I will not be until my feet are on solid ground. "How are you feeling?"

"Ask me when I am standing up."

I'm back on the platform.

I DID IT! I'm so proud of myself!

Chapter 25

As I come back from a run, I bump into my neighbor, Maria. Maria is an ESL teacher and has lived and visited many places all over the world. She is curious about my trip. "How were Australia and New Zealand?"

"Amazing!" I fill her in on the highlights. "I didn't like Christchurch much, though. It's so boring."

"Christchurch is the only place I have ever traveled to where I went to a movie theater. That's how bored I was."

Note to self: Never take advice from anyone who forgets about me twice.

I want to start a solo book project, but I don't know where to start. I have set a writing goal for a minimum of fifteen minutes each day to start a discovery journal and see if this leads me anywhere.

Hi Dad,

How have you been? I am starting to understand things better now. I know life isn't easy. I have a hard enough time taking care of myself. I can't imagine trying to juggle this with two kids and a spouse. I know you had addictions. And in hindsight, I think you were depressed. I know you and Mom did the best that you could with the knowledge that you had.

I'm sorry we weren't close before, but I am so happy that you are finally happy now and can be close now. I love it when you visit. I don't smell the smoke as much anymore, but I think that is because you stopped smoking. I see you in other ways, though. Mostly coins. I see a lot of change on the street. I always pick up a coin if I see it because I know that it is you. I also think I see you in birds. And sometimes in strangers, when they say or do funny things. Thank you so much for watching over me and taking care of me. Please continue to lead and guide me, and I will write you letters every day. I hope you are doing well. I love you.

JANUARY 26, 2020

I didn't wake up to go to the bathroom last night, so I didn't change my tampon. It was a bloodbath. As hard as I tried not to get blood anywhere but the toilet bowl, I got it on the bed, the floor, the rug, my shorts, and somehow in the shower. It's 5 a.m. I want to return to my dream where I am the Rock's girlfriend. At least rest my eyes. But here I am doing laundry and cleaning up the blood. Marc used to call situations like this Dexter, so mentally, I still call it that. I wonder if the neighbors can hear me doing laundry. I want to be invisible. This is the wounded inner child in me who fears upsetting Mom, who will withhold love if she is upset. The best way not to rock the boat was to be as quiet as possible. The whirring of the washing machine snaps me out of my dissociation.

I go to yoga. I don't like Sunday yoga anymore. The instructor, Summer, incorporates weights and things like mountain climbers, which is not yoga at all. Also, her soothing voice gets all high tempo and drill sergeant-y as she shouts the commands. I used to see yoga as a workout, but now I like it for the mindfulness aspect. This is not mindfulness. This is not yoga. I want it to be over. Finally, it is.

I go to the beach to relax. But first, I scroll through Instagram. Gary Vee posted a picture of Kobe Bryant. The caption is a bunch of broken hearts. I immediately close the app and open Google. Kobe Bryant died in a helicopter crash.

I try to relax, but the people next to me are talking loudly. They look like father and daughter, but they banter like a couple. The man's voice is perfect. I wonder if he is a radio DJ or voice actor.

January 27, 2020

The dread of waking up at 4 a.m. The zombie march to wash my face and drink some water before logging onto work. Work is draining my soul. What should my new career be? Universe, show me a sign! After work, I went to the beach. What a beautiful day! And so relaxing. There were two women next to me on beach towels, maybe in their sixties. They started bickering.

"Are you saying that you can't enjoy the beach without marijuana?"

"I'm just saying it's more enjoyable."

"You say that about everything. You need marijuana to make everything more enjoyable. You
clearly have an addiction."

"No, I don't. At home, I once went a whole month
without."

"But you can't go without here?"

"Oh no, not here."

"You have an addiction. You need help."

Are they friends or lovers? The righteous lady
stands up and sees the monk seal sunbathing on
the beach.

"Oh, I wonder if that's the seal that just had
a baby!"

That triggered me. That is totally something
that Mom would do, start an argument by nagging
and then sweep it under the rug as if it never
happened. I spent my whole life sweeping shit
under the rug to avoid anger and rejection.

JANUARY 29, 2020

I wake up to clouds and rain for the second day
in a row, which is rare in Hawaii. I need ground-
ing. I am craving yoga. My regular yoga class is
held outdoors. I Google for nearby indoor yoga
classes. Open Door Yoga. I've seen it before.
Riding high on last year's goal to get out of my
comfort zone, I sign up for the 8:30 a.m. class.
The description reads that it involves Sanskrit
chanting, philosophical teachings, flowing asa-
na sequences set to uplifting music, meditation,
hands-on adjustments, and closes with a deep re-
laxation. This sounds completely different than
anything I've ever done. New Me, fearless and
confident, happily signs up. Because I've been

chanting with Kahea, I feel like I will be prepared for this class. I am taking Kahea's chakra workshop series this year, and we just did the root chakra. Kahea taught us the chants to heal root chakra and prescribed a chant to recite one hundred and eight times per day. Omg. I hated it from the beginning. Who has time for this? My obsessive neurosis about numbers kicked in. I didn't want to count. I didn't want to mindlessly recite words that don't resonate with me. That is exactly why I don't like going to the Catholic church. I resisted. Kahea persisted. I agreed to try it the bare minimum of twelve times per day. I've been doing it, so I feel like an advanced-level chanter as I strut my way to Open Door Yoga.

We start the class with a chant. The teacher has already handed out primitive, spiral-bound books with hundreds of chants, each identified by a number. "Turn to page five, number fourteen," the instructor announces. She even has a little organ. By little, I mean it looks like a child's toy. It reminds me of a keyboard I had in fifth grade when I wanted to learn how to play the piano. And there are so many people crammed in the room that even the toy organ barely fits. She starts playing the keys, and the chanting begins. I have a hard time pronouncing the words. I don't understand the Sanskrit pronunciation. It would help if there was a phonetic guide. Or have Kahea here. But neither of those things are here, so I go from confident to fumbling my words. I'm embarrassed because everyone else seems to know the pronunciation. I start to mouth the words. Then, I feel something that my new confident self hasn't felt in a while. Shame. I regress to a child and start to dissociate.

I especially hated class performances. I always lip-synched. To my childhood logic, if I couldn't physically hide, I could vocally hide.

The reason why I was so painfully shy and hated to be in the spotlight was shame. I thought I didn't deserve to be loved, and I didn't want anybody to see me. I felt like people could see right through me. I cried a lot. I hid a lot. When I look back on how cringe-worthy my shyness was, I wonder:

Why didn't my parents notice? Why didn't they try to help me?

So here I am at Open Door Yoga, fresh off my New Zealand and Australia trip where I traveled ten thousand plus miles on my own, bungee jumped, among other badass things, with an established chanting practice, confident and ready to face the world, and I am lip-synching the chants because I am embarrassed about mispronouncing the words in a room full of people I don't even know.

January 31, 2020

I was walking down the sidewalk by the grocery store, and there was a street person with some kind of mental illness walking in the opposite direction. There was a guy on a bike, riding on the street, whizzing past us. The street person yelled to the guy on the bike, "What time is it?"

Without missing a beat, the bicyclist looked at his watch and replied, "A quarter till one!"

The street person thanked him. Watching this scene was so bizarre, yet like an orchestrated dance. Of all of the people to ask for the time, why the guy speeding by on a bike? How did the street person even notice his watch?

February 7, 2020

At the beach, I was eavesdropping on the trio behind me. They were tourists because they kept referring to their hotel. They are going to the Cannabis Expo tomorrow because the torso-tatted, overweight guy with the dreaded-French braid pigtails said their booth was "stupid cheap." That guy had a big personality in addition to his big body. The only female of the trio had hair that was more gray than blonde. She was on her phone for the entire two hours I was there. The big guy must have said at least three times, "She must have the best phone battery ever."

She did look away from her phone and speak up a few times. This is how I learned she had been invited on a date for drinks. She didn't say, but I assumed she met him on a dating app while on her phone because she could not confirm specifics about his looks. The quieter guy suggested she give them a bat signal, if necessary, and the guys could swoop in as Bosnian cousins to rescue her.

"I can't do a Bosnian accent," said the loud, big guy. "How about Australian? G'day, mate!"

I don't understand why they have to play roles. Why can't they go as themselves and rescue her? I got in the ocean. It was cold, so I practiced emotional regulation by submerging myself up to my neck. The gray-haired girl and the loud-mouthed guy were still arguing. He seemed mad that she was ditching them to go on a date. She got defensive and asked why he volunteered to save her. He denied that he ever wanted to do that. Unresolved sexual tension?

FEBRUARY 13, 2020

I've been exhausted all week. Tomorrow is Valentine's day. I have so much love in my heart and so much to offer someone else. Why am I still single? I don't know what to do to find true love. I am figuring it out. The universe shows me signs every day. Has any man ever really loved me?

FEBRUARY 15, 2020

I couldn't get the caulk gun to work today. I am always triggered (no pun intended) by home improvement tasks. I mean, it's a fucking gun. Why does it have to be more complicated than pulling the trigger? Oops, you have to puncture the tip of the tube. *That's* what the metal thing on the gun is for. Thank God for YouTube.

How did Dad know how to do all of this stuff? It's so hard, and Mom was always so critical of him. Like, she could *never* do it, and she had the nerve to criticize him when anything was less than perfect. Why did he put up with it? I hope I never become so dependent on someone that I can't leave when things get bad. I mean, I did it with Marc, but I hope I don't do it again. I'm glad that I am independent now. So that I can do all of this shit now when I am single and still know how to do it when I am married.

When I am married. I'm almost forty. Look how much work and money I have put into my healing. In a lot of ways, things are turning around. In other ways, I feel like I am going to be alone forever. I have so much love in my heart and so much to offer someone else. If there was a God, why would he want someone like me to be alone? I should be spreading this love. I still haven't started on my book. I have no idea what I'm doing, and my writing sounds like rambling. Who would read it?

CHAPTER 26

MARCH 2020

ON New Year's Eve, Air New Zealand had a fifty percent off sale, and I booked another trip for March. As my second trip to New Zealand is approaching, I have started hearing more stories in the news about countries closing their borders to prevent the spread of COVID. I Google about New Zealand. The Prime Minister is expected to decide within forty-eight hours.

I hope my trip doesn't get canceled. Maybe she will delay it a few more weeks.

Seven days before I am scheduled to leave for New Zealand, she announces they are closing the borders. Any visitors have to abide by a fourteen-day quarantine in their accommodations. My trip is only nine days, which would suck up my entire trip. I start crying.

It's not a big deal. It could be worse. Other people have it worse. I'm acting like a spoiled brat. Stop crying.

I switch my thoughts to have a more positive attitude, but there is more news about states on the Mainland U.S. instituting Stay-at-Home orders as the week goes on. Then, the Honolulu mayor declares beach closures.

WHAT?!? No!

The beach is my safe place, where I go to restore my energy. I mentally and emotionally need the beach. The beach is why I moved to Hawaii. How can they take it away? They can, and they wasted no time. Soon after, they implement a Stay-at-Home order.

But the ocean is still open. As I go on my daily walks near the beach, I see surfers getting into the water.

I wish I knew how to surf.

One of the goals in my 2020 planner is to get serious about taking surfing lessons. I took a handful last year but wasn't consistent enough to learn. Ozzy was cool, but I have enough self-worth to know I don't deserve to be forgotten about once, let alone twice. But the entire island is shut down, except for essential services. I want to take surfing lessons to enjoy nature in one of the few legal ways. I have Ozzy's cell phone number. Despite forgetting about me, he is chill, and I am confident that he would be willing to give me lessons during the lockdown. I text Ozzy. He texts me back immediately and suggests Sunday morning.

I have a pit in my stomach as I walk to meet Ozzy.
What if he forgets about me again?

I need these lessons to fill the void of the beach. It doesn't help that this whole lockdown is triggering my feelings of isolation from childhood. I grew up in a house with my parents and sister, but we were completely disconnected from each other. My recurring dream is being isolated. I hate being isolated. I also hate being restricted. This Stay-at-Home order is my worst nightmare. If Ozzy forgets about this lesson, I am going to have an emotional breakdown.

He's here!

He looks just like I remember him from last summer: skinny, weathered skin, crazy surfer hair, big, bright smile. We have so much fun during the first lesson! I remember some things, and Ozzy is as fun and funny as I remember. He tells me that his wife just went back to New Zealand to stay there indefinitely for COVID. He explains that it's because she doesn't have health insurance here and healthcare in New Zealand is basically free in case she were to get COVID. He is clearly very excited by this new arrangement, and I find that so odd, but their whole relationship always seemed strange.

Won't he miss her? Won't he at least miss the sex?

The following Sunday, Ozzy and I have another totally fun and funny lesson. I can't do this once a week. I need Ozzy's fun energy in my life during this restricted, isolated time. The only other people I see in person right now are my friend Sam who I work out with once a week at her house and my friend Kelly once or twice a month. I ask Ozzy if he could do two lessons each week. He agrees! I now have lessons on Sunday mornings and Wednesdays after work. Ozzy is cool because he keeps hot water jugs in his car to shower off after surfing. He starts packing an extra jug for me and giving me rides home. I like that he is taking me under his wing.

There is a hidden adventure to Ozzy giving me rides home. Every time we get back to the car, he loses his keys, and we spend at least ten minutes looking for them. This is something that would normally annoy me, but for some reason, I have a lot of patience with Ozzy. I like how he balances out my rigid side and teaches me patience.

"How about you start putting your keys in that cubby?" I gesture to a spot on the console. He begins to do this, and we no longer have to look for the keys. We joke that we make a good team.

THE COVID Stay-at-Home order brings back all the feelings of loneliness and isolation from my childhood. With everything closed, except essential services, this cuts off most socialization. I can't even go to the beach to recharge. I feel out of control and disconnected.

What is this teaching me?

I need to be more connected to myself and connect with others. For a first step, perhaps bold for the first step, I decide to make a phone call. The next day, I do something I haven't done in at least six months and call Mike. In the past, he picked up immediately whenever I called. The phone rings twice.

He doesn't want to talk to me.

He picks up on what is probably the last ring before voicemail. We casually talk for a while, even though I feel I am being awkward. Then, I let him know the reason why I am calling. "Listen, I called to apologize for being inconsistent with the book project. I won't make excuses. I am sorry for hurting you."

I know we were both equally inconsistent, and as much as I want him to apologize for his role in the dysfunction, I don't need an apology. I almost apologize for the email, but the truth is, I am not sorry for speaking my truth. I am sorry for the back and forth drama with the book, though, mostly because I should never have agreed to do the book when he reached out to me after the Guam trip. I hold my breath.

"No need to apologize. I wasn't hurt. I appreciate the apology."

He has to go, and we hang up. I have said my piece for closure. I know that I had been fighting tooth and nail for the friendship because I wanted to work on the book with him, so I didn't have to allow myself to be seen by writing a book of my own.

I won't be hard on myself. It was a learning experience.

Are you kidding me? You have no idea what you are doing. You don't know how to communicate or interact with other people.

I can't handle this Stay-at-Home order. This is only the beginning, and I am going crazy. When I am craving connection more than ever, it's being restrained on a global, institutional level.

*B*ECAUSE staying at home is so depressing and isolating, the only two things I look forward to all week are my two lessons with Ozzy. I don't even like surfing that much. I just love that we laugh so hard our stomachs hurt. The best part is, Ozzy thinks *I'm* funny, which is a huge honor because I think he is hilarious. And even though our conversations are funny, they are also educational.

"At least there aren't crocodiles in the ocean."

"What is the difference between an alligator and a crocodile?"

"I don't know."

It was an earnest question, but a funny joke pops into my head. "One you see later and one you see in a while."

After the lesson we laugh and Google the differences between alligators and crocodiles. Then, I tell him about another reptile.

One day on a walk, I discovered a house in the area with a pet tortoise, so as Ozzy drives me home, we drive by. We soon become obsessed with the turtle and drive by after each lesson. We can't figure out this turtle. It has hind legs like a tortoise and deformed sea turtle fins up front with snaggly toenails. One day, the owner is outside, and we learn that the turtle's name is Turtle. He's twenty years old and is out from 8 a.m. to 4 p.m. Otherwise, he sleeps.

SURFING with Ozzy is only two days each week. On the other days, I feel alone and isolated. I want to talk to Dad. I text Celeste. I know Luna doesn't do remote sessions, but maybe she has changed her mind since COVID has forced the world to operate as remotely as possible. She has! Celeste gets me on the schedule for the following week. Zoom-ing with Luna is like a breath of fresh air. I miss her positive aura so much. I hope that she has good advice from Dad.

She tells me that Dad calls me his "Sunshine Girl," which makes me happy to hear. The thing I love about Luna is that she is so on-point receiving messages. "Who's Rick?"

"That was my old manager at work. He quit in December."

She closes her eyes as she always does when getting a hit. "Your dad says 'good riddance.' He didn't like Rick. He didn't have your back, did he?"

"No." The fact that Dad is looking out for me in this way, a way that he didn't when he was alive, warms my heart.

"Who is Brian?"

"My new manager."

"Your dad likes him. You can trust him. Your dad is telling me something about parkour. Does that mean anything to you?"

"Yeah! When Stay-at-Home started, I started filming an Instagram story series called 'No Gym? No Problem!' It started as at-home workouts, but then I started making a joke out of it. One day, I filmed myself jumping over a discarded high chair in the street and called it parkour."

"Tell me about who you have been surfing with. I can't pick up the name. Your dad says it's a nickname."

"Ozzy."

"Tell me about Ozzy."

I light up. I tell her all about how we have been surfing, laughing, and having fun.

"Your dad says that Ozzy is your blueprint. What does that mean to you?"

"Well, he's very protective of me, so I feel safe around him and he is one of the only people in my entire life who has truly accepted me for who I am. I can be myself around him, and I love it."

"Keep him around and find people like him for your tribe. Your dad specifically used the word 'tribe.' He doesn't use words like that."

She's right, and I know that means he wants me to pay attention to the message.

ONE day, Ozzy strikes an offer. "I have so much fun in our lessons, if you are interested in adding another day, let me know, and it's on the house."

I love surfing with Ozzy, so this is amazing, but I don't want to take advantage of his time. "Are you sure?"

"Yeah, of course."

"Sure! I would love that! Thank you!"

Yay!

Now I have guaranteed fun and laughs three days each week. Surfing is fun, and I am making progress. I'm still a city person at heart, and I don't feel comfortable in the water yet, but Ozzy helps me feel safe and protected. He is aware of my ocean apprehensiveness, so doesn't push me to do something new if I am not comfortable with it. And he lends me a wetsuit jacket when the water is chilly. He has started introducing me to some of the regulars, so I feel even safer knowing more people in the water now.

Ozzy has also started packing two hot water jugs for each of us to rinse off post-surf. The ocean is still pretty cold, so this is a treat. My favorite part is that Ozzy always shares his second jug with me.

ON Mother's Day, I call Mom as I am walking to meet Ozzy for our lesson. As I talk, I hear the wheels of a skateboard rolling on the pavement behind me. I expect it to pass but it never does, and the sound of the wheels lingers behind me. I turn around, and it's a teenager riding on his skateboard behind me, taking a video of me walking in my bathing suit. My Chicago attitude gets activated. Even though Mom is on the phone, I lash out. "No! Delete that fucking video right now!"

In Chicago, this kid would not be intimidated by me, but this guy is scared, so I use it to my advantage. "Delete it right now!"

He fumbles around with his phone, pretending to delete it, but I know he isn't deleting it. Part of me wants to rip the phone right out of his hands and throw it into the street, but I'm talking to Mom and eager to get to my surfing lesson. I don't want him to follow me anymore. "Turn around and go the other way, or I am calling the police!"

He obliges. Still, I feel violated and uneasy. I go back to talking to Mom.

"What was that?"

"Nothing."

She continues talking about herself. When I meet up with Ozzy, I tell him about the incident. After the lesson, he gives me a ride home as usual, but when he drops me off, he strikes another offer. "I'll pick you up on Wednesday."

"No, it's fine. I can walk." I don't want to inconvenience him.

"No, I'm picking you up. I'll be here at 1 p.m."

I know he is offering because of the skateboarder incident. I like how Ozzy makes me feel safe and comfortable in and out of the water. My favorite part about spending time with Ozzy is that he creates a safe space for my authentic self to shine, and he wholeheartedly accepts me for who I am. This is one of the rare times in my life that I have felt both physically and emotionally safe.

One day during a lesson, Ozzy opens up to me that he was married before his current wife and has a son.

"How old is your son?"

Ozzy seems embarrassed. "Ang, you're old enough to be my daughter and hot enough to be my wife."

I am flattered that he thinks I'm hot, but not sure what any of that had to do with my question about his son's age.

"He's thirty-two."

I think I get it now. Ozzy's wife is thirty-one years old. Maybe he is embarrassed that his wife and son are the same age.

Ozzy and I are doing lessons three times per week. The lessons are technically only an hour, but we are usually in the water for about two hours, plus warm water jug showers and rides back and forth. I start to see him more as a friend than a surf instructor. I can tell he feels the same way, too, as we both start opening up more, including him confiding more about his marriage. He admits he and his wife have separated, which is why she went to New Zealand. He isn't sure if she is coming back. He also mentions that they only talk on the phone once every two to three weeks. Despite not talking on the phone, she texts him a lot. I know this because she has her own ringtone on his phone: sci-fi, spooky music. The first time I heard it, I laughed hysterically. He later told me that is her ringtone because anything that comes from her texts and phone calls is scary. I get a sense now, more than ever, that he feels trapped by her, but I still don't understand why. I don't pry. I enjoy Ozzy's company, and we have plenty to talk and laugh about outside of his relationship with her.

When he drops me off from lessons, I don't get out of the car immediately because we still have so much to talk about. One day, he tells me a riddle about paying for a hotel room, which leads me to giving him an accounting lesson on T-accounts, which are visual representations of accounting entries. Another day, we have a conversation about what his name should be in a foreign country. His real name is Robert, so he thinks he should say his name is Roberto if he goes to Spain. I tell him that his name is Ozzy, no matter what country he is in. A few weeks ago, Ozzy had told me how he texts pictures of cards and gifts to people for their birthdays, even his wife. I laugh because the thought of it is funny, but I would kill my husband if he didn't even get me a real card. It has gotten to the point that when he pulls up to my building, he automatically turns off the car because we are going to talk for at least an hour. It's odd because whenever I get out of the car, I want to hug him like I would any other friend, but I don't know if that would be crossing any boundaries, even though he is separated from his wife. But if we hug, he needs to be comfortable with it and make the first move.

BECAUSE the beaches are closed for lounging, the City and County of Honolulu are redistributing the sand on the beach. Ozzy and I still have to traverse the beach to get to the ocean, so the walk becomes somewhat treacherous with the uneven sand, especially while carrying surfboards. One day, as we are getting out of the water, I trip on a hard mound of sand. Ozzy and I laugh it off, but I am really lucky that I didn't fall. On our next lesson, we get out of the water, and I internally remind myself that I need to watch out for the lump so that I don't trip again.

But what's moving by that palm tree?

Thud

My foot hits the hard lump with more force this time. I struggle to catch my balance, but it's not enough, and I fall right into the sand in front of a bunch of people. I cannot believe that I have tripped twice in a row in the same spot. I start laughing while I am still on the ground. Covered in sand like Shake 'n Bake, I look up, and not only did Ozzy not turn around to see if I'm okay, but he never stopped walking. He continues to walk away.

I embarrassed him.

I feel something I haven't felt with Ozzy yet— shame. My feelings are hurt. I felt like he was my protector, and now he is walking away. We laugh about it later, but it still hurts my feelings.

FRIDAY after our lesson, Ozzy strikes a proposal. "Do you want to go to Sandy's?"

Sandy Beach is on the East Side. It's a popular place for boogie boarders. We have talked about going there before. I am somewhat hesitant because this would be our first time hanging out outside of lessons. I know that even though Ozzy's wife is away, and they are separated, he is married, so I don't want to cross any boundaries. But I love hanging out with Ozzy, and because of the Stay-at-Home order, there isn't much else to do. It's nice to have Ozzy as a companion, and now I consider him a friend. I agree.

On the drive out to Sandy's, Ozzy confides more to me about his marriage. It turns out the reason that they separated, and she is in New Zealand, is because they have been having problems for a long time now. Their main problem is that she wants to have kids, but not with him because of his age. She grew up without a father, and with him being sixty-one years old, she's afraid Ozzy would pass away while the child is still relatively young. She doesn't want her child to be fatherless at a young age. Plus, Ozzy already has a thirty-two-year-old son, and he doesn't even want another child.

Didn't they think about this before they got married?

Their marriage is still confusing to me. He continues to tell me that they are both having issues letting go. Him, because she co-owns his surf school business and he cannot do the back-end aspects. She is also the photographer. She doesn't want to let go yet because she doesn't want to have kids for a few more years, so wants to hang on to the relationship until she is ready to have kids. Wisely, he wants to make a clean break now. He wants to move out while she is away, but she feels that would be kicking her to the curb. He agreed to stay in their shared apartment until she gets back, but he tells her to start calling her friends for a place to live in order to have a game plan for when she gets back.

"When is she coming back?"

"I don't know."

This answers some questions about their relationship but opens a new set of questions. I have a feeling there is more to the story. After Sandy's, we grab a bite to eat. Since restaurants are closed, we have to take it to go. The restaurant is next to a marina, so we eat on a bench that overlooks the water. While we are eating, I confide to Ozzy about a conversation I had with my improv friend, Tony, a few months ago. Tony and I had lunch together, and he asked me where I saw myself in five years. I didn't have a realistic answer prepared, but I knew what my dream life entailed. I went on for at least five minutes describing how I wanted to be married, financially independent, be a writer, and travel with my husband. I went into detail about the travels and adventures I hoped to accomplish. After I finished, Tony zeroed in on one comment. "I didn't know you wanted to get married."

"Why do you say that?"

"You're so independent. I thought you wanted to be single."

I had spent the past three years recovering from codependency on Marc, that I swung completely in the opposite direction. That was extremely helpful feedback because I hadn't been getting approached or going on dates, so I felt like this explained why. When I finish telling this to Ozzy, he chimes in with his two cents on why he thinks I haven't been attracting as many men in Hawaii. "You need to lose the Chicago attitude."

At first, it stings, but I know he's right. Especially with him being a local, I respect his opinion, and I knew before he said it that I hadn't integrated into the Hawaiian culture. This is also helpful feedback, even though the initial impact was hard to absorb. But he softens the blow. "I think you are a catch. If I weren't married, I would be hitting on you."

I'm not sure why he is telling me this, but I find it flattering because I have started to look up to Ozzy and respect him. He gives off an amazing vibe, and I know he genuinely has a good heart. The conversation turns to all things love, falling in love, falling out of love, soulmates, and heartbreak. Ozzy looks me directly in the eyes. "Sometimes, you can't control who you fall in love with. Do you understand what I am saying, Ang?"

Meeting his intense gaze, I nod. I feel there might be a story behind that statement, but he doesn't elaborate.

*B*ECAUSE Ozzy and I have been bonding more outside of lessons, during one of our lessons, I open up to him. "When I fell that one day on the beach, it hurt my feelings when you walked away and didn't even check to make sure I was okay."

I am not sure why I am telling him this and don't expect him to care but he is genuinely upset that he hurt my feelings, and for one of the few times in my life, I don't regret speaking up about how I feel.

"Why didn't you tell me before?"

"I didn't think you would care."

"I walked away because I heard you laughing, so I knew you were okay. Listen, it hurts me to hurt you, so you need to tell me these things. Maybe we should come up with a signal."

"How about this?"

I put my hands together in the shape of a heart and then pull them apart to demonstrate the heart breaking. From here on out, when one of us says something the other is sensitive to, we use the hand signal.

We come up with another signal later in the lesson. I catch a wave but fall, and the water pulls my top down. I bob under the water to fix it. There is another wave coming. Ozzy wants me to catch it. "Get on your board!"

My boob is still hanging out of my top. The wave comes and goes, and I fix my top before paddling back out to Ozzy.

"Are you okay? Why didn't you get back on the board?"

"My boob was hanging out!"

We laugh like we always do and then come up with the OK hand signal for whenever that happens.

I have been trying to look on the bright side of the potential gifts of being restricted from my pre-COVID daily routines. I start posting Instagram stories that follow the "Yes, and" theme of improv. For example, yes, the gyms are closed, and I can find new ways to work out. Last week, the State of Hawaii extended the Stay-at-Home order until the end of June. I thought that meant the beaches were also going to remain closed until the end of June. Because I have started to enjoy the water, I ordered a big, pink flamingo raft on Amazon for when I don't surf. A few days later, the City announced the re-opening of the beaches, but I still want to do an Instagram Story with my flamingo, so I enlist the help of Ozzy to do the filming. We go to the lagoon in Waikiki after a lesson. Ozzy puts his face mask on the flamingo's beak, which I think is hilarious. Then, he starts filming and commentating as I rodeo the flamingo. "Okay, she's on it. Yep. Three more seconds! And it's a com—"

I face-plant into the water, which is funny until my leg gets caught in the flamingo's neck. Luckily, it is soft plastic, so I quickly and safely escape. Ozzy and I are doubled over in laughter.

CHAPTER 27

SOON after announcing the beach re-openings, they also announce that restaurants are re-opening for dine-in, at limited capacity. Unfortunately, the restaurant we chose on re-opening day has chosen not to open their seating, so we take-away like we have been doing and eat in a nearby park. We also get a slice of cheesecake for dessert. They gave us two forks, but Ozzy takes only one fork, cuts it into the slice, and feeds it to me. He then takes a bite for himself and alternates feeding it to him and me. I am enjoying getting closer to Ozzy but still confused about why we haven't hugged. After eating the cheesecake, Ozzy tells me a story about his son and how he wasn't close to him in his formative years. He starts tearing up. I find it endearing that he is comfortable showing emotion in front of me. I instantly feel even more fond of him.

Salons are also now open. I haven't had my hair professionally cut or colored since February, although I did trim and color it myself a few months ago. I am well overdue for a hair appointment. The day after my first professional cut and color in four months, I have a lesson with Ozzy.

"Do you like my hair?" I dramatically turn my head, so it flows gracefully.

"I do." And I can tell by the way he is looking at me, he does. When we get out of the car, Ozzy commands, "Turn around."

I turn around. I feel his fingers running through my hair. He takes his time alternating between running his fingers through my hair and grabbing it as though he is going to tie it in a ponytail. When he does this, it kind of turns me on. I like getting my hair played with and the sensation of him pulling my hair while being behind me is sexy.

The thing that is not sexy about Ozzy is smoking. He doesn't smoke a lot, but it bothers me when he does. He usually does it after surfing or eating, so I stroll away and wait for him to finish. I don't like that he is hurting himself, and it reminds me of how Dad slowly killed himself by smoking. I would hate it if anything ever happened to Ozzy.

Because my hair is now freshly colored, I want to protect it from the saltwater when we have lessons. I order Moroccan oil leave-in conditioner from Amazon, but I don't like the smell. I buy another brand I like a lot better. Because the Moroccan oil was not cheap, I don't want to waste it, so I give it to Ozzy. He has long, surfer's hair, and I know he doesn't care about protecting it, but it might give it a little shine. It becomes part of our pre-surf ritual for me to spray Moroccan oil in his hair. Now, I get to run my fingers through his hair. I like to examine his shoulder-length hair as I spray it with conditioner. It's mostly salt and pepper, but it has perfectly placed blonde, surfer highlights that women pay hundreds of dollars to get professionally done. I also like it because it has a wavy texture.

Because the beaches are now open, and Ozzy knows I like to go to the beach, he invites me to Bellows Field beach, which is part of the Air Force base and only open to the public on the weekends. I love the fact that Ozzy wants to introduce me to new places on the island. Ozzy isn't into relaxing on the beach, so he brings boogie boards. I also bring my inflatable flamingo. I have a hard time catching waves on the boogie board. Ozzy assists me by pushing.

"Don't touch my butt."

I hope he's not offended, but I don't feel comfortable telling him the real reason why. Although, after the hair-pulling, part of me likes the idea of him touching my butt.

"Maybe when you get more comfortable with me, you will let me push your butt. It's easier that way."

Ha, if he only knew the issue was I am a little too comfortable with him.

After boogie boarding, we surf with the flamingo. It is hilarious and extremely difficult, which is made harder by the fact that we are laughing so hard. After Bellows, Ozzy takes me around the coast to Kailua, where he grew up. He drives past his childhood home and the high school he went to. We then stop at a beach park to sit in the sand and chat. Ozzy tells me about a dog that he had when he was younger. He starts to tear up. I like seeing more of his sensitive side. We then go to Aloha Salads in Kailua to eat.

We love Aloha Salads so much that we start frequenting a closer location in Kahala Mall on our lesson days. There is also a gelato kiosk in the mall. We begin a habit of getting gelato for dessert. Our favorite flavor is strawberry cheesecake. We usually share, and sometimes Ozzy feeds it to me. He also lets me in on a secret dessert he likes to make at home: warm Pop-Tarts topped with ice cream. I tell him he should open a side business selling these treats. "You can call it Ozzy Tarts."

"Oz Tarts!" he replies.

I like the sound of that. So much so that I start calling him Oz Tart as a nickname. He starts bringing Pop-Tarts with us, and we make our own Oz Tarts out of the gelato. He doesn't let me make my own. He makes each bite himself and then feeds me every other bite.

THE City and County of Honolulu have started opening up Kalakaua Avenue on Sunday mornings to pedestrian and bike traffic. Since this is the main drag along Waikiki where Ozzy and I have lessons on Sunday mornings, we start skateboarding on Sundays after our lesson.

Another Sunday ritual that Ozzy and I have is eating breakfast Sweet E's, which is down the street from where I live. Because we are regulars, they know our names, what we like to order, including extra sugar and cream for Ozzy's coffee, and they know to bring out Ozzy's pancake on a separate plate because he always shares it with me. One of the waiters is a surfer, and since he knows we come from surfing, he always asks us about the surf conditions.

The Sunday free-for-all on Kalakaua is getting crowded, so Ozzy and I change up our routine to go to Sweet E's first and then skateboard on our own. Today, we are at a graveyard because Ozzy says it has a perfect grade hill for skateboarding. It feels weird and somewhat disrespectful to be here. Plus, I am a beginner, and the hill is too steep for me. We start down the hill, and I start screaming because I am going too fast. Miraculously, I pull off a turn at the bottom. Ozzy is laughing hysterically and smoothly meets me at the bottom of the hill, where he pulls out a cigarette and lights it up.

"Oz Tart, I don't want to be around you while you smoke, so I'm going back to the car." Then I make a joke out of it to lighten the mood. "Watch me, I'm speeding!" I try to sprint pedal uphill, but I end up tripping, luckily not falling. We are both doubled over in laughter. Ozzy cuts his cigarette short and I know it's because he knows it bothers me.

MY birthday is coming up. It's on a Wednesday this year and, lucky for me, Ozzy and I have lessons on Wednesdays! I am also taking the day off work, so we change it up and do the lesson in the morning. The week before my birthday, Ozzy has an important question for me. "What do you want for your birthday?"

Laughing and having fun with him three times each week is a gift enough. "You don't have to get me anything."

"But I want to. Think about it and let me know."

"Okay."

I don't think about it any further. Mostly because I don't need a gift from him, and because I am not looking forward to turning forty. I've been dreading this all of age thirty-nine. But when I wake up on my birthday, turning forty feels pretty badass. As I am waiting for Ozzy to pick me up for our lesson, I get a text from him. It's a picture of a birthday card. Since I know this is how he rolls, I am flattered. He then picks me up, and when I get in the car, he hands me a card.

"Oh my God! A real card!" I am so honored and overwhelmed with emotion. "Can I open it now?"

"Sure."

I open the card. A one hundred dollar bill falls out, and there are two Post-it note coupons. One is for a free lesson, and one is for a surf photoshoot with his friend Dana. The card says:

```
In these crazy times we live in, no one has
made me smile more or laugh harder than you have.
Thank you so much for that! Thank you for being
a friend!
```

"Oh my God! Thank you so much! This means so much to me! A real card and real gifts!"

"You're welcome."

My heart is so warm. We have our lesson and go to Sweet E's afterward. They are surprised to see us because it is not Sunday. I brought my beach bag because I have the day off and plan to go to the beach next. Ozzy offers to drop me off. As he pulls up to the beach, I realize that I want to keep hanging out with him because I am having so much fun and enjoying his company. The only problem is, I know he doesn't like relaxing on the beach as I do.

It doesn't hurt to ask.

"Do you want to come with me? I know you don't like—"

"Sure!"

He immediately pulls the car into the parking lot. It's heart-warming to me that he wants to hang out too. Usually, when I go to the beach by myself, I only stay for about an hour. I stay two hours max if I am relaxed or take a nap. Ozzy and I spend four hours at the beach talking and laughing, and time just flies by. While we are at the beach, Mom texts me happy birthday. This is disappointing because it's mid-day my time, and she is six hours ahead of Hawaii. She waited until late in the day, and she couldn't even pick up the phone to call me. I tell Ozzy how I feel.

"You deserve a phone call."

As we leave the beach, I have to go to the bathroom. The plan is that Ozzy will get in the car while I go to the bathroom and pick me up at the bathrooms, which are less than a quarter-mile down the road. Because I don't want to tote my bag with me, I leave it in his car. After I walk out of the bathroom, I look for Ozzy but don't see him. I wait. I wait some more.

Uh-oh, did I misunderstand the plan?

And the worst part is, he has my phone, so I have no way to contact him. My fear of abandonment kicks in.

Did he leave without me? What am I going to do?

My bag has my phone, my keys, and my credit card. I start panicking. I walk back to where the car was parked. It is gone. I start walking back to the bathrooms, and as I do, a sense of calm floods my entire being. Ozzy is one of the few people in my entire life who has made me feel both emotionally and physically safe.

Ozzy would never abandon me.

I sit on the curb and calmly wait. A few minutes later, I look over my shoulder and see Ozzy pulling up behind me on the street. He misunderstood and went to a different set of bathrooms. Afterward, we go to Banán, which is like ice cream except it's made out of bananas. My favorite part about hanging out with Ozzy is the simplicity that we can laugh and have fun anytime, anywhere.

This is the best birthday ever!

THE following week, for my birthday present, my friend, Kelly, treats me to a Yoni steam— sitting over a pot of boiling herbs to steam clean your vagina. Kelly has been to Yoni Steam before, but I haven't, so I have to fill out a new customer form. One of the fields is for emergency contact. For emergency contact, I usually use big brother Joe, but I put Ozzy for my vagina steam emergency contact and can't wait to tell him so we can laugh about it. As Kelly and I sit next to each other, draped in robes, wide-legged under steaming pots, we chat. Kelly brings up the day when she and her friend Nikita ran into Ozzy and me as we were skateboarding on Kalakaua.

"Nikita thought you guys were a couple. I told her, 'he wishes!'"

"Why do you say that?"

"I think he likes you. What's the deal with his wife? Is she ever coming back?"

"That's a good question. He doesn't talk about it much. All I know is that they are separated."

Instead of being rejuvenated the next day, I have a raging headache. I never get headaches. It must be the herbs from the vagina steam. Ozzy and I laugh about how that plan backfired. I tell him that I put him down as my emergency contact. He does laugh but then gets serious. "Who do you usually use as your emergency contact?"

"My friend Joe in Chicago."

"You need somebody local. From now on, you put me down as your emergency contact."

"Okay."

THE following Sunday, Ozzy and I shake things up and eat breakfast at a different restaurant. There is a picture on the wall from 1953. I take a friendly jab at him.

"That's only five years before you were born!"

Ozzy does the broken heart signal with his hands.

Oh no, I didn't think he would be offended.

"You know how you felt when I walked away when you fell?"

"Yes."

"That's how I feel when you point out my age."

He is teary-eyed, and I feel like an asshole. I didn't know he was that sensitive to his age.

"I'm sorry. I promise I won't do it again."

And I didn't.

SOME days after lessons, we go skateboarding on the bike path on my street. We have been skateboarding so much that I store my board in his car now. Today, we are playing a game where Ozzy pushes me from his skateboard so that I don't have to peddle. We are having fun, but when we get to one end of the road, Ozzy stops for a smoke break. It breaks my heart. "Listen, I know that you smoke, but I don't want to see you hurting yourself. From now on, whenever you smoke, can you please do it out of my eyesight?"

Ozzy looks at me with visible pain in his eyes. It's as if he is reflecting the pain I feel when I see him smoking. He takes the boundary a step further. "How about this? I won't even smoke when I am with you. If you catch me smoking or even sneak off to smoke, tell me to take you home. I don't want to cut our time short, so there is no way I would jeopardize it by smoking."

"Deal."

We continue skateboarding. After we are done, we start walking with our boards to cross the street. I don't see a biker that is quickly approaching us, and Ozzy pulls me out of the biker's way.

"You're my emergency contact, not my safety contact."

"Oh, so you wanted to get hit by a bike?"

We both laugh, and he continues, "From now on, I am both your emergency and safety contact."

These roles seem fitting because I always feel safe with Ozzy. We put the skateboards back in Ozzy's car, and then we sit in the car to talk some more. While we are talking, Ozzy's friend Gordon, who I know from surfing, calls. Ozzy answers on speakerphone. "Hey, what's up, Gordon?"

"Hey, Ozzy! You had a heart attack, right?"

"Yeah."

Um, what?!?

They continue talking. Gordon has to wear a heart monitor for a week and has questions for Ozzy because Ozzy is apparently an expert on heart problems.

He never told me any of this and we have talked about a lot of shit.

He ends the call with Gordon.

"When did you have a heart attack?"

"I didn't have a heart attack."

"What are you talking about? I just heard you."

"No, he said, 'you've heard of a heart attack, right?'"

Is he gaslighting me?

"I heard what he said. When did you have a heart attack?"

Ozzy sighs as he admits defeat. "About five years ago." He tells me the story.

I hesitate to ask, but I can't help myself. "Why do you still smoke?"

"I don't know. I stopped, but then I got stressed out a few years ago and started again." He pauses. "I promise I'll try to stop again. It will help now that I'm not smoking around you, and we have been hanging out a lot."

"I'm not trying to tell you what to do, but I don't want to see you end up like my dad. He died way too early. I would be really hurt if anything ever happened to you."

I see the pain in his eyes reflecting my pain. We talk for a little longer, and I get out of the car. As I ride the elevator upstairs, my heart is overflowing with love.

I love that man so much. I would be devastated if anything ever happened to him.

Shit, I caught feelings. And we still haven't hugged.

O
ZZY and I are talking, and he asks what I am doing for the upcoming weekend.

"I am going to Glenn's Nursery in Waimanalo to buy a plant."

"How are you going to get it home?"

"In my car."

"Your car is nice. You don't want to get it dirty. We'll go together. We can put it in my car."

I am not sure if this is a bid for connection to spend more time with me or if he really is concerned about dirt in my beige interior car. Either way, I would love to go with him, so I have no problem with it. We go to Glenn's on Saturday and Ozzy helps me pick out a plant. We go out to eat before he drops me off, and we do the usual thing where he turns off the car, and we talk for a while. Then, I retrieve the plant from the back. I am strong enough to carry it, but I want him to come up with me to chat more. It feels inappropriate to invite him up even though he is separated from his wife.

"Do you need help carrying it?"

YES! I mean no, but I want you to come with me.

"No, I'm good. Haven't you seen my muscles?" I flex my bicep.

"Text me a picture when you give it a spot."

I go upstairs with my plant, but it feels lonely without Ozzy. I enjoy his company. I am happy that we have a lesson tomorrow morning. The previous owner of my condo built out the lanai, so that area of the living space has windows that go from the ceiling to the floor. I put the plant in front of the open windows. I text a picture to Ozzy, and he responds.

> What are you going to name your plant?

> Roberto. It's Spanish for Ozzy.

OZZY and I just got takeout salads to eat in a nearby park. As we are getting out of the car, I notice a pack of cigarettes on the console. I hate seeing them, but don't want to nag him about it because I know that me being annoying to him about smoking isn't a reason that he would stop. To minimize my discomfort with the cigarettes, I attempt to cover it with humor and casually toss them out the open door. I laugh, but Ozzy is not amused. "Bitch."

I feel like he plunged a knife in my heart. He is not joking, even though I was. Chicago Angie emerges, Hulk-style. "What did you call me?"

He looks me dead in the eyes and says, "A bitch."

"Don't *ever* fucking call me that again! It's disrespectful."

I tear up, and we both get out of the car. Angrily, I throw the cigarettes back in the car and see that Ozzy is walking around to my side of the car.

I don't want to eat with him right now. I don't even—

Ozzy hugs me. "I'm sorry."

"Thank you, Oz Tart."

My heart melts. This hug feels so good and is so overdue. From this day forward, Ozzy and I now hug upon greeting and goodbye and every opportunity in between.

OZZY and I have been spending time every day together. I usually don't like spending this much time with other people, even with boyfriends. Part of it is a protective mechanism. I'm afraid that if someone gets to know me too well, they will reject me for who I am. And because there have been a lot of people who haven't accepted me for who I am in the past, I tend to mask my authentic self, and it's exhausting to keep up the charade long-term. It's also draining that I tend to pick up on other people's energy, and I need time by myself to recharge. But with Ozzy, it's different. He accepts me for who I am, so I am free to be my quirky self without fear of rejection or abandonment. And Ozzy's energy is so energizing that I don't need to recharge after spending time with him. The best part is that I feel emotionally connected to someone for the first time in a long time. And with all of the COVID social restrictions, I am not spending much time with other people, so Ozzy has become my best friend.

Ozzy and I are skateboarding on the bike path along my street. He has gout, and it is starting to flare up in his knee, so we sit in the yard of my building to chat instead. The sun has set, and it's breezy and kind of chilly. I don't want to cut our time short, so I suffer through the chill. Plus, I can tell he is uncomfortable with his gout and I want to comfort him. He motions to his knee. "Don't you have a little thing you can do for my knee?"

I am not sure what he is referring to, but my mind jumps to black magic. I don't skip a beat as I say, "Hold on." I walk to the building next door because I know they have a hibiscus plant. I pull off a flower. I take it back to Ozzy and perform an improvised ritual. At one point, I look up at him to see if he is enjoying it. He is looking at me with pure pleasure in his eyes, and I don't think it's gout relief. After I am done, he takes the flower from me and performs a ritual on me. He gently rubs the flower up and down my torso, pausing at my belly button and groin. Then he moves up to my lips. By this time, his face is close to mine. He pulls the flower away from my lips and gently grazes his lips against mine but does not kiss me.

Holy shit, I am so turned on right now.

He quickly pulls away and the ritual is abruptly over.

What just happened? Does he not want to kiss me? Did I do something wrong?

The night comes to a close with a magical hug, but I am confused about what just happened.

Chapter 28

J am burned out from work. I haven't been proactively taking days off because of COVID travel restrictions canceling my vacation plans. It's the beginning of July, and I have only taken two days off work this entire year. I think it's a good idea for my sanity to take three days off later this month so that I can have a five-day weekend. During conversations with Ozzy, we plan things to do together on those days, so now I am especially looking forward to the time off.

A few days before the five-day weekend, Ozzy and I go to the beach after I get off work. Things are more sexually charged since the almost-kiss over the weekend, and on the one hand, I am curious where this is going to go, but on the other hand, I don't care because all I know is that I love hanging out with Ozzy and I can't wait for this five-day excursion with him. It is getting hot in the sand, so we go into the ocean to cool off. When we get in the water, Ozzy commands, "Turn around."

This is what he said to me after I went to the salon to run his fingers through my hair, but my hair is pulled up. I don't know why he wants me to turn around. I trust him completely and oblige. I feel his hands around my waist. Then, they move to my butt. He gently cups my butt and then quickly pulls away. My ass is my arousal station, and he totally activated all systems. I pull in closer to him, but he moves away.

Okay, I get it. He's not interested.

But now I'm irritated because he did the almost-kiss, and now he grabbed my ass and left me hanging. It's not okay to tease me.

We get back to the beach, and I assume the reason is because of his wife. He doesn't talk about her much, but from what I know, they are still separated, and when she gets back, which is who knows when, they are going to be living together for a few months until she finds a place of her own. Because Ozzy and I are so close now, we probably won't be able to hang out while he is living with her. This thought is devastating to me.

"Listen, I love hanging out with you, but it's probably not a good idea for us to hang out outside of lessons anymore because when Sarah comes back, we won't be able to hang out at all, and that's is going to hurt really bad. It's probably best if we draw a boundary now, so it's not so painful later." This hurts tremendously to say right before our five-day weekend, but I know it's going to be more painful later if we don't pull back now. I should have said this sooner. My heart sinks.

Ozzy considers what I say and takes a moment before responding. "The decision has been made that we are splitting up. When she comes back, we are dividing everything up, moving out, and moving on. I am going to tell her where I am going and who I am going with when you and I hang out. There is no reason for us to stop hanging out. You are my best friend. We are not going to stop hanging out, especially not right before our big weekend."

I don't know anything else other than to trust him. I am so relieved to hear that we don't have to stop hanging out. When we leave the beach, Ozzy puts his arm around my waist as we walk to the car. I can't wait for our long weekend together.

On the first day of our extended weekend excursion, we eat breakfast at a place other than Sweet E's. Every time we try to go to a different place, it's never as good as Sweet E's. But Ozzy always shares his pancake, which shows a thoughtfulness that I love. Then we go to Sandy Beach. The waves are big and strong, so I don't even like to put my feet in the water for fear of getting swept out to sea. Being a born and raised Hawaiian, Ozzy is not afraid of the ocean We don't have boogie boards, so he goes swimming. Ozzy stands up to go into the ocean. "Do you want to go?"

"Oh my God, no!"

I watch Ozzy in the water. It's amazing how he swims with ease, just how he looks when he is surfing. I hope one day to be as comfortable in the water as he is. We grab dinner, and then as Ozzy drops me off, we do the thing we always do where he pulls up the car and turns it off so we can talk. We plan our North Shore excursion tomorrow. We get out of the car, and Ozzy embraces me in a big bear hug. His face lingers right in front of mine as we pull away, our lips almost touching. Then, it happens. He kisses me. It's soft at first, but then we slide our tongues in each other's mouths. It's as amazing as I imagined. The only problem is that we are standing on the sidewalk outside of his car and people are milling around. I would love more privacy. "Do you want to come upstairs?"

Ozzy has never been to my home before. This is the first time we have kissed. Hell, we just started hugging a few weeks ago. I am afraid he is going to say no.

"Yes."

We go upstairs and continue making out, which leads to getting naked, which leads to…nothing. Not because neither of us doesn't want to. He can't.

"I'm so sorry. You're so fucking hot."

I don't know if it's because of his age, or if it's me, or what, but as always, I love being with Ozzy, so I don't mind. I can tell he is embarrassed though. "I don't care. I just want you to be comfortable."

"I'm not like you. I've passed my sexual peak."

I've passed my sexual peak too. That's why this doesn't bother me. I just want to enjoy Ozzy. I don't say any of this because he continues talking. "If I can't please you in bed, then there is no us."

"I don't care about it as much as you think I do."

He seems irritated, and I assume it's frustration from not being able to perform. I don't know what he means by "us" because even though he is separated, he is still married. I don't even know where this is going. I simply want to enjoy his presence right now.

WE drive to the North Shore in my red convertible with the top down. This part of the island is less developed, with expansive fields instead of the urban Honolulu homes and businesses filling up the land. It's much less tropical, but still has a rural island feel. My favorite part of the drive to North Shore is driving past the pineapple fields of the Dole Plantation.

Our first stop is Waimea Bay to jump off the rock. The Waimea Bay rock is an approximately twenty-five-foot tall rock along the shore. Ozzy brought his GoPro to film me jumping. I am scared, so he agrees to jump off with me, which means I have to jump twice— a warm-up jump with Ozzy and a jump with the GoPro. I thought that because I jumped off a cliff almost twice as high and went bungee jumping in New Zealand, I would be over this fear of heights and free falling by now. Unfortunately, I am just as scared as I was on that trip. The difference is that, now, I have my metaphorical rock, Ozzy, as a safety net to do it with me. As we climb up the rock, I am fine. It's not as tall as the one I jumped in New Zealand. Plus, the water is not freezing here. We get to the top and look over the edge. My heart is now in my stomach. Ozzy does not seem afraid at all. He looks over at me. "Tell me when you are ready."

"I'm never going to be ready."

"On three. One…two…three!"

We jump at the same time. I scream as free-falling consumes my body and drives my heart deeper into my stomach. Then, I hit the water. It's warm and refreshing.

That was fun!

I pop up to the surface and Ozzy has already emerged. We laugh.

"Ready to do it again?"

I nod my head.

"Let's go get the GoPro."

We retrieve the GoPro out of my bag on the beach. Now, I have to climb the rock while Ozzy positions himself in the water.

I just did this. Why am I so nervous?

I get to the top, and Ozzy is ready to go. "When you're ready!"

Again, I'm never going to be ready, and I don't have anyone to do a countdown.

What the hell. I'm doing this!

I jump. I scream as free-falling consumes my body and drives my heart deeper into my stomach. Then, I hit the water. It's warm and refreshing. Ozzy swims up to me and tries to untie my bathing suit bottoms. This is a welcome pleasurable moment after two terrifying jumps. We make our way out of the water, grab our bags, and go further down the beach to relax. After chatting on the sand for a little bit, we need to cool off in the water. We get in the water and my legs automatically wrap around Ozzy's waist. He embraces me and we make out in the water. He gets hard.

Oh good, maybe today is the day we have sex.

As we walk back to my car, Ozzy embraces me and we make out. He pulls away to ask, "Are you ready to go home?"

I don't know what this means, but I hope it means sex. "Yes."

I drive back to my house with the top down. On the way, Ozzy writes a message with his finger on my leg.

`I want you so bad.`

We get back to my place and sex is clearly happening. Usually, my first time with any partner is not that great and sometimes awkward, but it gets better in time, most of the time, much better. But the first time with Ozzy was good. This is exciting to me because this means that it will get much better sooner!

ECAUSE the last two days we were on the go, today we surfed in the morning and are now relaxing on a local beach. My favorite part about going to the beach with Ozzy is that it is always an adventure. Sometimes we play games in the water, sometimes we play word games in my journal notebook, sometimes we joke around, and sometimes we have intellectual conversations. Today, while playing hangman in my notebook, my co-worker Devin texts me.

`You have probably already heard by now that I got fired.`

What?!?

I haven't heard anything. I have been completely unplugged from work, enjoying the time with Ozzy. I call Devin. He had a one-on-one with our manager and was let go. He didn't seem clear on why, other than his position is no longer necessary, which makes me super nervous because I have a one-on-one with our manager Monday when I get back. I am one of the few members remaining from the old management regime after the new CEO cleaned house. After my former manager left in December, I thought for sure I would be next, but I still have a job. Maybe.

Shit, it's only Friday. I was supposed to have five relaxing days off from work, but now I am worried that I am getting fired!

I express my concerns to Ozzy, and his laid-back voice of reason calms me down. "There is no use in worrying until Monday."

We go back to my place and make love. Afterward, I start worrying about getting fired. I start crying. "I've been through so much the past few years, and I'm tired of going through the struggles of life on my own."

Ozzy is lying on top of me and wipes my tears, which melts my heart. "You don't have to go through anything on your own. You can talk to me. I'm here for you."

My heart is overflowing with love. I have never trusted anybody so much in my entire life.

THE next few weeks are amazing. I didn't get fired, and Ozzy and I surf and have sex a lot. Before or after sex we shower together and have more sex in the shower. Between the sex, and washing each other's hair and bodies, we take extremely long showers, but it's intimate and fun. I get the impression he is starved for affection, and I love giving it to him. I also enjoy doing sexy dances in and out of the shower for Ozzy. He loves it. We also give each other massages, and I enjoy giving him manicures and pedicures. At first, I thought he would think it was cheesy, but his eyes always light up when I offer, and he finally admits that he loves being pampered.

I also cook for us. I am not the best, but luckily Ozzy enjoys my cooking. One night, I make chicken burgers. As we are eating, Ozzy spills ketchup on the beige cloth seat of my barstool. His face is horrified because he knows I like things tidy. Normally I would freak out, and his reaction would be warranted, but I am calm because I have some top-tier stain remover that I know will take care of the ketchup. I'm also calm because Ozzy brings out patience in me that I didn't even know I had. He dutifully cleans up the ketchup, thinking I am mad at him, but I tell him I am not mad, and we have a good laugh.

I have been doing his laundry since he doesn't have a washer and dryer in his unit, and I do. I notice one of his pairs of board shorts has a hole, and I sew it for him. I normally wouldn't invest this much effort into someone I am not in a relationship with, but with Ozzy, everything feels so natural and I have never felt this unselfish before. I don't know where this is going, but I enjoy it.

Chapter 29

*J*T's Sunday morning, and Ozzy and I are surfing as we usually do. Our pre-surf ritual for Sunday morning is to put on our wetsuits, and then I spray Ozzy's hair with Moroccan oil. Because he picks me up, we usually don't hug until we get out of the car so that we can have an intimate hug. Today, we get out of the car, and he goes straight to the back of the car to get our surf supplies.

He forgot the hug.

I assume he is distracted, so I proactively go in for the hug. He pushes me away. My heart shatters. One thing about me is that my face always reveals what I am thinking, and Ozzy has done a great job of learning to interpret my facial expressions. He can tell I am hurt, so he tries to play it off like he is joking. But he wasn't joking. He pushed me away.

What the hell is going on?

As we walk to the water, I deliberate within my head if I should say that my feelings are hurt. I mean, he did tell me after he walked away when I fell on the beach that I should be open with him when my feelings are hurt. The broken heart hand signal has worked great in other situations. But he seems so distant and cold right now. I have a bad feeling that if I bring it up, he will get mad. We get in the water and the vibe is different from any other time we have gone surfing. Usually, we laugh and have fun the entire time. This time, as we paddle out, we are silent.

Fine, if this is how it's going to be, then I will say something.

Ozzy beats me to it. "Is something wrong? Why aren't you talking?"

"It hurt my feelings when you pulled away from the hug."

Ozzy contorts his face and loudly expresses a grunt of disgust. "Are you kidding me? That wasn't a big deal. Why are you mad about that?"

Where in the hell is the Ozzy who cares about hurting my feelings?

I am speechless. I don't know how to respond, and I want to start surfing, but all I want to do is cry, so I'm having a hard time. I haven't been standing upon any waves, which is child's play at this point in my surfing journey. I advanced past standing up months ago. I have fallen every single wave. I fall again. All I wanted was a hug.

I'm done.

I start paddling to shore. I don't even care about telling Ozzy where I'm going or why. I don't want to be around him right now. I have no idea what the hell is going on with him, but it is not okay for him to treat me this way. I get to shore and turn around. Ozzy is paddling to a different spot on the shoreline. I don't know where he is going or where we go from here, but I don't care. I pull my board into the sand and then lay on my back in the sand and rest my head on the board. I am exhausted. Between work and Ozzy and I hanging out non-stop, I haven't been getting enough sleep. I rest my eyes and am so tired that I could fall asleep, especially with the white noise of the waves crashing on the shore and the wind blowing through the palm trees.

Maybe I am overreacting. I have been tired lately. Maybe he was joking. It was just a hug. Am I making too big of a deal?

When I wonder how long I should lay here before looking for Ozzy, I hear a familiar voice speak up behind me. It's just as distant and cold as when we were paddling out. "Come on, let's go."

Oh great, he's pissed now. But wait a minute, why the hell is he pissed? I just wanted a hug.

I am covered in sand, so I get in the ocean to rinse off. While I am in the water, Ozzy collects my surfboard and leash. Since he has the equipment covered, once I get out of the water, I start walking to his car. Because I walk faster than him, I purposely walk far ahead. We get back to the car and, usually, we take warm water jug showers, but I just want to go home by myself and take a real shower. And now I'm even more pissed because I'm hungry, and we usually go to Sweet E's for breakfast on Sunday, so now I have to go home and eat something boring there. Ozzy gets out a jug, and I assume it's for his shower, so I start packing up the car to leave.

"Don't you want a shower?" he asks.

I am freezing, so, yes, a hot water jug shower sounds amazing.
"Sure."

I reach out to take the jug from him, but he pulls me close to him and pours the water on me. To finish off the container, he pulls away my bathing suit bottoms from my butt and pours the warm water down my bare butt. It's kind of sexy. Then, he teases me. "You want a hug? I'll give you a hug." He gives me a huge bear hug and says music to my ears. "Come on, let's go to Sweet E's."

Okay, our first fight was about a hug and wasn't that bad. I assume he is in a bad mood today and brush it off.

"Chim chim cher-oo!"

O ZZY and I are surfing, and we run into his friend Ian's girl-friend, Hannah, who ignores me and speaks directly to Ozzy. "You didn't respond to my text. Are you coming out to eat with us tonight?"

Ozzy and I always go out to eat together after we surf. Because Ozzy is not divorced yet, we are keeping our lover status a secret. I understand why I wasn't invited, but I am confused about why he didn't tell me he was going out to eat with them.

"No, sorry, I can't tonight."

I don't want him to feel obligated to eat with me if he wants to go with them. Hannah paddles away, and I turn to him. "I don't mind if you go out to eat with them. We can go out to eat tomorrow."

"Oh, now that hurts *my* feelings. Are you saying you don't want to hang out with me?"

Is he for real?

"No, I do want to hang out with you, but I don't want you to feel obligated to hang out with me if you would rather go out to eat with them. I was trying to give you the freedom to do what you want. Never mind…"

Ozzy relaxes. "I see what you are saying. I would rather hang out with you."

I think things are fine, but after that, every little thing I say, Ozzy gets combative. I feel like I have to put up my dukes with every single subject change. I am not having fun surfing anymore.

Who is this man? Did I do something wrong?

But then there are other things that I start to notice that my fun, loving, protective, emergency/safety contact Oz Tart would never do. He continues to be combative in conversations. He starts rolling his eyes at me, even though I tell him I feel disrespected. The worst part is that he has been violating our smoking boundary. He doesn't smoke in front of me, but he will sneak off to smoke as if I don't know what he is doing. I don't know what is worse, the fact that he is insulting my intelligence because he thinks I don't know what he is doing, or that I am not enforcing the boundary because I want to enjoy the small scraps of joy that we still have.

After a few weeks of this, I'm sick of it. I miss loving, protective Ozzy. I'm tired from not getting enough sleep, and I don't have the emotional or physical energy to put up with this new version of him. I wake up Sunday morning, and where I was once looking forward to lessons, especially Sunday morning lessons when we go to Sweet E's afterward, I am dreading a lesson today. I don't even want to talk to Ozzy. I send him a text.

> Hi Ozzy, I am going to take today off. I don't feel like having a lesson with you today.

A few minutes after sending the text, I walk out the door to go for a long walk. I don't know where I am going, but I need to burn off some energy. I don't bring my phone because I want to totally unplug. I walk about three miles, crying most of the time. I walk around my usual running route that partly circles a local canal waterway, and the other half wraps around a golf course. I find the water section peaceful, except I am wearing slippers and have tripped a few times on the raggedy asphalt. The struggle of walking at a Chicagoan pace in slippers matches how I feel about life right now.

What the hell happened? Did I do something? Did I say something?

I get home, and I have two texts, two missed calls, and a voice-mail, all from Ozzy. I check the texts first.

> Are you okay? Is something wrong?

> I just tried calling you. I am go-
> ing to go surfing in the country.
> I'll call you later.

The first missed call is from shortly after I left for my walk and the second call and voicemail are from about ten minutes ago. I listen to the voicemail.

"Hellloo Angie. I'm leaving a message. I'm gonna see if you're going to call me back. Anyway, I hate you being mad at me. Um, sorry, sweetie. Um, I'll try to talk to you later. Okay. Have a nice day. Bye."

I feel bad for avoiding him, so I call him. He's driving. I take a deep breath. "I didn't want to go surfing because the dynamics between us are different now. I feel like you are combative with everything I say, and it hurts my feelings when you roll your eyes at me." I hold my breath. Any other time I have spoken my truth, it has been met with anger and defensiveness.

"Sweetie, I'm sorry. It's just that I have a lot of things to figure out, like my business and where I will live in the future, so it's been stressing me out."

I release my breath. Finally, we are having a mature adult conversation. I don't understand why we haven't talked about this before. We hang out every day and talk about a lot of things, and he never brought up how stressed he is. We end on a loving note, and I have hope again for our friendship, even though I am still not sure where this is headed with so much uncertainty around the timing of when he is going to wrap things up with his marriage. Part of me wants to set another boundary about not hanging out so much, but Ozzy is so special to me, and there would be a huge void in my heart from not seeing him every day. I've been doing weekly workouts with a small group of friends and hanging out with Kelly more, but I would still miss daily laughs with Ozzy.

The next time we go surfing, he drops me off but doesn't come upstairs. My heart sinks. We sit in his car talking like we did back in the day before we were hugging, kissing, and lovemaking. It feels different this time because the dynamics are so different. I feel so disconnected from Ozzy now.

"There is something in this car that makes me think of you. Do you know what it is?" Ozzy asks.

"Me?"

He laughs. "It makes me think of you when you're *not* here."

I look around his car. "I don't know."

He picks up a dried hibiscus flower off his dashboard. It's the black magic flower.

I have prescription Clonazepam that I take for anxiety attacks when I can't calm down on my own. My doctor in Chicago prescribed me twelve pills a year. It's a nervous system suppressant and too strong for me, so I usually only take a half pill, which means twelve pills are twenty-four pills and that lasts me at least a year. When I asked my doctor in Hawaii for a refill, he gave me thirty. The problem is because I have more now, I feel like I have been more reliant on them, especially with the uncertainty and restrictions of COVID. And now, with Ozzy's changed demeanor, I have been taking a half pill almost every night. It helps me sleep through the anxiety, but I have been feeling groggy during the day. I haven't been able to mange the anxiety without the pills. I need to take back control of my life. I text Ozzy before I go to bed.

> Hey Ozzy, I'm about to lose it with life in general, and I was think-ing last night that, even though there are things out of my control right now, there are some things

for which I do have control over and need to step up and take accountability.

I need to take a few weeks off from surfing lessons. I'm not good at surfing, and I'm not catching on, therefore not enjoying it, and it's adding to my frustrations. I'm at the point where I don't even think surfing is for me, but I'm also too overwhelmed with my feelings right now to be able to make that decision. I'm open to re-grouping in a few weeks to see if I am ready again.

Also, I was thinking about what you said last week about needing time to sort things out for yourself. I completely respect and understand that, and I am here to support you as a friend, but I can't be friends with benefits anymore. One of the things I am working on is being authentic, and I'm disrespecting myself by giving myself to someone who is not a "fuck yes!" about me. And I'm not just talking about sex. I can't do your nails or give you massages or cook or do laundry anymore. I feel ashamed and embarrassed that I have been pouring into you without acknowledging your feelings for me, or lack thereof. I am a passionate person. Casual doesn't work for me.

That being said, I care about you so much, and I'm okay with hanging out with you, but I need a few weeks off from that too. My feelings for you go far beyond friendship, and I need a cooling-off period before I am ready to hang out again. Also, because I am not catching on to surfing, it adds to your frustrations with me and I am already sick to my stomach about how your demeanor toward me has changed from totally loving to disconnected, so I think the time off is beneficial to both of us.

The reason I texted is because I express myself best through writing, but I am open to talking this afternoon if you want. I totally understand and respect your decision if you don't want to.

I hold my breath as I hit send. That was a long-ass text. Anytime I have spoken my truth this deep, it has been met with negativity. I am positive that he hates me now, especially since he doesn't respond right away like he normally does. He responds the next morning.

Good Morning Angie!!!

I have read what you said, and I'm not like you. It will be a while before I can articulate what I feel and put it on paper, but I want you to know that you are more than just a friend to me, and you are a big part of my life.

I don't like that you are hurting right now, and it is because of me. I really appreciate all the things you do for me, and you do make me feel very special. I feel bad that you are embarrassed by pouring out your feelings for me. I want you to know that I will be super bummed that you won't be in my life. I understand the way you feel, and I don't want you to change who you are. I love you just the way you are. It's not you. I think you are an awesome person. I am scared of falling in love right now, and if you haven't noticed, that's what is happening. As far as surfing goes, I'm sorry you are not having fun. I understand if you don't want to see me anymore.

Please know that if you ever need someone to talk to or have a meal with or ride the rails with or go boogie boarding with or go out for a paddle or rodeo with the flamingo, please call me. I will be waiting for your call. I will always be your friend, emergency contact, and hopefully, one day, your soulmate. I do have so much love for you. Hopefully, I can get it together. Even with all of your beautiful quirks, I would love to give us a true chance at making it one day. Love you xoxo
Missing you already ♥

He has never told me he loves me before. This is heartwarming yet confusing at the same time.

Why did he tell me over text? Why did he not say this to my face? Do I tell him that I love him now?

I mean, I do, with all my heart, but I don't want to do it over text. This is all so weird and confusing. Nobody has ever accepted me this unconditionally before. I have no idea what the hell is going on or what to do about it except continue taking my Clonazepam every day to manage the intense anxiety this situation is bringing up.

KELLY is on the mainland. I miss her and want to tell her what has been going on with Ozzy. She knows that Ozzy and I are best friends and that he is married, but she doesn't know we crossed the line of friendship. I text her that I want to talk to her because I had a falling out with Ozzy. Naturally, she is shocked, so we plan a phone call. I tell her everything. She reminds me of famous wise words. "Hurt people hurt people."

Kelly offers to let me borrow one of her boards when she gets back so that I don't have to be reliant on Ozzy for surfing. I like the sound of that, and even more, I like having Kelly as a friend.

OZZY sends me a sweet text that he misses me. I miss him too. Maybe we can just do the surfing lessons and keep it as a teacher/student relationship. Except for the times that he has been mean to me, I am able to compartmentalize my feelings in the water because I am focused on surfing. I text him to see what he thinks. He suggests a Sunday morning lesson, but because he thought we weren't doing a lesson or going to Sweet E's, he scheduled another lesson. He offers to do my lesson, and I can bring my flamingo floaty and float in the lagoon while he does his other lesson. Then, we can go to Sweet E's.

When Sunday rolls around, I am excited about our lesson. It starts well, but then Ozzy keeps getting irritated with me because

I don't turn my board around fast enough when a wave comes. Therefore, I am missing out on paddling for waves. After a while, I ask him if we can work on turning, but each time a wave comes, he grabs the nose of my board and turns me around himself. This isn't helping me, but I can tell he is getting frustrated with me, so I do not speak up. I start catching waves with his help turning around, but I feel like I am not doing anything right because he keeps criticizing me.

"Bend your knees!"

"Why aren't you bending your knees?"

"Why aren't you doing anything you've learned?

After the lesson, as I am relaxing in my flamingo in the lagoon, I realize I don't want to continue the vibe of the lesson at Sweet E's. I love him so much, but this is so awkward. He hasn't even told me he loves me to my face, and I am too afraid to tell him that I love him because he has been so damn mean to me lately. If I go to Sweet E's with Ozzy, I'm afraid I will start crying or get an attitude when he starts in with his un-loving demeanor. I want to get back to his car before his lesson is over, so I get out of the water and head to his car as quickly as possible. I have his car key, but I know he hides an extra one under the car, so he still has a way in if I lock this key inside of the car. As I walk back, I draft a text. Then, I remember a journal page I had written at the beach one day about all of the things that I appreciate about him. It's only one page, but I could have gone on for several more. When I get to his car, I put the key and journal page in the middle console and lock up the car. As I walk away, I find a ten-dollar bill in the street. Dad usually leaves me coins, but not paper. I am so thankful that Dad is looking over me, big time this time. When I get out of sight of the parking garage, I hit send on the text.

Hey Ozzy! I changed my mind about Sweet E's. The key is in your middle console. Also, I found a page in my notebook from one day I was journaling about all of the things I appreciate about you. You don't

have to respond or reciprocate.
Just thought you might like to have
it. Journal page is also in the
middle console.
I'm sorry I ditched you for breakfast. Sometimes I get flooded with
feelings, and it's overwhelming,
and I need time to myself to re-
set. I was frustrated with surfing because I don't feel like I am
catching on. Also, I can tell when
you get impatient with me for being
a slow learner. I really am trying
to paddle hard, bend my knees and
turn faster, I don't know why I'm
not getting it.
And overall, I am still really hurt
by how you started something with me
that you couldn't finish. I am still
struggling with my emotions around
that and some days are better than
others. It digs the knife deeper
that your demeanor has changed from
loving to disconnected. I thought
it was better to spend time apart
instead of me getting more triggered at breakfast. I miss Sunday
breakfast with you.

I am scared that he is going to be mad at me. I am scared that he is not going to respond. By the time I get home, he responds.

Hi Angie
I'm sorry if you think I was getting short with you. I'm sorry
that I can't give you all of me
right now. Sometimes I know I get
a little frustrated, but I, too,

am struggling with our relationship. There is a huge part of me
when I see you just want to grab
you and kiss you all over. And
when I have to leave, I want to
go upstairs so bad and make out
and shower and all the beautiful
little things you do for me. I'm
sorry. But please know that it is
definitely not you. I think you
are so kind and so thoughtful,
and that's why I haven't read your
journal page. I know it's just going to make me feel crappy. But I
will read it. Thanks for all you
do for me!!!

I get what he is saying, but this is hurting me. It hurts that we can't be lovers, it hurts that we can't be friends, and it really hurts that we can't even figure out a way to do lessons without him getting frustrated with me. I can't do this anymore. I'm sick of taking my Clonazepam every single day. I keep going back and forth with him, but if he can't give me what I deserve, I need to move on for my emotional well-being. I send him another text, and it breaks my heart so much, but I don't know what else to do.

Hey Ozzy, I totally understand and
appreciate that you have things you
need to figure out but being around
you hurts me really bad, and I can't
handle it. I need time to heal. I
am going to do my own thing and take
lessons from someone else. I really
appreciate all that you have taught
me and done for me. When you figure things out and if it involves
a loving friendship like we used
to have, let me know, otherwise, I

> wish you the best, and you will
> always have a special place in my
> heart ♥

He probably hates me. I have been so back and forth, but in all fairness, I've been on a roller coaster of emotions. I feel like he doesn't even care. Right now, I feel confident in my decision. Even though I would like him to respond, I am okay if he doesn't. I want him to be happy and feel comfortable. He responds about an hour later.

> I am so bummed right now, but I understand completely. I want you to know I feel like I lost the best thing that has happened to me. I am truly sorry for everything. I want you to know the pain you feel goes both ways. You have been my best friend for what seems like forever and not having you in my life to laugh with, talk about all kinds of stuff from silly to enlightened conversations and somebody to just hang out with and eat with is really going to hurt, but I see the pain in your eyes when you look at me and I feel so bad that I'm the one that caused it. The thing that keeps me going right now is that we might have a shot at true happiness later, although I'm super scared that you might find someone else. I hope you don't, at least right now. But if you do, I truly wish the best for you. You have been so awesome, and I will always cherish and appreciate the times we spent together. If you need

anything, anything at all, if I
can help, please know all you have
to do is ask. I am proud to call
you one of my best friends, and
I will always be your emergency
contact. Writing this is bringing
tears to my eyes. I have so much
love and respect for you. I hope
this is not the end of us. I love
you Angie!!!! ♥

This is still confusing to me.

What is he not telling me?

For the next week, Ozzy initiates a loving text to me every day. Going even one day without him is so hard. I thought I would feel better if we weren't talking, but I am still taking my Clonazepam every night to manage my separation anxiety. He enhanced my life so much. Everything seems so boring and uneventful now, especially with the ongoing COVID restrictions. His one text a day keeps the love in my heart going.

Chapter 30

HELLO Angie!!! I don't know where to start, so I might be all over the place with this. I want you to know that I never ever intended to hurt you, but I am sorry that right now, I cannot give you what you deserve, someone that is going to give you 100%. I should not have started something until I took care of all my other stuff going on. I should have known better. I'm sorry, believe me, but it is hard being with you because I am in love with you, so I have a hard time not holding you and kissing you. The things I love about you:

You make me laugh.

You make me feel special.

You are such a bright, beautiful person, and you make me feel good about myself until recently.

You think about me, patches for my shorts, oil for my hair, lollipops, all the little things you do for me. I love our talks. You teach me so much.

You take care of me. It shows in all the little things that you appreciate when I help you.

The things I don't like about me: That I have hurt you because I was selfish and didn't have the courage to let you go thinking I would lose any chance of being with you and by doing that I might have lost you forever.

By rushing things, I don't have my best friend to talk to.

Angie, I am truly sorry. I want you to know that I will always be your friend, and you have made me smile again. I used to look forward to seeing you. I thought about it and got mad at myself for letting my best friend down. I can't say I'm sorry enough. Please don't feel like you are the only one hurting here. You have been my sunshine for a while now.

I hope you don't hate me, Angie. I'm going to take a little time and figure some things out. I miss you so much already. Fuck, this hurts. I hope, in time, we can go surfing and ripping the rails. Thank you for being my best friend. If you ever need anything or if you need someone to talk to, please give me a call. You are so special, and hopefully, one day, we can be special together. Sorry

Fuuuuuuck.

I was not expecting that. Now we aren't even going to text. My heart feels like lead.

Why does it have to be so complicated?

This further increases the need to medicate myself to sleep. I am a crying, anxious mess. I have no idea how much time he needs to figure things out or when I am going to hear from him again. From what I know about Ozzy, he isn't the greatest planner, so it could take a while. I mentally prepare myself to move on and not think about it.

KELLY is back from the mainland but in the mandatory fourteen-day, self-isolated quarantine, so we are catching up on a Zoom call. As we are chatting, she mentions Ivy, who she met through Ozzy when he gave Kelly a lesson over the summer. Ivy is friends with Ozzy and Sarah. Kelly has become friends with Ivy. Therefore, Kelly knows something that I don't. "I was surprised to see on Instagram that Sarah is back."

I can feel my heart thudding in my chest. "What?"

"You didn't know?"

"No, Ozzy didn't tell me."

I feel betrayed. I feel heartbroken. I feel angry. I take an entire Clonazepam to go to sleep. This is why Ozzy can't text me anymore.

But why didn't he tell me the truth?

Is he getting back together with her?

The next morning, Ozzy sends me a text.

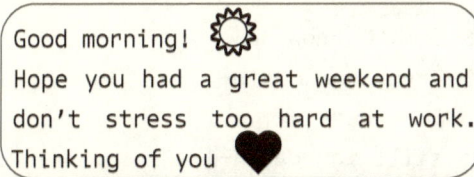

I can't believe he is pretending as if everything is okay, especially since I thought we weren't texting anymore and he still hasn't told me that Sarah is back. Where is my best friend Ozzy, who hates to hurt me? I am so confused, and my survival instinct is to put up the armor around my heart and push him away. I opened my heart to him, and he's been completely careless with it.

> Hey Oz Tart, thank you for the sweet message. I talked to Kelly yesterday, and she told me that Sarah is back. I understand why you wouldn't want to tell me, but I was extremely hurt and disappointed to hear it from someone other than you. I was hurting before, and now, on top of that, I feel numb and broken. I love you so much, but for my emotional safety, I would appreciate it if you left me alone until you get your stuff figured out. I respect whatever you decide, and if you decide your future does not involve me, you will always have a special place in my heart. And if we never talk again, I just want you to know that I appreciate you so much, and I am especially thankful for how you always accepted me for who I am, even if I wasn't the most pleasant to deal with and bringing so much joy into my life. Sending lots of love to you right now ♥

> I'm sorry Angie didn't know how to tell you I'm renting a studio in Waikiki. Been here for 3 days now. She is still in quarantine. I couldn't help myself and not say hello to you. I also have

so much love and respect for you and I have been lonely 🥺 and thinking of you a lot 🖤 I want you to know that I don't think you should change a damn thing about you. I fell in love with you just the way you are. I will not reach out to you till I figure out what the future looks like for me but I want you to remember that I am always thinking of you and if you ever need help with anything please just ask. Miss you. Sending so much love your way. Please be safe. Thank you for bringing so much joy into my life 🖤 🖤 🖤

*J*T's been three days, and I have not heard from Ozzy. My anxiety is sky-high. Sometimes, I have been taking a whole anxiety pill at night. I feel so groggy when I wake up, though. I don't know if it's the pills or stress, or both, but I haven't been able to think clearly lately. As much as it hurts to not be talking to Ozzy, I assume that he has probably gotten back together with Sarah. The thought of this hurts me tremendously, but I want him to be happy. My phone vibrates with a text notification.

Good morning Angie!! Sorry it's taken me this long to respond. I've got a lot of things going on right now and haven't been in a good head space. You are never far from my thoughts. I've made a lot of progress and have settled a lot of issues with me going forward in life. At least

I have somewhat of a plan. I hope
you are doing better. I miss you a
lot and hope you have a great day.
I'm thinking that maybe we can go
surfing on Sunday and maybe we can
have a talk about things. I understand if you don't want to. Please
think about it. ♥ ♥

All I can think of is that he wants to tell me that he wants to give it another shot with Sarah. For a minute, this doesn't sit well, but deep in my heart, I want him to be happy, and I am willing to accept whatever he tells me. Or so I think. I text him back that Sunday surfing and talking is fine for me. Hopefully, we surf first so that after the bad news, I can go straight home and cry and don't have to miss out on surfing one last time with him.

I have been waiting all week for this weekend, but now that it's Saturday, I am filled with dread about talking to Ozzy tomorrow. The good news is Kelly is finally out of her fourteen-day quarantine at 1 p.m.! I am at the beach, and she has plans this afternoon, but we have agreed to meet at her place at 1 p.m. when I am on my way home, and she is out the door. As I leave the beach, the excitement about seeing Kelly in person distracts me from Ozzy.

Kelly and I chat for about twenty minutes. It's so refreshing to have her back. I tell her that Ozzy seems to have something specific that he wants to tell me. She seems just as unsure about it as I am. Whenever I leave Kelly's, I usually Biki home because there is a station right next to her building. My intuition nudges me to walk home instead. Her building is on the same side of the street that I need to walk on to get home. But the crosswalk light is red in my direction, so I cross to the other side of the street. Instead of Biki-ing on the same side of the street as I normally would, I am walking on the opposite side of the street. A few blocks away from Kelly's, I hear a car honking its horn behind me. I am wearing skimpy Brazilian bathing suit bottoms, so I assume it's a pervert honking and ignore it. Then, the car pulls up next to me, and I hear a voice I would recognize anywhere. "You need a ride?"

I'm mad at Ozzy for not telling me that Sarah is back, but I can't wait until tomorrow to see him. Instead of surfboards on the surf rack on the roof, they are in the car, which means I have to sit in the backseat, behind him, like an Uber ride. Also like an Uber ride, we make small talk until he pulls up to my building. Then, he asks the question that I am dreading. "Do you want to talk now or tomorrow?"

I am hungry, but I wouldn't miss this conversation for anything. "Now."

He begins speaking. Before this conversation, I had never heard him say anything positive about Sarah, but I had never heard him directly badmouth her— until now. He explains that their marriage is very loveless, and they haven't had sex in over a year and a half. He reiterates that she wants to have kids, but not with him because of his age. They have been growing apart in other ways too. He continues to paint her as a nagging, disrespectful adolescent, who is codependent with her evil, man-hating mother. He is so distraught over her immaturity that he exclaims, "I am never getting into a relationship with a younger woman again! You're forty, so that includes you."

My heart drops to my stomach and I feel my entire body tighten up. Thankfully, we are having this discussion Uber-style. Otherwise, I would have exited the car at this point— running away out of fear, like I always do. He goes on to tell me that Sarah didn't seem to understand that they would be living separately once she returned home, which I find extremely confusing because he explained that to me crystal clearly five months ago. After he picked her up from the airport, he told her that she needed to find a place to live. She had a complete emotional breakdown because, apparently, at thirty-one years old, she seems to have never lived on her own, or at least doesn't seem to have enough of a handle on life to live on her own. The first thing she did was call her mom in a tizzy and, to help her out, her mom gave her two hundred and fifty thousand dollars to "get on her feet."

Ozzy continues. "I have a plan for the future. She has a green card, and we need to be married on paper for two more years so that she can get her citizenship. I am going to stay at the house for two more months to help get her on her feet. During that time, you and I will be friends. In two months, I am going to move out and she and I are going to live separate lives. After I move out, you and I can be in a relationship. We can finally hold hands in public and be open about our relationship. After she gets her citizenship, she and I will file for divorce."

He stops talking. He has been talking for almost an hour, verbally dumping a lot of shit I don't want to hear. It is a lot to process, especially considering the shocking nature of most of it. I don't even feel connected to my body. My head is spinning and my heart is racing. Every inch of me wants to escape the car, but I reel myself in and force myself to face this difficult conversation. I can tell he is waiting for me to say something, but I am speechless. I am confused, angry, and everything in between. I suddenly become aware that my fingernails are digging into my thighs, and my jaw is clenched so tight that it is sore. Ozzy speaks first, looking directly at me through the rearview mirror. "You look like you are about to punch me in the face."

My Chicago attitude uncontrollably bursts out from behind the curtain, guns blazing. "That's because I am! I don't even want to be friends with you right now! What you just told me is a bunch of bullshit and drama! I don't do drama, even as friends!"

He is silent. I can tell he is surprised by my reaction, and in all fairness, I am coming at him hard right now. He is brave enough to interact with Chicago Angie. "I don't understand why you are so mad."

"What part of ANY of this did you think I would be happy about?!"

"I know it's not all hunky-dory, but I didn't think you would be this upset."

"Also, I am totally confused. You just told me twenty minutes ago that you don't want to be in a relationship with a younger woman and you specifically said that includes me."

"You were supposed to interrupt me and try to change my mind."

This triggers the shit out of me because Marc would always try to manipulate me with statements, expecting me to respond a certain way. When I didn't respond according to his expectations, he would blame me for taking his manipulative statements at face value instead of interpreting them how he wanted me to. I'm not a fucking mind reader. Not then. Not now. "It broke my heart when you said that!"

He is getting frustrated that I am not happy. And as I process more of what he told me, I become even more pissed off. He is offering me a side chick position. I am not a side chick. The next sentence flies out of my mouth with the most confidence I have ever had in my entire life. "I'm not interested in being in a relationship with someone who is married."

I have never stuck up for myself like this before. I am newly accustomed to speaking my truth, but even then, I usually have to deliberately plan what I am going to say and half the time I don't even believe what I say. But right now, my knee-jerk reaction is knowing that I deserve to be with someone who chooses me as number one. Old Me would have settled for scraps, not knowing that I deserved better. He has no idea that he is dealing with New Me. And that is very clear from his next statement. "The marriage is for Immigration, not anyone else. You're being selfish for not even considering it."

"Oh, so I'M being selfish for having a standard for myself and sticking to it?!" I think I hear canned applause in my head. I have no idea where the hell that sentence came from, but I am so damn proud of who I am right now. Ozzy doesn't seem to appreciate my self-love. He squirms in his seat and says, "Can we please get out of the car and talk outside?"

At first, I didn't like this Uber arrangement for our conversation, but since it is providing an emotional barrier for me, I am perfectly comfortable here. If I get out of the car, I am afraid I am going to do the thing I always do where I run away from anything that is emotionally painful. Since we are in front of my building,

I can easily go upstairs right now, but I am dying to finish this conversation, and the only way this is happening is through the rearview mirror. "No."

"Why?"

"Because I am comfortable right here."

He sighs heavily. "Can you at least take off your sunglasses?"

I don't know why he wants to see my eyes, but I am afraid if I take off my sunglasses, I will start crying, and I want to wait until I am upstairs and alone.

"I never told you I was getting divorced."

I think back to the conversation where he told me they were splitting up and finalizing everything when she came home. He's right. He never used the word 'divorce.' And now, I realize that he intentionally did not use that word for the purpose of a conversation like this. The knife digs deeper into my heart. I cannot believe that my best friend withheld so much information from me.

Has he been dishonest about anything else?

I don't want to ask because I don't want to know. My entire body is tense, which isn't helping my emotional state. I cannot control my reactivity. "Withholding information is dishonesty! By not telling me any of this, you were trying to control my feelings and prevent me from making important decisions because I would never have gotten involved with you if I had known any of this upfront! And you KNEW that!"

"Oh, so you're a psychologist now? I never told you I was leaving her for you."

"You told me you were leaving her! THEN, we got involved! I never thought you were leaving her for me!"

I want to continue my attack, but I feel defeated and betrayed. His verbiage up until this conversation has been intentionally manipulative and now he is throwing it all in my face. I am too emotionally exhausted to engage. It doesn't help that I wanted to eat almost two hours ago, so I'm hangry on top of being an emotional wreck. There is silence for about a minute, but it feels like an eternity. I am not looking in the rearview mirror anymore because my fingernails will shred my thighs if I look at him. I remind myself to breathe, but I can only handle short and shallow breaths.

After a long pause, Ozzy says with an irritated, tone, "The only thing that has kept me going through with ending things with her, has been the hope for a future with you."

What the hell?

This is the first conversation we've ever had about a future together. It's not my responsibility to give him hope for the future while he chooses to cling on to his miserable marriage arrangement for two more years. I would love to respond, but I'm speechless. It's possible that I'm out of words for the rest of this conversation. Ozzy finally says in a soft, shaking voice, "I can't believe you don't even want to be friends."

I look in the mirror, and his eyes are tearing up. My heart softens. I love this man. Acting out with a Chicago attitude is not how I wanted this conversation to go. I soften up, but in doing so, my voice cracks. "I'm not saying I don't ever want to be friends. It's just that I care about you so much more than a friend. I need time away from you before I can be just friends."

Now the waterworks have started. I take off my sunglasses and wipe the uncontrollable waterfall coming out of my eyes. Now we are both crying, and Ozzy sees it as an opportunity for the connection that I imagine he originally envisioned for this conversation. "Come here." Ozzy turns in his seat and holds out his hand. I take his hand, and it feels good to hold hands. I rest my chin on the top of his seat back and look into his eyes.

I love this man so much. Why does it have to be so complicated?

Ozzy speaks next. "I love you. My heart is with *you*, and I want to be with *you*. I'm older, and I've been with a lot of women, but nobody has treated me better than you have. You know how to treat your man. When I am with you, I feel so appreciated and...special."

"You *are* special."

His face softens, and his eyes glaze over with love. I am floored. He has never told me he loves me to my face before. Also, I'm surprised. He's been married twice before. Did his wives not treat him well? This makes me feel proud that I was able to demonstrate how much I cared for him through my actions and words. He continues, "I was thinking one day, 'I think she is my soulmate.'"

"You don't believe in soulmates."

"I do now."

My heart is melting. His vulnerability makes me want to share something that I was thinking about the other day while I was floating in a raft in the ocean. Because I am so independent and have been hurt so much, I feel I tend to be on the selfish side. I am afraid if I sacrifice for others, they will end up leaving me, and I will be hurt. "For what it's worth, I was thinking the other day. If we were in a relationship, because you are twenty years older than me, I would have to sacrifice my elder years to take care of you as you age. I thought about it and decided that I would be willing to take care of you."

"Why are you telling me this? It doesn't matter now because you don't want to be in a relationship with me."

He says it jokingly, but I can tell it stings him. To be honest, it stings me too. I never in a million years would have guessed that this is what the conversation would be about.

He starts kissing me. Given what we just talked about and me speaking my truth, it doesn't support my truth, but I can't help it. I will never say no to a kiss from Ozzy. When we are done making out, I tease, "How did you think we were just going to be friends for two months?"

"I didn't think through that part of the plan too well."

"So, what are we going to do?"

"Let's just be friends for the next two months and go from there."

"Okay."

I agree, but in my head, I know I don't want a relationship with a married man. But I don't want to lose Ozzy. He has only been in my life for six months, but it feels like we have been best friends forever. I know this is a bad idea in my heart, but I want to milk the next two months of friendship with Ozzy before we have to say goodbye.

Where is the confidence that I just had a few minutes ago?

Before I exit the car, he looks at me straight in my un-sunglass-ed eyes. "I love you."

"I love you too."

"Sometimes, you can't control who you fall in love with. Do you understand what I am saying, Ang?"

CHAPTER 31

THE next few days are up and down. One minute, I am happy that Ozzy and I can be friends for the next two months, and the next minute, I am heartbroken that he still wants to be married to his wife for Immigration and have me on the side. And by next minute, I mean that my moods are changing from up and down so fast, it seems like every minute. It's hard to concentrate at work. Going to the beach is usually a great way to rejuvenate, but I find myself too agitated to relax or crying so hard I can't breathe. The worst part is that there is no in-between. This is too draining. My phone vibrates with a text notification.

> Hi Angie
> I'm sorry that I am the one causing you all this grief. I'm really depressed lately and only happy when I'm with you. I stumble through the days trying to keep myself from feeling miserable. The only time I'm not thinking about my stupid situation is when I am in the water surfing, but that is such a small part of my life. I think of you a lot and am sad that I can't be with you now. Thank you for understanding. Please know that I am not happy right now with you not in my life,

and hopefully we can be in time at least friends although I want so much more than to be friends. I LOVE YOU ANGIE ♥ 💔 ♥ 💔. Goodnight 😘

ᏔORK has been draining, and I'm having trouble concentrating with the Ozzy drama, so I am taking Thursday and Friday off from work. On Thursday morning, Kelly and I are going for a hike, and Friday morning, Kelly, Kelly's friend, Katrina, and I are going surfing.

Kelly ran into Ozzy while surfing yesterday morning, and she mentioned that we had plans to hike today. I just got home from the hike, and my phone vibrates with a text notification. Ozzy is asking how the hike was. I tell him about the hike and then mention that we are going surfing in the morning. Ozzy has a lesson at 7 a.m., so he says he will see me in the water. I let him know that I am meeting Kelly and Katrina at 6 a.m. in the water, so we probably won't see him unless we run into him while getting out of the water.

ᏦELLY, Katrina, and I are walking to the beach to surf. I am using one of Kelly's boards, which locked up in a locker a few blocks away. The plan is for me to get the board and meet Kelly and Katrina in the water. As I am paddling out, I see someone sitting next to Kelly. It's Ozzy.

I didn't think his lesson was until 7 a.m. He must be getting his own session in before the lesson.

But after chatting for a few minutes, some sets of waves come in, and Ozzy immediately starts pushing me like he does when we are in a lesson. On the one hand, I like it because I am not comfortable surfing on my own yet, but on the other hand, it feels kind of awkward. After all, I don't want Kelly and Katrina to think that I invited him to our girl trio because I didn't. Luckily, he only stays for about fifteen minutes and then heads to the shore to get ready for his lesson. After he leaves, I start ripping it up on my own! This is the best I have ever surfed on my own. It gives me the confidence that I don't need him for surfing.

After surfing, we walk back to Kelly's, where Katrina's car is parked. I explain to them that I only mentioned to Ozzy what time we were going to be there and did not invite him. I still feel embarrassed because he was slightly stalking me. I don't hear from him for days. I go through the roller coaster of emotions. But I find that the downs are lasting longer and the ups are shorter because we aren't even being friends right now, which I thought was The Plan for the next two months. Naturally, I send another psycho, emotional message. In all fairness, if he didn't keep responding, I wouldn't keep sending them. Okay, maybe I would. Taking all of this Clonazepam is giving me brain fog, so I don't even understand the consequences of my actions anymore. Or if I do, I don't give a shit.

This hurts so much 💔 What hurts the most is that I lost my best friend. Every day I want to tell you the funny stories about the things that happened that day and even more so I miss the deeper conversations and the word games we used to play. And of course eating and hugging and kissing and all of the things. I understand you need time but during this time you and I are growing apart by not having normal, healthy interaction and quality time. You asked for time and it's not as simple as time. It's asking me to live with the feelings of intense heartbreak and sadness that you are living with your wife and we can't hang out and bond anymore. It's asking me to feel like I am going crazy because I am so confused and so up and down about everything. I know you are dealing with a lot right now but at this point, I feel like I am disrespecting myself, which adds to the emotional roller coaster. I know you have a lot going on right now so me crying to you about heartbroken I am isn't helping anything. I'm sorry Oz tart 💔. I wish I could hug you 😢

Hi Angie

I too miss all the things we used to do. My nails are getting long. I have nobody to play word games with at the beach. I miss swimming at Kaimana with you. I really miss the hugs and kisses and the lunches and breakfast at Sweet E's. I know you are going to have guys lined up to ask you out. I cannot ask you to put your life on hold for me. I want you to know that my heart is with you. I feel lonely and trapped but it is my fault. I think about you every day. I saw someone with a flamingo and it nearly brought tears to my eyes. I miss you sooo much and love you. I too wish I could just hold you in my arms. Sending you hugs and kisses 💔

This doesn't resolve anything. His heartfelt messages are turning into just words that I am not even sure if I believe anymore.

MY phone vibrates with a text notification.

Good night 😴

I know I shouldn't respond, but I do.

I'll be dreaming about you

My dream is better

Mine is more X rated and involves special dances you don't even know about yet 🔥

OMG LOL One day I will experience that very dance and then I will know

Haha, then you will definitely be dreaming about it. I love the idea of doing special dances for you one day so you have plenty to dream about

Now I'm all excited

I wish I could take care of that

Miss you and want you too

I miss you so much. This has been hard for me

I know sweetie. I miss you too big time

Shit, I got caught up in the moment, and now all I feel is shame and heartbreak.

Oz Tart, I feel really used and abandoned right now and regret this entire conversation. I really didn't want to cut you off completely but I'm having a really hard time being without you and getting over you and this is just tearing up my heart even more. It's best if we don't stay in touch at all for a while. I need time to heal and move on with my life. My heart is hurting enough, please stop teasing me and making it worse. Now when you dream about me tonight you can dream about me crying on the floor.

Aaah, Angie so sorry really am. I'm not going to text and say hi to you anymore because it just makes you more mad at me. I don't know what life will have in store for me but I do know that it won't be as fun and fulfilling without you in it anymore. I think about you all of the time and in such a short time you have made such an impact on my life, bringing so much happiness into it. Just want you to know that you were not just filling in the blank spaces in my life. I always looked forward to

seeing you and now there is such a huge void. I also know that as much pain that I feel right now that I would not have traded those times with you for anything. Every time I see a flamingo or go down turtle road or pass Sweet E's or look at pop tarts or think of Aloha Salads the memories of you come flooding back. Every time I see a small red car my heart skips a beat until I realize it's not you. When I paddle out at Canoes, I find myself looking for you. Your black magic flower is still in the car. I can't throw it away and so much more. Just so you know you aren't the only one on the ground crying at night. Sorry but I miss and love you can't help the way I feel. Please take care of yourself and want you to know you are a very special person!!! ♥ 💔
♥ 💔

I'm not mad at you about texting hi. I'm hurting because you were my best friend and now you kicked me to the curb and are living with your wife. What I don't understand is if what all you are saying about how you feel about me is true, why do you consider me second rate and offer me a side chick position in a situation that in your words you describe as "depressing, lonely, and trapped." Something doesn't make sense. I find it hard to believe you are crying on the ground when it is your choice to lose me. I feel like I have been used all along for the emotional support that you aren't getting from your marriage. That is why it bothers me when you text me now that you are living with her. Go to your wife if you need love and connection. You shoved me aside. It's not my responsibility. I honestly thought we were friends, but lately, I have felt like I got played for a fool. I'm resentful that you intentionally dragged me into your drama without being upfront about it and having no regard for how it would affect me. I'm sorry that I sound so mean, and I am really trying to find loving things to say. I'm in so much emotional pain that I can't stand it and can't think of anything other than I really do love you and miss you and was really hoping we could at least be friends, but there has been a lot of damage here. I wanted to be there for you, and all you have done is push me away. Now that I'm away, you want to say hi. So yeah, you could say that makes me mad at you because it brings up all of the heartache, and I'm exhausted from it. My dark secret is that I hit rock bottom three years ago and

tried to kill myself. Not succeed-
ing was the best gift ever given
to me, and I have spent the last
three years digging myself out of
that hole. I promised myself that
I would never let anyone ever dim
my light ever again. My light is
dimming right now because I don't
feel respected. And this whole text
turned into emotional bullshit, so
I'm sorry. I don't want to move on
because my heart is still with you
but I love myself more than I love
anybody else and it's best for me
in the long run to find someone who
wants me as #1. And I deserve that

Why am I acting like such a psychopath?

I have instant regret after I hit send. That was way too long and emotional. It saddens me even more because we don't even talk anymore to be able to have these conversations in person. I hate doing this over text.

He doesn't respond. Two days go by.

I finally pushed him away with my long, psychopath texts.

I feel sick to my stomach. Naturally, I cover the pain by taking more Clonazepam. I am going to need a refill soon. I have almost blown through these thirty pills in the past few months.

IT's been two days since I texted Ozzy. He still hasn't respond-ed. It's Sunday, and I miss him the most on Sundays because we used to spend the entire day together. Kelly and I are surfing this morning. The waves are big— much bigger than I am used to. At some points, I am really scared and wish Ozzy were here to help me. I feel like such an asshole for messing up with my psycho text messages. It's just a bunch of emotion that lives in my head, and he doesn't deserve to have it dumped on him, but I have no idea how to communicate and he isn't communicating clearly with me, so I have no idea what to do.

After we are done surfing, Kelly and I paddle back to shore. Kelly is looking toward the shore and says, "There's Ozzy."

"Where?"

"He's paddling out to us."

Shit. I sent him that shitty text, and he didn't respond. What is he going to say?

As he approaches, I don't look at him. Then, he is right next to us and I look at him. I speak first. "Hi."

"Hi."

It's awkward as hell, and luckily, Kelly has a high emotional IQ and starts paddling to shore as she says to me, "I'll meet you onshore."

"Okay."

I turn to Ozzy. He usually wears a wetsuit in the water, but he has his shirt off, and his hair is all tasseled. My heart melts. I still don't know what he is going to say, so I speak first. "I'm sorry."

"Don't worry about it."

I gaze lovingly at him, not knowing what to say next. He says, "Sweet E's?"

Um, YES!

We haven't hung out in what seems like ages, and we haven't gone to Sweet E's in weeks, which feels like years. I nod my head with much less enthusiasm than I am feeling. Then, I remember that my belongings are locked in Kelly's car, and my phone is at home. "I have to go with Kelly to get my stuff and my phone is at home. I will text you when I get home."

"Sounds good."

We both paddle in separate directions, and I can't wait to get home and shower off the ocean water for Sweet E's. Ozzy picks me up, and we get our usual table outside. Luckily, they still remember us, even though we haven't been going on Sundays. The entire time at breakfast, I gaze at Ozzy with gaga eyes because I miss him so much. I have no idea what he is thinking or if we are doing anything after this. I brought my beach bag in case we go our separate ways, and I have to lounge on the beach alone.

We make small talk the entire time at breakfast, catching up on what has been going on since we don't hang out every day or even talk and text like we used to. He is living with his wife now, but he tells me that even though the original plan was that she would move out because she used to hate their apartment, now she can't decide and goes back and forth every day. Ozzy can't deal with the indecision, so he has decided that he is going to move out, and she can do whatever she wants. I don't like talking about his wife because I am head over heels in love with him, but Ozzy is generally not good at making solid decisions, and I am proud of him for making that hard decision. He tells me that he is going to move into our friend James' rental property in Waikiki on November 1st, over a month away.

"Why are you waiting until November?"

"She needs help getting on her own feet."

She's thirty-one years old. Why do he and her mom treat her like a baby?

As we leave Sweet E's, we get in the car. I am nervous because I want to ask him to go to the beach, but I don't know if he wants to or if that is even appropriate. Luckily, he speaks before I have to figure out what to say. "You want to go to Sandy's?"

Um, YES!

I notice how long Ozzy's fingernails are as we drive to Sandy Beach. Because we don't hang out anymore, I haven't been giving him manicures and pedicures. When we park at Sandy's, I pull out my nail file. If I can't give him a manicure, I can at least get the length down, so he doesn't peel them like I know he does when they get long. We continue talking as I file his nails. I am only partially through one hand, and he pulls me over to the driver's seat with him, holds me in his arms, and says to me, "I miss you so much."

I want to be stubborn, but I don't have it in me. "I miss you too."

He holds me tight as we talk. He explains his need to end the marriage amicably. He had told me before that his first marriage did not end amicably, and his first wife took him to the cleaners, and I know his biggest fear is being broke, so I get it. I don't understand how we can only be "friends" for the next two months if we love each other so much and, as of right now, we aren't even being friends because we don't hang out every day like we used to and the dynamics are so different. He strokes my hair as he talks. It's getting really hot in the car, but I never want to leave his arms. Then, he asks, "Why me?"

I know we seem like an odd couple. I am twenty-two years younger than he is, I make more money than he does, I am way more of a neat freak than he is, and he is way more laid back than I am. Visually, I think he's beautiful with a captivating smile, but I know some people would look at us and think I'm out of his league. The other day when I was journaling at the beach, I was trying to decide if it was worth it to be in a relationship with Ozzy while he was still married for Immigration. I still am not sure. But I know the answer to 'why me?'

"Because you are such a good person. I love how the simplest moments with you, like Sandy's and Sweet E's, are always so magical. I love laughing and having fun with you. I like how I feel safe and protected with you. I love how you truly accept me for who I am, quirks, flaws, and all. I love how you call me out on my shit. It helps me to grow and be a better person. You bring out patience and unselfishness that I didn't even know I had. You have helped me understand my ability to love and be loved. And you're the first person where I don't feel like I need you. I want you, but I don't need you." I pause and realize how far I have come, even though it feels scarier to want someone and not need them. I continue, "I guess that last one is more of a 'me' thing."

He agrees. We get out of the car and hang out on the beach for the afternoon. Then we grab a bite to eat. I am curious if his wife keeps tabs on where he is. I don't hear the spooky music ringtone, but he might have turned it off, so I don't hear. We plan to go surfing on Wednesday.

OZZY picks me up after work on Wednesday. At Sandy's, he had told me that he left a message for James about renting his vacation rental in Waikiki, but he had not heard from him.

On our way to the beach, I bring it up. "So, did you hear back from James on the rental?" He hasn't, but we conveniently run into James when we get into the water.

"There's James. You can talk to him about rental."

I figured he would take him off to the side and talk about it, but he brings it up to him right in front of me. "Hey, James! How much for your place?"

"It's usually fifteen hundred, but for you, one thousand. It's available tomorrow."

"I don't need it until November first."

I don't understand why in the hell a thirty-one year-old needs so much time to get on her feet, especially since her mom gave her two hundred and fifty thousand dollars. I smell a rat. He tells me how lonely and miserable he is living with her, yet he wants to live with her another month. I bring it up again on the way home. "Why does she need another month to get on her feet?"

"I feel pressured when you keep asking questions about it."

I can't handle this anymore.

CRYING on the floor, I decide that this is the last time I cry on the floor for Ozzy. This whole situation is so fucked up. I thought I would ride out these last two months and be friends with Ozzy, but it's taking its toll. I'm depressed, anxious, heartbroken, and ready to snap. We aren't even friends right now, which was part of The Plan. I used to take my Clonazepam once or twice a month, but I have been taking it every night. I have to stand up for myself.

Chapter 32

J type a psycho, emotional text and delete it. I send something else.

> Can we please talk sometime? I just typed a long ass text that sounds like more emotional vomit, and I don't think we communicate well over text anyway, so I would rather talk on the phone or in person.

He wants to meet in person tomorrow and offers to pick me up after work. I like to have time to deliberately think about what I am going to say because, in the moment, I am too emotionally overwhelmed, and my mind goes blank. I'll come up with a plan tomorrow.

Work has been busy today and honestly, I have no idea what I want to say. Ozzy picks me up and asks where I want to go. I just want to be outside. "A park or the beach."

The black magic flower is missing from his car. I feel like I am going to throw up. "Where's the black magic flower?"

"What? Oh, I don't know."

He's bullshitting. He threw it away so Sarah wouldn't ask about it.

We ride to the beach, mostly in silence. We wait until we are set up on the beach to talk. We both lay on our stomachs, facing away from the water. Ozzy rests his forehead on his hands and with his face down. "I'm listening even though my head is like this."

He probably thinks I'm about to lay into him, but I still don't know what I am going to say, so I just start talking, and as soon as I open my mouth, the tears start forming. I hate how difficult it is to talk while crying. "When we first started surfing in March, I was in a good place where I was improving my life and myself. And then I started hanging out with you, and you enhanced my life so much." I choke up even more. Ozzy puts his hand on the small of my back. I love how Ozzy is always affectionate and comforts me when I cry. It's one of the things I love about him and makes this even harder to say. "But for the past couple of months, I've been in a lot of emotional pain, and I feel like my soul is dying. I can't handle it anymore. I want to be friends with you, but I still have feelings for you, so I just need some time away from you now so that we can be friends in the future."

I start crying harder. I sit up. Ozzy sits up and puts his hand on my leg. He tells me that he knows what I want and deserve but can't give that to me now. He goes on to say more things that just sound like he is filling space with words. This is much different than The Plan conversation a mere three weeks ago, where he adamantly told me he loved me and wanted a relationship with me.

Did his feelings change? Or is it because he knows I'm not interested in a relationship with him while he is married?

It's hot and humid for the beginning of October. We are both sweating profusely, adding to the discomfort of the conversation. Suddenly, Ozzy stops rambling. "Do you want to get in the water?"

I know he's intentionally changing subjects, but I am so hot and just want to get in the water. "Yes."

We get in the water. This is dangerous territory. A lot of flirting and fondling has been had in the same area of the ocean. Ozzy changes the subject from our sad conversation on the beach about some new stocks he just bought. As he's talking, I look at his beautiful face.

Ozzy has been such a special person in my life. How can I let him go? This is going to destroy me.

A mere few minutes after having that thought, Ozzy abruptly stops his story, suddenly embraces me, and starts kissing me. I know I should enforce the boundary I was brave enough to enforce on the beach, but I don't want to stop. Not long into the kiss, he pulls his penis out of his shorts. I touch it. The hardness turns me on. I pull my bathing suit bottoms to the side, and he slides it somewhat smoothly in me. I am turned on and want to get into it, but there are a lot of other people there, namely kids, and I don't want the lifeguard to kick us off the beach.

How did I go from being brave and telling him that I need time away to no boundaries and letting him put his dick in me?

This is why I like to have a script. Then, Kelly shows up at the beach. Ozzy freaks out, pulls out, and gets out of the water to run away from her.

Why is he freaking out?

He knows Kelly knows about us. Kelly gets in the water a little further down with some friends. I go over to say hi and explain that I am here with Ozzy. After meeting her friends, I say goodbye and get out of the water. Ozzy re-appears but is ready to leave. He drops me off at home. We usually eat after hanging out, but he has to go to Costco to buy an air conditioner, presumably for his wife, so my heart drops. This is why I should have enforced the boundary. We plan to surf on Wednesday because I am not ready to say goodbye to Ozzy yet because it is going to totally devastate me, and sweeping shit under the rug is what I am programmed to do.

"Good luck will rub off when I shakes hands with you!"

SURFING today has been fun! I feel like I am making more progress, and Ozzy and I are catching waves together. Ozzy is coaching me along the wave, which is helpful to me. As we talk between waves, we make plans to spend the day together on Sunday, which is his birthday. Then, he gets weird. "Hurry up, we need to catch one more wave, and then I have to drop you off by 2:50."

I am having fun and want to stay longer. "What time is your lesson?"

"I need to drop you off by 2:50."

"What time is your lesson?"

"I need to come back here early and set up stuff."

"I can stay here and walk home when I am done."

"No, I am driving you home."

"Why are you acting all suspicious?"

He pauses and says, "I have to go home first and pick something up."

Sarah. If she is taking pictures for the lesson, in which selling photos is part of their business, then the something he is picking up is her. If that's all it is, it's no big deal, and no need to act suspicious.

So what the hell is going on?

This is another reason why I should have stuck to my boundary on Monday. My heart sinks. Just a minute ago, I wanted to surf for another hour, but now I want to go home. Ozzy drops me off and because he's in such a rush to get home, he gives me a hasty kiss through my COVID face mask that I have proactively put on to go into the building.

*J*T'S 6 a.m. on Friday. I am on a boring conference call with my co-workers. My phone buzzes on the countertop next to me with a text notification. My intuition immediately identifies it as Ozzy. I can't wait until after the conference call, so I pick up my phone. It's Ozzy! I read the message preview.

> Hi Angie, I've given this a lot
> of thought...

Fuuuuuuuck. This is not good.

Like a punch in the stomach, my heart goes from radiating love to sinking with dread. I read the full message.

> Hi Angie
> I've given this a lot of thought,
> and I am sorry, but I don't think
> I can see you till after I move
> out, I don't think it is fair to
> you or Sarah as long as I am stay-
> ing here it doesn't look right. I

> know you have told me this but it is hard to just be friends when I see you. I know you will be mad at me and I don't expect you to wait for me. I just need to get my shit together. I'm sorry that I dragged you into my mess of a life but when I see you all my feelings for you come flooding back. I need some time to sort things out on my own. Pls understand and that I do wish the very best for you. I cannot keep putting you thru this till it's over on this end I'm sorry and do miss and love you

I'm numb. This doesn't even sound like Ozzy. There are no emojis, Bitmojis, or exclamation points and he never calls Sarah by her name. Something is up. I am so hurt and angry that I have no response. Ozzy was my rock, my protector, and now he is abandoning me just like everyone else I've ever loved.

I go surfing in the afternoon and hope with my raw heart that he will paddle out to talk to me, but he doesn't. I don't even see him in the water. The next day, the day before his birthday, I take all three hundred dollars worth of the birthday presents that I bought for him and the one hundred dollar coffee maker that I bought for him to have at my place and throw them away. I am willing to throw money away instead of drawing out the pain by returning them. Sunday is his birthday. On Wednesday, he asked me to surf with him on Sunday, and I was honored that he wanted to spend his birthday with me. But here I am, all alone.

He doesn't care anymore that he is hurting me, which hurts the most. He used to protect me with every ounce of energy he had. The numbness in my heart is replaced with the familiar raging, emotional pain of abandonment, shame, and loneliness. All of the pain that Marc stirred up and took me three long, painful years to overcome is back. A few weeks ago, Ozzy told me he loved me and wanted to be with me. He said I was The One.

J survived a week, but I am barely hanging on. In the past six months, Ozzy and I have never gone this long without contact. With each day, the emotional pain gets more intense. After our Friday morning workout, my friend Sam starts unloading her trauma about her boyfriend. He's a piece of shit she has been with on-and-off with for eight years. He's a total psychopath who has broken into her apartment, trashed the place, keyed her car, and sabotaged her friendships. I told her over a year ago to kick his ass to the curb, but just like my toxic relationship with Marc, she has a trauma bond and thinks that a part of her is missing when they are not together. I'm already in an emotionally delicate place, and here is Sam unloading on me about her toxic boyfriend. She's upset because earlier that morning, she was crying to her roommate, Terri, and apparently, Terri said, "Fuck him! I wish he would die!" Sam starts crying. "I don't want him to die."

I feel like I am talking to my thirty-seven-year-old self about Marc. Between my raw pain from Ozzy and total compassion and empathy for Sam, I start crying too. "It's because it hurts us to see you hurting."

We both have a good cry and hug. Sam thinks I'm such a strong person and has no idea how bad I want to die right now.

I log off work around noon. Kelly had been thinking about surfing with me this afternoon, but she texted back that she can't go surfing but could walk with me to the water so we can chat and catch up. I have been trying to be strong in front of Kelly, but I can't hide my pain when I meet up with her. I start crying. "I can't believe he did this to me. He was my best friend."

Kelly hugs me, and it's loving and supportive, but it's not enough. I want to escape this pain.

I get in the water. The ocean is always so comforting, but not now when my heart is so raw that I can't stand it. All of me is hoping Ozzy will do the thing that he always does, at least used to do, where he shows up unannounced where he knows I am going to be. He doesn't. He used to hate it when I was mad at him. Now I am dead to him. I would rather him say, "I hate you," to my face than give me the silent treatment. The silent treatment kills my soul and uncovers my Marc trauma, like a swamp monster emerging from the sludge of the deep, murky waters.

I'm not important.

I don't deserve to be acknowledged.

I don't even deserve to be loved.

I can't do this again. I've been through too much hell since February 2017 without a break. After I get home from surfing, I grab the bottle of Clonazepam. There are two left in this bottle. It's 4:30 p.m. It's Friday, so I have tomorrow off work and can sleep in. Maybe if I sleep for over twelve hours, this emotional pain will go away. I take both pills. I am convinced this will knock me out until tomorrow morning.

I wake up at 11:30 p.m. and promptly run to the bathroom to throw up. The emotional pain rages in my chest like a vice gripping my heart. The physical and mental anguish is too much. In the past three and a half years, I have had to deal with Marc leaving me for Julia, Dad dying, moving from Chicago to Hawaii on my own, the flood, buying a new wood floor, health issues with my tongue, the difficulty of walking away from important friendships, having trouble making new friends, Grandma dying, the struggles with Mike and the book project, the constant stress at work and fear of getting let go through the management changes, the horrible Guam and Denver trips, the restrictions and isolation of COVID, and now Ozzy abandoning me. Ozzy was the only true love and connection I have felt during this entire time and the only person in my entire life with whom I felt one hundred percent unconditionally accepted and emotionally safe, and it was ripped away from me with the swiftness and ease of turning off a light switch.

I grab the brand-new bottle of thirty pills that I refilled last week. The warning on the side says do not mix with alcohol, so I take two shots of tequila to ensure that it is. I put my pillow and blanket in the shower. I split the bottle of pills into two piles on the bathroom counter because all thirty seems like too much to swallow at once. I have a brief moment where I hesitate out of fear, but I know the pills will knock me out before I die. There is no hope for the future. This is the only way out.

Dad, please don't save me this time.

I swallow pile one, followed by pile two, and wash them down with a final swig of water from my red water bottle. I lay down in the shower. I am hoping to lose consciousness immediately, but it feels like forever. It's probably only a few minutes, but when you are expecting to die and scared that something painful could happen before you lose consciousness, a few minutes feels like an eternity.

There was no pain or discomfort. Just like you don't remember the moment before falling asleep, I don't remember blacking out.

CHAPTER 33

MY heavy and swollen eyelids slowly open. The sun is up. I'm laying in the shower with my head on my pillow and my blanket neatly on top of me.

Fuuuuuuck.

I can only remember one thing right now. I am supposed to be dead. I panic because I am alive. I quickly stand up, but I am so high I can barely walk. I take the five steps to my bed and collapse. I'm scared. My brain is not working. The room is spinning. My hands are shaking uncontrollably.

Am I dying?

I blackout.

I remember talking to Kelly on the phone while laying on my bed, but I don't remember what was said. I have a vague memory of being in the passenger seat of her car and staring at the dashboard. The next thing I remember is waking up in a hospital bed with an IV and a bunch of wires taped to my chest. I am hungry as hell but still very high from the pills, so it feels like a dream. Because I am on suicide watch, there is a nurse stationed beside me.

"Can I have some crackers?" My appetite needs way more than crackers, but it's a hospital, so I figure I should ask for something they have handy.

"Let me go check."

I blackout. I am in and out of consciousness for who knows how long. Each time I wake up, there are no crackers. Each time I wake up, I ask, "Can I have some crackers?"

"Let me go check."

And around and around we go. At one point, a nurse approaches me with Ozzy's first name and phone number on a piece of paper. Either I told them who my doctor is, or it is in my medical records, but they called my doctor, and Ozzy is my emergency contact. The nurse has questions. "What is Ozzy's last name?"

"Don't call him."

"What is Ozzy's real name?"

"Don't call him."

"How do you know Ozzy?"

"Don't call him."

I am so embarrassed. He let me down so badly that I cannot rely on him as my emergency contact. That is why Joe was my emergency contact because he would have gotten his ass on a plane and done whatever he needed to do to help me. Although, he probably would be disappointed that I did this to myself again, even worse this time.

I blackout. I wake up with total raging hunger. I don't know what time it is, but it's probably been about twenty-four hours since I last ate. The nurse has still not brought crackers. I am hangry and high as shit. Another nurse walks in and asks, "How is everything?"

"I'VE ASKED FOR CRACKERS LIKE TEN FUCKING TIMES AND NOBODY HAS BROUGHT ME CRACKERS AND I JUST WANT TO FUCKING GO HOME!!!"

I say more, but in my brain cloud, all I know is I am saying words. I am so inebriated that I have no control over what is coming out of my mouth. I am a total emotional wreck and verbally annihilating this nurse who came to check on me. Unfortunately, this person is responsible for deciding whether or not to admit me to the psych ward.

"We are going to keep you in the psych ward until Monday."

"NOOOOOO! I CAN'T STAY HERE FOR TWO DAYS!"

More words are coming out of my mouth, but it's all a blur. Although, I'm certain I just called her a bitch. I am not helping my case. I feel so helpless and alone. I am still so messed up from the pills and just want to go home and sleep in my own bed. The hospital is so institutional and emotionally cold, just like my childhood home. I cry. Not the quiet kind, but the hysterical, ugly crying, only adding to their desire to admit me to the psych ward. Just like the pictures of Little Angie crying in the photo album, my emotions are intolerable to others when all I need is to be comforted.

I blackout on the transition to the psych ward. I arrive in a wheelchair, and I have to stand up to get out, but I cannot stand up without assistance from the two nurses who transported me here. It is nighttime. The lady at the admission desk greets me cheerily. "Would you like some Clonazepam to sleep?"

Why is she offering me more when I still have an alarming amount in my system?

"No."

They lead me to my private room. It is small, all-white everything and nothing but a bed. No clock. No window. No nothing. I don't even have my phone. They must have confiscated my purse at some point. The worst part is, there are truly crazy people in here, so I fall asleep to the sounds of screaming and yelling.

I sleep until morning. I am still overwhelmingly high and stumble to the bathroom. I can't believe they put me in here without medical attention. I can barely function or think straight. The meals in the psych ward are communal so that we can be monitored while we eat. I slept through breakfast. I ask for food, and I am told that I have to wait until lunch. I ask one of the nurses when I can go home. She says the doctors start making rounds at 9 a.m. It is 8 a.m. I stumble back to my spartan, white room with no clock. I start sobbing uncontrollably. I have never felt so alone and helpless in my entire life. I feel like a prisoner that nobody cares about. My worst fears of being abandoned and unloved are all coming true right now, and I am too emotionally unstable to handle it.

I blackout. I sleep through 11 a.m. communal lunch. A male nurse comes to check on me. Through crying hysterically, I ask, "Can I please have food? I am so hungry."

"Hold on."

He comes back with an egg salad sandwich without the wrapper because he is not supposed to bring food to my room, and there can be no trace. I think this male nurse is my guardian angel. I inhale the sandwich as if it is the most delicious thing I have ever eaten. I feel like a stray dog manically eating out of a trash can. I go back to bawling uncontrollably. I have never cried so much in my entire life.

Is it possible to dehydrate from crying?

I blackout. Two doctors knock on my door. They are here to do the exit interview! They introduce themselves, but my brain is too focused on trying to stand up without falling to retain anything they say. They take me to the common area to sit down at a table. I am trying to keep it together because these guys are my keys to go home, but I am an emotional wreck and start crying hysterically again. "I just want to go home!"

"We will make sure you're safe enough to go home," says the nice doctor. It's like a good cop, bad cop scenario. The younger Asian gentleman is nice and asks me questions in a soothing voice. The old man with white hair is acting like he is interrogating a terrorist. The whole conversation feels like a dream. All I know is that I am crying violently. "I just want to go home!"

Bad Cop steps up. "Well, you certainly don't seem like you are in a safe emotional state to go home."

I gesture around the room full of psych ward patients. As if on cue, one of the patients starts yelling obscenities, and a few are already talking to themselves, which helps set up the scene. "In all fairness, this isn't the safest environment for my emotional state!"

I am extremely proud of myself because this is the most logical sentence I have said during this entire hospital excursion. Bad Cop silently concedes, and I can tell by his softened facial expression

I have won this battle. But have I won the war? He speaks again. "We're concerned you will go home and try to harm yourself again."

It's a fair statement, but my emotions and the high take over and I become hysterical again. "First of all, I don't have any more pills because I took them all! Second, even if I did have more pills, I wouldn't take them to kill myself because I already know it doesn't work!"

Through my hysterics, I am proud of the second most logical statement I have said during this entire hospital excursion. And I seem to be gaining credibility with both of the doctors. They ask if I own any guns or weapons. I don't. Then they wrap up the interview and send me back to my room.

"Can I go home?"

"We will make a decision and get back to you."

I go back to my white room with no sense of time and sob uncontrollably until the male nurse knocks on the door and says, "You are cleared to be released."

Yay!

"It will take up to two hours to complete the paperwork."

WHAT?!?

I can't stop crying. This whole experience is a total nightmare. I am imprisoned, physically and emotionally. Time is a weird thing when you are in a room with no windows, no clock, no phone, no TV, no radio, no laptop, and high. It feels like forever, yet the time is also going by fast since I was brought here last night because I keep blacking out between emotional breakdowns. Finally, the male nurse knocks on my door. He hands me a folded-up pair of olive green cargo pants and a red T-shirt. "Will these fit?"

I stare at him blankly because these are not my clothes, but my brain can't seem to form those words.

"Your clothes are in plastic bags and, due to COVID, you can't open the bags until you get outside. Will these fit?"

My eyes can't fully focus on the folded-up clothes, but I am so desperate to leave that I will walk out wearing these whether they fit or not. "Yes."

I change into the T-shirt and realize that I am not wearing a bra because I was admitted wearing a sports bra, and they took that off. The pants fit perfectly, which is the only twist of luck I have received here because cargo pants require a specific fit, like jeans.

I black out again as I am being discharged. The next thing I know, I am standing on the curb outside of the hospital, holding two plastic bags containing my real clothes and purse. I am barefoot.

This is it? They were sooooo concerned about my safety that they just dumped me on the street, still high as shit, barefoot, and no ride home?

Once again, I feel disrespected and abandoned.

Why didn't I die? I don't want to be here. I hate this.

I open the plastic bag containing my purse. I turn on my phone. It starts blowing up with text messages. I order an Uber and then start going through my text messages. A few are from Kahea. She is having a workshop tonight to wrap up our yearly series about healing our chakras. I need to tell her I can't make it. I read her texts. They are from yesterday.

> You didn't tell me you weren't coming to the workshop

> Are you okay?

What is she talking about? The workshop is tonight.

The most recent series of texts are from today from my esthetician, Hazel. I have an eyelash tint and eyebrow wax appointment with her tomorrow.

> Are we still on for 1 today?

> Are you okay?

> Do you need to reschedule?

I text her back before reading my other texts.

> Yes, we are still on for 1 tomorrow. We do Monday's remember?

I look at my phone to see what time it is. It's 2 p.m. I see the date.

Oh. My. Fucking. God.

It's Monday. I took the pills on Friday night, which means that the day I woke up was Sunday, not Saturday, which means I was unconscious in my shower for a day and a half. The realization hits me like a ton of bricks, sobering me up for a moment, then fades when I feel my phone vibrate. It's Hazel calling.

"Hello?"

"Are you okay?"

"No, I just got discharged from the hospital and I thought it was Sunday, but it's Monday!"

"Where are you? I'm picking you up."

"I already ordered an Uber to take me home, but I can have her drop me off somewhere else."

"Meet me in front of the zoo."

"Okay."

My phone vibrates with an unknown number as I disconnect from Hazel.

"Hello?"

"Hi! It's Paula, your Uber driver!"

Shit.

Usually, I am obsessed with the thrill of the estimated arrival, license plate, and make/model of the car, but I forgot the next step of ordering an Uber because I am so high. Paula has not forgotten. "Where are you?" she asks.

I just found out what day it is. I have no idea where the hell I am, other than outside of the hospital. I notice that I am standing on the curb of a pickup/drop-off area, so I walk toward the side street to which it is connected. Immediately, a black Acura SUV pulls up. I don't even ask her what kind of car she is driving because this car seems eager to pick me up and I am eager to get the hell away from the hospital. I get in as I disconnect the call.

"Hi, Angie!"

Oh good, it's Paula.

"Hi! Hey, can you drop me off in front of the zoo instead of the address I gave you?"

"Sure!"

I like Paula. She is the first nice and happy person I have seen in days. And I like that there is no Uber bureaucracy around where she has to drop me off. She continues to talk. "How are you?"

"Fine. Listen, I just got out of the hospital, and because of COVID, they gave me these weird clothes to wear home, but these cargo pants are too stifling. I am going to change into my real clothes back here."

"Oh sure, I don't mind. I won't watch."

I don't care if she watches. I am free from the walls of the hospital, and that is all I care about right now. We continue to make pleasant small talk as I unapologetically disrobe from the weird hospital clothes and into my own. I am not wearing a bra or underwear, so there is a point in time when I am completely naked in Paula's backseat. We stop at a red light, and I am pretty sure the car next to us is watching. I don't give a shit. I am so thankful I am free. I open up the second plastic bag with the clothes I wore to the hospital. They didn't return my slippers. After all of this, I am still barefoot.

Paula cheerily drops me off at the zoo, where I meet Hazel in hysterical sobs. We sit on a nearby bench. The irony of this is that the outside of the Honolulu Zoo is a popular congregation hotspot for a lot of mentally unstable, homeless people. Since I am in the middle of a hysterical, emotional breakdown, under the influence of drugs, barefoot, with two plastic hospital bags, and haven't showered, brushed my teeth, or eaten in three days, I fit in perfectly. I ramble the entire story to Hazel, including how deliriously high I still am.

The thing about Hazel is that I don't trust her. I started going to her about a year and a half ago for eyelash lifts and tinting. There were red flags from the beginning. She overshares. A lot. And rarely does she ask about me. But her prices are extremely cheap and she does a great job. She also waxes my eyebrows for free.

The trust thing all started last Thanksgiving. She invited me to Thanksgiving at her house in Kailua, which she shares with her boyfriend, Drew, and their roommate, Kenny. She told me there would be people coming in and out all day long. She also told me that it started at noon and we could go paddle boarding afterward. Admittedly, I went because I wanted to paddleboard, and it seemed like there would be a lot of people, so it wouldn't be awkward.

Wrong. The only two people besides Hazel, Drew, Kenny, and I were her two boring, snooty neighbors. Also, because Hazel told me the food was going to be served at noon, I didn't show up until 2 p.m. because I didn't want to eat. I wanted to paddleboard. And I thought there would be more people, so it wouldn't matter what time I showed up. Wrong. They were waiting for me to show up to start eating. The whole "casual" affair was contingent on me. I didn't even really know Hazel that well, and this was the first time seeing her outside of the lash studio.

After we ate, we sat around for what felt like forever, watching *Saturday Night Live* reruns that Drew and Kenny laughed at hysterically, even though I guarantee they had seen the episodes at least a gazillion times. Finally, Hazel asked me if I wanted to go paddle boarding.

Um, YES.

It was fun, but since it was so late in the day, it was kind of cold and, overall, anticlimactic. After the Thanksgiving incident, I kept Hazel at arm's length. I began to notice that she never speaks of any female friends. There is usually a reason if females do not have female friends. And it's never a good reason. A few months ago, Hazel was having relationship issues with Drew and seemed sad. I referred her to surfing lessons with Ozzy because he was so much fun to surf with and I thought that would cheer her up. Fortunately, it did! For some stupid reason, after Hazel met Ozzy, during one of our lash appointments, I confided to her that my relationship with Ozzy had turned romantic.

"First of all, Ozzy is *old*, and he is *married*."

Wow, not your typical, empathetic female listener.

In later conversations, she made more judgmental comments about the situation, although interestingly enough, there were times I sniffed a hint of jealousy. After our last appointment, I vowed never to tell her anything about Ozzy again.

So here I am, sitting with Hazel in front of the zoo, high, hangry, and hysterical, spilling my guts about how I tried to kill myself when Ozzy dropped me on my ass. Not surprisingly, her reaction is cold and way too harsh for my fragile, emotional state. "You need to move on and get over him."

No shit, Sherlock.

I was trying to eternally get over him, but now here I am with a whole new host of problems. I instantly regret confiding to her. I was so starved for connection after being unconscious and in the cold, institutional hospital for the past three days that I was desperate to be around anybody. In my inebriated state, I made a serious mistake by meeting her. If only the hospital would have discharged me even an hour earlier, I could have realized what day it was and told her something came up and rescheduled.

Hazel drives me home and gives me a snack pack of cookie wafers that I inhale. They are the quality of an airplane snack, but the sweetness of the cookie on my tongue is like fireworks exploding in my mouth. It's Monday afternoon, and this is the second thing I have eaten since Friday afternoon. I get home, and there are dishes in the sink. I never leave dishes in the sink. I look at the frying pan, and it is charred so badly that it is ruined. I must have tried to make something when I was blacked out. I log onto work. I missed an entire day of work without putting my out-of-office on my email or letting anyone know.

Surely they are worried about me.

I scroll through my emails and despite not showing up for three conference calls that I hosted, nobody seemed to notice that I was gone.

I'm not important.

Nobody cares if I am missing.

I call Kahea, who I know from her texts was concerned that I didn't show up for the workshop yesterday.

"I was in the hospital."

"Hospital? What happened?"

"I overdosed on my anxiety pills."

"Well, don't try to kill yourself."

I know she is kidding, but I have to tell her. "That's what I was trying to do. I had a total emotional breakdown."

"You didn't have a breakdown. You had a breakthrough. What happened?"

I take a deep breath and give her the Cliff Notes version of the Ozzy developments because we haven't talked in a few weeks and I am tired of rehashing the drama. I end with defeat. "I feel so rejected."

"No, *you're* the one who rejected *him*."

I am still high, so my brain needs a few extra seconds of processing time to fully understand what she is saying.

But wait, she's right.

The Plan was a proposal for me to be in a relationship with him while he finished his marriage agreement. For the first time in my entire life, I confidently and firmly stood up for my worth by telling him that I didn't want a relationship with someone who was married. I fucked up because I had zero boundaries around the two-month friendship period. It was going to end after then anyway, but I was milking my time because I didn't want to let go.

Kahea and I continue to talk, and I tell her about how many pills I took and how I can't believe I survived.

"It's not your time," she says.

A cold chill runs through my body. A lot of people don't get second chances, especially with life. But I'm still here after taking a lethal dose of Clonazepam and lying unconscious for a day and a half in my shower. I am here for a reason, and I have no idea what my purpose is, but I resolve to figure it out.

CHAPTER 34

$\mathcal{I}$ am working and hear my phone vibrate on the countertop next to me. I look at the screen. It's an unknown caller. I can function after being released from the hospital yesterday, but I still have a low-grade high, and my judgment is impaired, as I normally wouldn't answer a call I don't recognize.

"Hello?"

"Is this Angie?"

"Yes…"

"Angie with the red hair?"

Did I give some thirsty dude my phone number when I was high at the hospital?

"Yes…"

"I know you from surfing with Ozzy, and I have some information about him you probably want to know."

My blood runs cold. "Who is this?"

Pause. No response.

"How did you get my phone number?"

"It doesn't matter. Listen, Sarah found out about you and Ozzy."

I sober up a little bit. I don't dare ask any more questions because I want to hear more.

"He can't contact you right now because her mom is giving him money to stay married to her so she can get her citizenship. Sarah and her mom have threatened him not to see you or talk to you, or they are cutting off the money. And there is someone else involved. They know about you, and they know about the money, so they are blackmailing him."

My head is spinning. I'm pissed because I just got out of the hospital yesterday. I'm hungover, emotionally and physically, and this is a lot of shit I don't want to hear. "Why are you telling me this?"

"I thought you might want to know."

On second thought, knowledge is power. I should be thanking him for going through the effort to track down my phone number and having the courage to call me.

"Thank you."

"You're welcome. Have a nice evening."

When does the drama stop?

*J*T's Saturday, five days after being released from the hospital, and I am hiking Koko Head. I find a secluded ledge and have a hysterical breakdown by myself at the top. I don't want to be alive, but I know I have to be. There is no going back. I have to keep moving forward. But I don't know if I have the strength. I feel more helpless and alone than I did before I took the pills. My withdrawal symptoms are intense and adding to the emotional spiral. My hands are still shaking uncontrollably. I haven't slept more than one or two hours each night, and when I do sleep, I sweat uncontrollably. I'm never hungry and have to force myself to eat. Worst of all, the heartbreak is squeezing my chest, which feels like a black hole.

It's only been a week. How am I going to make it another week? One day at a time.

After Koko Head, I catch up with Kelly on her lanai so that she can fill me in on all of the things that happened with her while I was blacked out. At one point, she starts crying and comes over to give me a huge hug. "I thought you were going to die."

I feel like such an asshole. I didn't realize how much my actions would hurt other people. I wanted to kill myself to end the pain, but now I realize that the pain doesn't go away. It gets transferred to the people who remain.

Why was I only thinking about myself?

"What is your game plan to recover from this?"

I love that Kelly keeps me accountable. I tell her about my conversation with Kahea and how I am determined to figure out my purpose. I can't do it alone, though. Kahea offered to help with spiritual healing, but I need to work on my brain in addition to my soul.

The first thing I do is reach out to Pablo. Pablo is a personal coach that I met through the Neil Strauss intensive. I have wanted to reach out to him for a while about coaching, but his niche is coaching men with dating. But I know from following him on Instagram that it's not pickup artist bullshit. He teaches men how to be authentic and have confidence in themselves. This is what I want to work on— my inner game. I like Pablo's style, and he is my first choice for a coach. If he doesn't want to work with me because I am not his target market, I will find a different coach.

I used to be timid when reaching out to people like this, but I just survived an overdose, so I have nothing to lose. I send Pablo a text message. He responds that he would love to set up a call and talk! We set up a time to Zoom. Pablo is just as cool as I remember. Talking to him feels like talking to an old friend. I tell him about how I want to write a book.

Why are you still telling people this?

Because I have never been more certain about anything in my entire life.

At first, I don't want to get too personal and tell him about the overdose, but we are developing great rapport, and I feel like he should know in case it prevents him from wanting to work with me. It's scary as shit to be vulnerable with him, but he's an empathetic listener and wants to work with me. I sign up for a six-month package.

Before our first coaching call, even though I am still highly emotional and break into random crying fits throughout the day, I have a newfound hope. I am going to find my purpose. After my first coaching call with Pablo, my homework assignment is to write about my dream life one year from now. "Dream big!" he instructs. I know what this assignment is because I have done it before. What I write is going to manifest as reality.

Over the weekend, I have another breakdown, crying-fit at the gym.

Why does Ozzy hate me now?

Why do I have to endure another heartbreak?

Why doesn't anybody ever love me?

Focus on the future.

I take my journal to the beach and write out my assignment:

> October 28, 2021
>
> Pablo arrives at HNL wearing a black hoodie and shorts. I pick him up, greet him with a lei, and immediately make fun of him for wearing black and a sweatshirt in Hawaii. I was afraid this might happen, so I offer him an Aloha shirt instead. We drive from the airport straight to the beach in my convertible with the top down, blasting hip hop. The weather is beautiful and sunny as usual, so we head to Waikiki to go surfing before lunch. Pablo has been practicing surfing in California and has advanced to standing up. We'll see how he holds up in these waves. I have also been practicing, and I can now hang ten. Pablo has brought black board shorts, so we have to stop in Billabong to buy a brighter pair to fit in with the locals. We surf for an hour. Pablo stands up! I hang ten! I introduce Pablo to some of my friends in the surfing community who I have met over the past year.
>
> We then go to Duke's for lunch. A few rainbows appear as we sit down. Since COVID is over, there is a live band playing reggae music. I get the rib and chicken plate because it reminds me of Chicago, and I miss Chicago food. Pablo gets the

Korean street tacos because he's a city person too. Then, I fill him in on what's been going on with me for the past year.

I have been working on my spiritual health and meditating and tapping into my intuition so that I can listen to my gut and make better decisions. I have also been working on personal growth, putting down the wall I have around my heart, and always being my authentic self no matter what. These things have helped me meet amazing groups of people and formed more of a community.

Now that COVID is over, I am hanging out with my improv friends again. We have regular improv jams, which are fun and hilarious.

Last, but not least, I have been in a loving, committed, healthy relationship for nine months. I pull my huge diamond ring out of my purse and put it on my ring finger to floss my bling for Pablo. He congratulates me on my engagement and puts on his sunglasses because the sun's glare on the extremely large diamond is blinding.

My fiancé and I are taking our time planning a wedding date because we are working on some relationship issues. Unlike in the past, when I would shut my partner out to protect myself, we are learning to communicate better. Also, the sex is amazing. We are living together. I just moved into his place, and now we are going to rent out my condo for rental income.

Last October, after my rock bottom, I asked my manager for a raise and got a twenty-five percent raise and an extra bonus. My partner is financially independent, so I don't have to work once we are married if I don't want to. I have been working on my book this past year and am ready to publish it. As part of the marketing campaign

my fiancée and I put together, we are going to
travel the country and do storytelling events,
David Sedaris style.

    We also have international, first-class, five-
star travel planned to Thailand, Sydney, Rio de
Janeiro, Costa Rica, Morocco, Spain, and Sri Lan-
ka. We are forming an idea where we form a community wherever we travel to spread love and keep
the world connected through this love.

    I graciously thank Pablo, as all of this was
accomplished due to his coaching. Regardless, I
still make him pay for lunch.

For the first time since being released from the hospital, a sense
of hope comes over me.

I will make it another year. Things will get better.

I get home from journaling at the beach and I see a text notification on my phone. It's Ozzy. My stomach fills with dread.

Hi Angie

I know you must hate me right now,
and I'm sorry that I just cut you
off like that. I do miss you but
can't talk to you without wanting to spend time with you, and I
can't do that while still in the
house. I will be moving out on the
7th, and don't blame you if you
don't want to ever talk to me. I
do understand if that's the case.
I do wish you all the happiness
in the world. Hopefully, we can
at least still be friends in the
future. Miss you and still have
lotsa love for you 💔 💔 💔

I am reduced to a crying mess.

How am I going to make it another week, let alone another year?
With Pablo's help. Keep doing the work.

I am at a lash appointment with Hazel. It's the first time I have seen or talked to her since I was released from the hospital last month. She opens the conversation as if the zoo incident never happened. "How is your surfing going?"

That's odd. She never asks me questions.

I tell her how my surfing is going, and then I quickly realize that the only reason she asked me about my surfing was so that she would have a segue to talk about her surfing. "My surfing is going great! Ozzy and I have so much fun! We talk and laugh…"

Why in the hell is she telling me this?

I feel a pang of jealousy. I miss the days when Ozzy and I used to talk and laugh while we were surfing. Hazel isn't done. "You and I should go to Sweet E's sometime."

I catch my breath.

What the hell?

Hazel and I have never been out to eat together. There are a gazillion restaurants on this island. Why did she specifically say Sweet E's? Ozzy must have said something to her about us going there. A big part of me wants to pull out my Chicago attitude on Hazel because I am pissed that she mentioned Sweet E's. But I know that Hazel would dish it right back, and I don't have the energy for it.

"Ozzy and I used to go there all of the time. I'm not ready to go back yet."

"Well, now I can rub it in his face that you and I go together."

What is going on? Why would she invite me to do something with an ulterior motive of rubbing it in his face?

I'm trying to heal my broken heart. I don't need this petty bullshit. "No, thank you."

There is no counteroffer to go to another restaurant. I leave the appointment with a huge sadness in my heart. My next stop is Whole Foods. I always seem to find parking in the lot next to the store, but this is the first time I have ever seen this lot full, and I have to park on the roof. Parking on the roof means that I have to walk through the mall to get to Whole Foods. As I walk through the mall, I see Aloha Salads and the gelato place. It reminds me of the good times with Ozzy. Tears form in my eyes.

Why did I let Hazel pull that manipulative bullshit on me?

I text Hazel that I can no longer come to her for my lashes and eyebrows and briefly explain why. She never responds.

I am still in a down mood after my appointment with Hazel yesterday. It doesn't help that I am still not able to sleep more than four hours each night. I wake up in the middle of the night in a hypervigilant state, too anxious to go back to sleep. I think I have PTSD. I go to the beach after work to cheer up. It doesn't work. I walk home to clear out my energy. It starts to drizzle. My heart is so heavy. The weather matches my mood. As I approach my building, a big, bright rainbow appears. It's one of the bright, solid ones with bold colors. My eyes appreciate the sight, but my heart is way too raw to enjoy it. When I get home, I pull my phone out of my bag. There is a text.

Oh, that's probably Kelly. I forgot that I texted her at the beach.

It's Ozzy. My heart pounds as I hold my breath.

Hi Angie
Just saw you walking home. I was too shocked to even beep the horn. I know you hate me right now, so I didn't have the guts to turn around. I think about you all of the time and miss you so much. I hope one day we can sit down and talk. I want you to know that you mean so much to me, but I can't give you what you want right now and when I see you I can't just be your friend right now. I'm still figuring out what the future is going to be like. I hope you are doing well. You looked really

> good. Hope work isn't so stressful
> and want you to know that I think
> you are great just the way you are.
> Miss you and love you 🖤 🙁

I always thought Ozzy's love was unconditional, but it was just as conditional as everybody who has ever loved me.

I can't do this anymore.

No, I got this. I'm doing so well with the work with Pablo. I have been working on a lot of shame stuff, and this is triggering it.

I hug my shadow self. She needs a lot of love right now.

I am on my way to a dentist appointment to get my teeth cleaned. My dentist is next to the neighborhood where Ozzy lives. Or, at least where he used to live. While I am in the dentist's chair, my heart fills up with love. I miss Ozzy so much. I wonder if he moved. I wonder if he forgot about me already. I wonder if I will ever talk to him again.

I leave the dentist and ride a Biki down Turtle's street. Our street. Ozzy and I used to drive down this street all of the time. I haven't been down here much, but every time I am, I think of Ozzy, just like I am now. Halfway down the street, I see a familiar car approaching me on the other side of the road. I hear a beep. I look up. It's Ozzy.

It happens so fast that neither of us has time to react. He is looking at me straight-faced, but I can tell that seeing me has sparked some emotion in him. What that is, though, I don't know. The rest of the bike ride home is short, but my heart is thumping, and all of the memories come back. I can't help it. I text him.

> Hi Oz Tart, it was nice seeing your
> face. I miss you so much. 💔

I don't expect him to respond, and he doesn't, which triggers me because the silent treatment reminds me of Marc. I send another text.

> I don't understand why you can't
> tell me what happened or why you

don't care about how much you are
hurting me.

Why are you being psycho?
Because I miss him.

You fucked up. He doesn't miss you. He's giving you the silent treat-ment, and you are acting like a needy little child. Haven't you learned anything? You are wasting your money on Pablo. You don't deserve a life partner, and you don't deserve to be loved.

I feel miserable about texting Ozzy yesterday, especially since he didn't respond. I text Pablo that something came up that I would like to talk to him about on our call today. He responds that he will add it to the agenda. Then, I go to the gym to clear my head. As I am working out, I think about a recent session with Pablo where we came up with value statements to contradict my shame statement of "I am not enough."

I am enough if I allow myself to be seen.
I am enough if I speak my truth.
I am enough if I am being authentic.
I am enough if I have an open heart.
I am enough if I am courageous.

By texting Ozzy that I missed him and venting my frustration, I allowed myself to be seen, spoke my truth, was authentic, acted with an open heart, and was courageous. I start feeling a sense of pride about putting myself out there.

By the time I talk to Pablo about it, I am feeling a lot more comfortable with it. He takes it a step further by telling me about connecting without attachment— energetically sending love to someone without actually contacting them. I love this concept and resolve to do it in the future because I have a feeling I will run into him again.

I am so burned out from work and not being able to sleep that I need a vacation, but due to COVID travel restrictions about re-entering the State of Hawaii, it's not practical to travel right now. I don't even know where I would go. I don't feel up to visiting Mom. My delicate mental state isn't capable of dealing with the dynamics. I haven't even told her about my hospital excursion. I was afraid that she would want to come here and stay with me in her attempt to control the situation and make sure I don't physically harm myself while brushing the severity of the emotional distress under the rug. All that would do is create more anxiety because I would feel suffocated and controlled, not loved.

However, I'm excited because I'm taking the entire week of Christmas entirely off work to unplug. At first, this seems like a lonely concept because I don't have family here, but Kelly planned a surfing bender all week with a small group: Kelly, Kelly's other friends, Jon and Hoku, and me.

We surfed Sunday morning and yesterday afternoon. It's Tuesday morning, Hoku is not coming, and Jon is running late. Kelly and I walked the beach together, and we are standing on the beach, zipping up our wetsuits, getting ready to go in the water. I turn around to attach my leash to my board, and that's how I see Ozzy talking to someone about fifteen feet behind me. He is intentionally ignoring me. My blood runs cold. This is the first time I have seen him since we went surfing together the first week of October. The shame is exploding in my chest. I can't breathe.

Escape! Run! Why are you still standing here, you fool!

I need to get in the water now. I try to get Kelly's attention, but I can't say anything because he is right there. Plus, she is now attaching her leash to her board. That is how she sees him too. She tries to warn me but doesn't realize that it's too late. "Don't turn around."

"I know. I already saw."

Get in the water now! He hates you! You don't even exist to him. Get in the water to escape this painful shame!

I am practically running into the water and hit the water paddling. Kelly is right along with me.

He intentionally ignored me. I want to cry, but I am too numb.

Don't worry about him right now. Just worry about surfing.

Jon meets us in the water, and after we are done, Kelly, Jon, and I walk back to Kelly's, where Jon has parked. Jon offers me a ride home. I want to cry so bad, but I just met Jon two days ago and don't feel comfortable having an emotional breakdown in front of him. As he puts his stuff in his truck, I briefly turn to Kelly while tearing up. "He didn't even acknowledge me."

She hugs me. "I know on some level that he is hurting too."

"Why? I didn't hurt him."

"Because he lost you."

It warms my heart that she would say something so loving, but a big part of me truly believes he doesn't care about losing me. If he did, he would have done anything in his power not to. I get home, and I can't stop crying. Luckily, I have a call with Pablo in an hour. I text him that I have something I want to talk to him about that just happened. We spend two hours talking about it. I bawl my eyes out the entire time, but what I love best about Pablo is that he holds the space for me to feel how I feel without trying to cheer me up or change how I feel. He also doesn't respond to Ozzy's behavior by trying to analyze or decode it. Now, I feel accountable for myself and am not even worrying about him anymore. My goal is to recover from this situation as quickly as possible. For my homework, Pablo wants me to come up with a game plan for what to do the next time I see him. I have a lot to think about.

But first, surfing.

TODAY we are on the West Side, so there is little chance of seeing Ozzy. I am catching the biggest waves I have ever caught! I am being courageous! This week of surfing has made me realize that I can have fun without Ozzy, and I don't need him to surf big waves.

I think about my homework assignment, and the next time I see Ozzy, I am going to initiate a "Hi" without expecting anything in return. I don't care if he ignores me. I don't care if he doesn't reciprocate. I don't care if he hates me. I don't care. Because saying "Hi" is allowing myself to be seen, having an open heart, speaking my truth, being authentic, and most of all, being courageous. I don't need or want anybody's approval.

I am enough.

TODAY is Saturday, the last day of the bender. I haven't heard from the surf crew on the group text. It's chilly and raining, but a big part of me wants to surf for a little bit to fulfill the seven-day commitment. I message the group text that I am going to our regular Waikiki surf spot, but only for a little bit. I arrive, and the waves are fun! I was only planning on staying out for about thirty to forty minutes, but I have been out for a little over an hour.

Okay, two or three more waves, and then I am going in.

Then, I see Ozzy closer to the shore, giving a lesson. He is lined up with the lifeguard stand, just like me.

Escape! Go in now!

Noooooo. I already decided that I am going to catch a few more waves. Plus, if I catch a few waves with him right there, I am allowing myself to be seen.

Good point. But it's way too terrifying to say "Hi."

I am not going to worry about that yet. I am going to have fun and catch some waves. Oh, and make sure I look hot and sexy while I do it.

For one of the first times in my life, I am not running away from my fear. I am going to catch a few more waves and allow myself to be seen. As I am catching a few more waves, I have another decision to make before I go in.

Am I going to say "Hi?"

Um, yes! That is the game plan. It's terrifying, but how amazing would it be if, on the very next call with Pablo, after my two-hour crying meltdown last week, I am able to tell him that not only did I come up with a game plan, but I had a chance to do it in person AND fucking nailed it!

I notice a shift in how I am responding. I used to let anxious thoughts control my actions, but now I am listening to them, almost as if I am an observer. My chest doesn't feel tight, and even though there is a lot of chatter in my brain, I am thinking clearly.

I chicken out on a few waves because I am procrastinating. I need to do this. A wave is coming.

I can do this!

I catch the wave and ride it toward the shore. As the ride is ending, I look up, and Ozzy is right in front of me with his lesson. His signature captivating smile is sprawled across his face, and he is looking directly at me.

"Hi, Angie!!!"

"Hi, Ozzy!"

The wave dies, and I jump into the cold, refreshing water. When I bob up to the surface, I paddle to shore, my heart racing.

Look how that works! When I let go of expectations, he said "Hi" to me first! And he was smiling! I am so proud of myself for allowing myself to be seen!

I walk home, ecstatic to tell Pablo. And I have to admit, as much as I was crying about how he ignored me, it hurt just as bad to see him smiling at me.

How did it get so messed up? We used to have such a beautiful friendship.

But I am so proud of myself!

I can feel the shift from when I first started working with Pablo after I got out of the hospital and now. At times, it has felt like watching grass grow. I'm still sad about the loss of the friendship with Ozzy, but I am determined to move on. New Year's Eve is tomorrow, and this week is the perfect week to let go.

My friend Erin is on-island visiting her parents, and we have plans to go surfing today, the last day of 2020. As we walk across the beach with our boards, Ozzy is getting out of the water. Because Erin doesn't know who Ozzy is, she continues walking. I stop in front of him.

Escape!

There is nowhere to escape, plus he sees me and is smiling. I got this. Remember the script. Say "Hi."

He speaks first. "Merry Christmas, happy new year!"

My response is not as cheerful because it feels fake to have this exchange where there is nothing merry or happy between us. "Merry Christmas, happy new year."

He leans in and kisses me on the cheek. He lingers for what seems like forever with his lips on my cheek. He finally pulls away and asks what seems like a rhetorical question. "How have you been?"

Motherfucker, how do you think I have been? You cut me and left me bleeding, so I overdosed on my anxiety pills, resulting in the worst months of my entire life!

Breathe. Love. Compassion.

I take a breath. "Okay." I should probably ask how he has been to keep up the cordial facade, but I don't care how he has been.

I think he senses how I am feeling and he speaks again. "We need to talk." He says it in a loving way that shows he knows it is long overdue.

"Yes, we do."

He starts muttering about how it will be soon and he needs to take care of a few more things. I tense up.

How much more time could he need? It's been three months.

He senses my frustration. "I just need a little bit more time."

I relax. "I know."

He shows me his fingernails. They are long. "I've been saving them up."

"Saving them up for what?"

"You."

He does think about me.

I don't know how to respond. He speaks again. "Your surfing has improved a lot. You look really good out in the water."

A lot of people have been complimenting my surfing lately, but to hear this compliment from the man who taught me how to surf is one of the most amazing things I have ever heard.

"Thank you."

He looks me dead in the eyes with a loving gaze. His eyes are so beautiful. "You look really good," he says.

"Thank you. So do you."

"I miss you."

"I miss you too."

"We'll talk soon. I promise."

Breathe.

"Whenever you're ready."

I walk over to Erin and let go. I don't need closure or an apology anymore.

CHAPTER 35

*T*ODAY is New Year's Day, and I am hiking Koko Head to clear my mind and elevate for the upcoming year. Surely, it has to be better than last year. When I get to the bottom, I check my phone. I have a text from Mike.

> Hope you're ready to have a beautiful new year. We'll definitely have to catch up. Are you still trying to write?

Something seems off.

My intuition is on alert, and something tells me he is reaching out to me is because he wants me to write for him again. Whether it is the book or something else, I don't know. I mean, we never talk anymore. I had asked him for feedback on one of my coaching assignments for Pablo several months ago, and after agreeing to do it, he fell through and never got back to me. If he was busy, all he had to do was say so, but I haven't heard a peep from him until now. I am tired of sweeping shit under the rug and pretending everything is okay.

> Hey, Mike, wishing you a beautiful new year as well!
> I have been writing a book. I got sidetracked from my goals last year, but hired a personal coach a few months ago and have gotten back on track with the book and everything else.

> When you said you were going to
> help me with feedback on my coach-
> ing homework and then didn't, I
> felt disappointed. I know we have
> had our ups and downs but out of all
> of the people to not follow through
> on their word, I never would have
> expected you. Because of this, even
> though I would love to catch up, I
> don't feel totally comfortable with
> it right now.

Immediately after hitting send, my phone vibrates with a text notification.

> Sounds good. Have a good one.

I feel hurt that his response is so cold, especially since I was vulnerable with him. On the other hand, we're not at the same place in our lives. I know the only other reaction he can respond with is anger and I don't want to bear his wrath again. I feel calm with an acceptance that this friendship has run its course.

I just logged off work, and Kelly and I are walking to the beach to go surfing. As we walk up to the shore, I see Ozzy ahead.
Remember the script. Say "Hi."

He sees us approach. He beats me to it. "Hello!" Kelly and I are both here but he is looking directly at me.

"Hi, Ozzy."

"Did you get a new wetsuit?"

"Yeah."

"How many do you have now?"

You seem to know more about my wetsuits than I do, so why don't you tell me?

"Five."

"It matches my Two Crows surfboard."

I mean, they both have blue in the color scheme, but other than that, they don't match at all.

He continues the interrogation. "Did you get a new watch?"

Maybe you should be concerned about how fucked up my sleeping habits are since you dropped me on my ass four months ago, instead of my goddamn watch.

"Yes."

"Is it a tide watch?"

Why are we pretending like nothing is wrong? A month ago, you said you would reach out "soon" and haven't, so now you are sweeping that under the rug and dissecting my attire.

"Yes."

"What brand is it?"

Who gives a shit?

"Nixon."

"I like your hair. Is that a different color of red?"

I'm surprised you noticed because you never fucking see me anymore.

"Yeah, I added a semi-permanent red to the color and developer."

Why am I telling him this? He doesn't even know what that means.

"I like it. What's on your nails?"

I show him my fingernail art as Kelly joins in the awkwardness. "Hey, I have friends coming in a few weeks. I'll refer them to you for lessons."

"Sure, sounds good."

Wait, why is she referring business to the person who broke my heart?

Finally, we say goodbye as Kelly and I go into the water. I want to be strong because I know Kelly is tired of me crying about Ozzy, but I can't help it. I am internally berating myself because I wasn't prepared for anything beyond saying "Hi." He threw me off with the barrage of questions.

After I get a hug from Kelly on land, I head home. I muscle through my normal afternoon stuff: writing my book, journaling, cooking, and laundry. But as I wind down and start my evening routine of journaling, I can't hold it in anymore and start crying. I don't even know what I am crying about, and I feel a feeling I recognize. Anger.

Why did Kelly offer to refer her friends to him? Does she not remember driving me to the hospital?

I text Kelly.

> I'm going to be honest. It hurts my feelings that you offered to send Ozzy business. I would never support anyone who totally disrespected you and broke your heart.

> Thank you for being honest. I just felt like it was normalizing the conversation. Just to chat through the awkwardness. I meant no disrespect nor real intention of sending them. I'm sorry. I would never intentionally hurt you.

Shit, she's right.

That entire conversation was so weird and fucked up. I see where she is coming from now. I know she would never intentionally hurt me, and I am glad that she is cool enough that we feel comfortable having these exchanges. One of the good things that has come out of this situation is growing closer to Kelly.

My emotions turn to sadness. Conversations with Ozzy used to be happy and lighthearted, and now they are awkward as hell. I sit on the floor and start crying. Crying turns to bawling, and sitting turns to the fetal position. It feels like a cruel joke that after making progress with healing, I met someone who created a feeling of physical and emotional safety that I have never felt before. Then he abandoned me, savagely shoving the self-hate and belief that I don't deserve to be loved right back up to the surface. Mom has only shown me love when I am acting in accordance with what she wants, Marc only showed me love when I was being who he wanted me to be, many other boyfriends and many platonic friends have only shown me love when it was convenient for them, and Ozzy only showed me love when his wife, who he was allegedly separated from, was in another country.

Nobody will ever love me unconditionally.
There is something wrong with me.

I don't know how long I am on the floor, but there is a puddle of tears on the floor when I sit up. I try to go to sleep, but I can't. This isn't anything new. I haven't slept much since getting home from the hospital. I sit in my chair facing the window and cry for hours. There is police activity on the street, and the lights on the cop car are seizure-inducing.

Great, I can't even sit in my favorite chair and be miserable in the middle of the night without something interrupting me.

I go back to crying on the floor, probably leaving another puddle, but I can't see because the lights are off.

I am on my weekly call with Pablo, and I am telling him all about the awkward scene from yesterday with how I froze and went along with Ozzy's inspection of my wetsuit, watch, hair, and nails.

"If you could go back and do it again, what would you say?"

"Why are we pretending like everything is okay?"

"There. That is the second line in your script after saying 'Hi' when you see him again."

I like this script thing. I feel prepared. Not so fast. Pablo has a caveat. "But be careful of using a script for everything. For now, just have those two lines for your script, and your approach for the rest of the conversation is to be real."

Pablo is so smart. I don't know what I would do without him right now. I've come so far in the past four months.

I am driving to the North Shore where I rented an Airbnb for the weekend to have uninterrupted writing time. I want to nail down my book outline and make serious progress on the content. As I drive, I decide to also use this time for resetting and letting go of Ozzy. I have started moving on with my life by hanging out with other friends, writing for my book, learning new surfing skills, and self-development with Pablo. I respect his boundaries if he doesn't want to reach out to me. Even though it would be nice to have closure, he is not responsible for my healing. I can do this on my own. Once at my Airbnb, I put away my phone and work on my book for three hours straight. I don't even look at my phone before going to bed.

I wake up early to the call of roosters. I still have rooster PTSD from Guam and abandonment PTSD from Ozzy, so I don't even try to go back to sleep because I know it's pointless. I get out of bed and grab my phone to connect it to the charger. I have some texts. One is from Ozzy. My heart thumps through my chest.

> Hi Angie!! I'm pretty sure that you hate me right now, and I don't blame you, but I would like to talk to you, preferably over dinner tomorrow if you don't have any plans. I would totally understand if you don't. Ozzy

Is this a joke? Of all weekends to text, it's my uninterrupted writing weekend.

I take a few deep breaths and think about what I want to do. First of all, I cannot let this interfere with my writing weekend. I booked this months ago in anticipation of working on my book. Old Me would have been so desperate to talk to him that I would have driven down to the South Shore or invited him up here to talk, but I will not. Also, I will not talk over dinner. What if I start crying in the middle of the restaurant? There is no what if. I definitely would start crying in the middle of the restaurant.

But do I really want to know what happened? Do I want to tell him what happened to me?

I decide that I need to practice having difficult conversations. When we had The Plan conversation, I was totally reactive. Working with Pablo, I have become much more responsive, so I want to redeem myself by being more responsive this time. And I don't have anything to say, but if he has something to say to me, I will create a loving space for him to share. I don't need an apology. I don't need to tell my story. I will go to listen. I text him back.

> Hi Ozzy, I've thought about it, and I am open to talking with you, but I am not available today because I am on the North Shore all weekend. I can be available during the week after work or next weekend. I don't feel comfortable having this conversation over food. Let me know what works for you.

> Hope you have fun on the North Shore just let me know what works for you.

> How about Monday after I log off work?

Luckily, this brief exchange doesn't interfere with the rest of my writing weekend.

I am in my childhood home. There are other people in the house, but we are not interacting. I am in my bedroom. I see a spider with a body the size of a rat. I run to another room. It follows me. I run to another room. It follows me. Even though there are other people in the house, I feel helpless, and the responsibility to solve the situation is on my shoulders. I run to another room. It follows me. Then, I realize that even though I cannot change the situation, I can take control of it. I run outside. The spider follows me and escapes into the trees behind the house. I feel empowered. I'm not helpless.

I wake up.

It may not always be easy, but I have control of my life now, regardless of the circumstances surrounding me that I cannot control.

CHAPTER 36

*J*T'S finally Monday, and I am oddly calm because I usually worry about everything. Plus, this is a conversation with Ozzy, the man who hung me out to dry four months ago with no explanation, and we haven't talked since, other than the beach incidents. I wonder what he is going to say. And I wonder if he is going to ask what has been going on with me. I don't want to talk about the overdose. I have moved on and am doing so much better now. I used to yearn to talk to him, but I'm not even excited.

We aren't meeting until later, so I have time to go to the beach and meditate after work. If he asks about me, I am not going to be able to simply flat-out tell him the story. There are too many details to remember. Not to mention, I am going to start crying. I need a strategy. I want to create a PowerPoint deck, but I don't want to take my laptop to the beach. I go old school and bring my sketchbook. I draw a comic strip about what happened. I can't even draw the story without crying.

I don't know if this is a good idea.

Ozzy picks me up at the beach. I have no idea where we are going to talk. He starts driving. I am afraid it's going to be awkward talking to him. The conversation is pleasant, other than the fact that I'm bothered that we are sweeping shit under the rug again, but I understand it is only temporary until we find a place to talk. Ozzy merges on the H-1.

"Where are we going?"

"I don't know."

He doesn't have a plan?

He keeps driving, and I realize we are going to Sandy Beach, which is on the other side of the island. I start to panic.

There's no escape. What if I want to run away?

I take a few deep breaths. I am not Old Me and don't need to run away. Ozzy parks, and I have to go to the bathroom before we find a spot on the beach. I hand him my beach bag to hold while I am in the bathroom. It's heavy because I already had a bottle of water in it, and Ozzy brought two more water bottles. He feels the weight of the bag as I hand it off. "Did you bring a gun?"

Ahhh, he thinks I'm mad at him. Wait until I show him the inner game skills I have been working on with Pablo.

I come back from the bathroom and he hands me my bag. I still feel oddly at peace. Now that I am in his company, I miss the old times. A part of me hopes that he still wants to be friends.

But will it ever be the same?

We find a spot, and I set up my blanket. I sit across from him and wait for him to start speaking. He does, but not in the way that I expect. "Let me have it."

There was definitely a time I would have loved to rip his head off by telling him how much he destroyed me and how I almost died. But that time has passed. "I don't have anything to say. I came here to listen."

"You don't have anything to say?"

"I mean, I *can* talk, but I came here to listen."

"Why don't you talk first?"

"I *can*, but I don't *need* to talk unless you want me to."

"I want to know what you have to say."

But does he really?

I reach for my sketchbook in my beach bag. "I came prepared just in case you asked me to talk. I'm not good at this." I walk him through the pages of my sketchbook. It starts with us being happy and in love back in October. There is a picture of me pushing him in a wheelchair because I used to want to grow old with him. I drew an electric wheelchair so that I could walk beside him and hold his hand. Then, it turns to me crying on the floor next to my plants. I was hoping I could hold back the waterworks until later in the presentation, but my voice cracks. It's too late now.

Then, it moves to the day at Kaimana when I told him that I couldn't take anymore and needed time away from him, but then we ended up having sex. I take accountability for not having boundaries. The story moves to the devastation I felt when he ghosted me with no explanation and how I swallowed all thirty pills and laid down in the shower with my blanket and pillow to die. Ozzy grabs my arm, mouth gaping open from surprise, preventing me from turning the page.

Oh no, motherfucker, we're not finished.

For the first time during my presentation, I look directly at him. "I'm not done." I turn the page. "Plot twist! I wake up, and it's morning…"

Ozzy is visibly distraught, but he wanted to know what I had to say. It took a lot of effort to draw pictures of me in the hospital because these are more intricate since I was hooked up to machines, so I want to make sure we get through the whole thing so my artwork is not a lost cause. I get to the part where the ER nurse comes to me with Ozzy's information as my emergency contact, but I tell her not to call him because I couldn't trust him. I look directly at Ozzy again. "That's why Joe was my emergency contact. He would have immediately got his ass on a plane to fly nine hours to rescue me from the psych ward."

Ozzy buries his head in his hands, clearly ashamed. I don't have empathy. I move through the pages and arrive at the part where I get the mystery phone call telling me how Sarah found out about us, and her mom is giving him money. Back when I wanted to tell him this story, I always envisioned that when I told him, I would inspect his every reaction to try to determine if he was lying, but at this moment, I don't give a shit. I know my truth, and that is all that matters. I just want to get through the rest of the story because it's painful to relive it. I continue through the rest of the pages and arrive at the last page, a picture of me with a huge heart in my chest and an electric aura around my entire body. I cry even harder. "I'm doing a lot better now—"

Ozzy cuts me off. "Come here."

He pulls me toward him and gives me a huge hug. It feels so good. I have wanted this for the past four months. Neither of us let go and he says, "I miss you."

"I miss you too."

We pull away. Unfortunately, this conversation is not finished. I still want to know what the hell happened.

"Sarah did find out about us. There was a video on the Go Pro."

Oops.

We were testing out a feature, and he just happened to be naked on my couch when I was recording. I thought I deleted it. He continues, "We had a huge blowout argument, and I couldn't handle everything, so I needed time to sort things out on my own. But I moved out a few months ago, and I only see her and talk to her when she takes pictures for lessons. I don't know about the rest of the stuff you heard. Her mom doesn't give me money."

Something seems off.

He couldn't talk to me for four whole months because of an argument? And it seems weird how nonchalant he acted when I told him some random guy called me to tell me scandalous gossip. I mean, if he would have told me that a random person called him and told him things about me that were untrue, I would have some serious questions about the details. This conversation is generating more questions than answers.

We get cut off by the lifeguard announcing that a movie is being filmed on the road behind the beach and everybody has to leave by 4 p.m. Otherwise, we will be trapped at the beach all night, as they are closing the road for filming. Ozzy looks at his watch. It's 3:45. We have been here for over an hour, and this is the first announcement they have made. There are people in the water. There are people with tents and grills set up that have been here all day. There are people on the beach who did not even flinch when they heard the announcement. Ozzy and I, on the other hand, have no desire to spend the night on the beach, so we are the only people who immediately get up and leave the still full parking lot.

I am starving. I had a small snack earlier at the beach, but I need another feeding. Ozzy knows that I can only go two to three hours without food, or I start to get hangry. I would prefer to eat smaller, controlled meals to prevent binging in one meal. Ozzy has a good memory and has not forgotten this about me. "Are you hungry?"

"Yes."

"Do you want to get something to eat?"

"Yes."

Even though I don't feel like everything has been resolved, I still feel comfortable around Ozzy and enjoy his company. Plus, I need to eat soon. We have dinner at a nearby Greek restaurant. As we eat, I tell him about my coaching with Pablo. His reaction is not what I expect. "Even though I know it's not my business anymore, I feel a tug at my heart that another man helped you through that."

"I needed help. He's a professional. I paid him to help me."

"I know, but I feel a little jealous."

That's interesting.

After dinner, he drives me home. I'm not sure where we stand. We talk for a little bit in the car, just like the old days. As I wonder how this evening is going to end, Ozzy reveals a preview. "Can you please reconsider adding me back as your emergency contact?"

"No!"

Doesn't he understand how bad he messed up that role?

I think this is the first time I have been reactive with him today, but I still feel unsafe with him as my emergency contact. He needs to earn that trust back. I end the conversation by saying goodbye and getting out of the car. Ozzy gets out too and gives me a hug. When we pull away, he says, "I want to give us another try."

"What do you mean?"

Exasperated that I don't understand, he exclaims, "Us!"

This is covered in bright red flags. I still don't think he understands how careless he was with my heart. He interrupts my pause by saying, "I deserve a second chance."

"I already gave you a second chance. You forgot about me twice. I gave you a second chance by taking lessons with you again."

"I'm a baseball person. You get three strikes in baseball."

"As long as you're still married, I can't afford to lower my standards."

"What about friends?"

"I don't know. I don't want to risk getting hurt again."

"You can't live your life afraid of getting hurt. Otherwise, you never experience life."

He's right. That sounds exactly like something Pablo would say.

I am trying to work on having an open heart. Maybe this is the test that I need.

"I'll think about it."

*B*ecause I am blacklisted in Hawaii from prescriptions in the same or similar class as Clonazepam, the strongest medication I can be prescribed now is Ambien, which I need because I still can't sleep. I took it for the first time tonight and, in the middle of the night, I have woken up, but I am still dreaming. It is not like lucid dreaming where you are half awake and half asleep. I am both fully awake and dreaming at the same time, which is scary because I can't turn off the dream. In the dream, I am scrolling through Google Calendar on my phone. I stop in October. An alert for October 17th keeps popping up. Because I am awake, my logical brain is working.

It's not October.

But the October 17th reminder keeps barraging me. Then, I snap out of the dream. October 17th was a Saturday. It was the day of my life that I completely missed out on because I was unconscious in my shower.

Never again.

I stayed silent before to keep the peace, but I did not survive a day and a half in the shower to continue sweeping shit under the rug. From now on, I will speak my truth and never betray myself again.

Chapter 37

*I*t's been six months. In October, Ozzy left me to bleed with no explanation. Only a few months ago, I found out it was for selfish reasons. After the conversation at Sandy's, I gave in and trusted Ozzy as a friend. It turned romantic, but it was a lot different than before. He acted distant and guarded, and I soon became suspicious that something was up. I had asked him for the truth but the questions pushed him away. I had been practicing tapping into my intuition, but I was only getting vague hits like "he feels trapped" and "he's suffering."

But why?

Finally, after getting more vague hits, I made a specific request. *Please give me a crystal clear sign of the truth.*

The next day, I went surfing. My surfboard is stored in a locker on the beach. Someone else had mysteriously put a lock on top of my lock, preventing me from removing my surfboard. I needed to call the locker manager, but I didn't bring my phone. I walked over to the beach to see if I could find someone I knew to use their phone. Lo and behold, Ozzy was on the beach, getting ready to take out a lesson. I explained the situation and asked if I could borrow his phone. I walked back to my board and called the locker manager, who had never heard of anything like that before, and arranged a time to meet him the next day so he could cut off the lock. After the call ended, I was standing on the sidewalk, unable to surf, with nothing else to do, and Ozzy's phone in my hand.

I checked his phone. His wife, who he told me he never saw or talked to outside of lessons, he actually talked to a lot. Her texts were all lovey-dovey, and his responses were very deadpan, void of the emojis, Bitmojis, and exclamation points he usually sent to me. It seemed as though she was hoping for something more with him, and he was definitely not doing anything to shut down that idea. It was creepy how her texts read in a baby-talk type of way. It made their dynamic seem more like a little girl trying to gain her father's approval, especially since his responses were so flat and did not reciprocate. It was also creepy what a dominating presence her New Zealand mum plays in their marriage, as if she is their manager or something. At one point, Sarah referred to her mum as "evil," so it was clear that she didn't like it, but I assume they tolerate it because Mum holds the purse strings. There were frequent references to "gifts" that Mum gave to Ozzy. He lied about talking to Sarah outside of work and he did that thing where he intentionally manipulates his words to deceive me. Her mom didn't give him money. She gave him gifts. From what I pieced together, it seemed as though he is trapped with Sarah because of the money Mum gave to her and she shares with Ozzy, the money Mum continues to give them, and because of Sarah's role in the business that they own together. The straw that broke the camel's back was that Sarah made a comment about the size of his bed when he cut off the text thread for that day to say he was going to bed.

Awww, your teeny weeny cute little bed.

How the fuck does she know what his bed looks like?

I had seen enough. I marched back to the beach, hoping Ozzy wasn't there because I was so angry that I probably would have killed him with my bare hands.

If he wants to choose money over me, that's his loss. I'm priceless.

I thought I could wait until evening to talk to him on the phone, but I couldn't. I sent him a series of crazy texts, telling him that I saw his phone and he was dead to me. A few days later, after I calmed down, I decided to break the cycle of deceit and bullshit. True to my vow to never again sweep anything under the rug, I wanted to tell Sarah the truth. Like Julia in the Marc situation, I would want to know if I were her. Unlike the Julia and Marc situation, I was one hundred percent confident in my decision to speak the truth. Plus, Ozzy is charming. He can find someone else to replace me and do his manipulative bullshit again. But not on my watch. I almost died over their illegal marriage arrangement shenanigans, and I wanted to do my part in preventing this from happening again.

I tried to look Sarah up on Instagram, but she had blocked me, presumably when she originally found out about me and thought I would reach out to her. But you can never really block someone. I have a second Instagram account for my writing blog. I found her easily, and her account is set up as a business account so there is an incredibly convenient option to email. I sent her an email and told her that she deserved to know the truth. I let her know that Ozzy and I had been seeing each other and were being intimate. I attached some screenshots of Ozzy's "I love you" texts. I didn't tell her I almost died. From what Ozzy has told me about her, she seems desperate for U.S. citizenship. I honestly don't think she would care if I died as long as she could live in Hawaii. She probably swept the email under the rug anyway. It doesn't matter. I brought the truth to light to prevent anybody else from going down with their sham marriage, not for any reaction or action from her. In hindsight, I realize that the lock on my surfboard locker was not a fluke. It unlocked a crystal clear message of the truth.

Ask, and you shall receive! That shit still works!

Cutting off Ozzy and emailing Sarah seemed like a test from the universe.

    Angie, how have you used what you learned in the last six months?

    Hi Universe! Thanks for asking.

    I acted with an open heart ✓

    I was authentic ✓

    I spoke my truth ✓

    I allowed myself to be seen ✓

    I was loyal to me ✓

    I did not sweep anything under the rug ✓

> I did not give one fuck about what anybody
> else thought because I was acting according to
> my values ✓

Coming back from the overdose was the hardest thing I have ever done in my life. Some days I cried and questioned why I survived because I didn't want to be here, but I realize that Ozzy's gift to me was the chance to work with Pablo and uplevel my life exponentially. I am starting to understand my purpose. Most importantly, I understand how to create internal happiness. I not only survived, but I am thriving. Kahea was right. It wasn't my time.

I have no fear of skydiving today. I don't know if it's from working with Pablo or if almost dying does that to you, but I feel a sense of peace and calmness. As our plane takes off, my eyes well up with tears. I can't believe what a different person I am today than I was six months ago. I am confident. I am courageous. I am still learning.

"Are you ready?" Chris, my jumper, has snapped me back into the reality that I am about to jump out of a plane.

"I'm getting scared."

"You're in good hands. You already saw that I have a lot to live for."

He is referring to his two-year-old son, whom I met on the ground. I trust Chris. We wobble to the door. The air is so cold. My heart is beating out of my chest, but like all of the things I feel so deeply, it makes me feel alive. We lean. We fall. I surrender.

It feels like flying. Between falling and the cold air, every one of my senses is stimulated. My mouth is unintentionally open and falling at this speed in cold air dries my mouth out instantly. I taste the dryness. I smell the air. I see the beautiful ocean. I hear the wind rushing through my ears. I feel ecstatic and grateful in every inch of my body.

I'm so proud of myself!

THE END

ACKNOWLEDGMENTS

Words can't express the gratitude I have for the beautiful souls who have helped me along this book journey.

Thank you, Mom and Dad, for all of the experiences, even though I didn't appreciate them at the time, because they have helped me learn and grow as a human being. Dad, thank you for always visiting and protecting me on the other side.

Thank you, Pablo Rosario, for improving my life exponentially and helping me courageously evolve into a functional adult.

Thank you, Hollay Ghadery, Kelly Maurica, Brian Henson, Pablo Rosario, Kim Strickland, Bob Schram, and Kelly Gunn for peer editing and providing valuable feedback.

Thank you, Hollay Ghadery, for editing the content and encouraging me to go even deeper.

Thank you, Nicholas Lawrence Carter, for performing the final editorial review.

Thank you, Andy Bridge, for the cover design.

Thank you, The Second City Chicago, for accepting me in the sketch comedy writing program. That fun-filled year gave me the hope I needed during that time and, most importantly, re-ignited the dormant writer inside of me.

Thank you, Maria Guardino, for being a friend, neighbor, walking buddy, and sounding board for book opinions.

Thank you, Joe Wilson, for always being a big brother of choice.

Thank you, Kahea Bencke, for the insights, guidance (conscious and unconscious), and unconditional friendship.

Thank you, Jess Abner, for teaching Shakti, which was the springboard to becoming my authentic self.

Thank you, to my loyal @sowhathappenedhere Instagram followers, especially @ralphwalin, @storieswithsole, @rephael_epstein, @haikugrammer, @theothernye, @frodowrote, @dilo922, @pebbles28below, @elverum51, @wander._.words, @postcards-fortherapists, @mikehauser56, @kellymaurica.writes, @loriwrites1, @threegoatshenanigans, @present_journey_art, @gigifs72, @can-dkwords, @lily.g.17, @the_nuclearcowboy, @a.t.flowers, @steven_flint, @schram_i_am, @cairo770, @a.celt.abroad, @krista.lukas, @ocdisorderly, @mentalmonopoly, @philrydes, @milesouthwest, @belindablogs, @starwarspoetry, @hanswyser, @nancydeesculptures, @cystarkman, @luchainroyal, @gp_bell, and @david_kammer-zelt_writes_stuff. Because of you, I have always felt supported in my writing journey.